DATE DUE

DEC 7 1982		
DEC 9 1982		

INFORMATION, INFERENCE AND DECISION

THEORY AND DECISION LIBRARY

AN INTERNATIONAL SERIES

IN THE PHILOSOPHY AND METHODOLOGY OF THE

SOCIAL AND BEHAVIORAL SCIENCES

Editors:

GERALD EBERLEIN, *Universität des Saarlandes*

WERNER LEINFELLNER, *University of Nebraska*

Editorial Advisory Board:

VOLUME 1

INFORMATION,
INFERENCE AND DECISION

Edited by

GÜNTER MENGES

University of Heidelberg

D. REIDEL PUBLISHING COMPANY

DORDRECHT-HOLLAND / BOSTON-U.S.A.

Library of Congress Catalog Card Number 73–91432

Cloth edition: ISBN 90 277 0422 8
Paperback edition: ISBN 90 277 0423 6

Published by D. Reidel Publishing Company,
P.O. Box 17, Dordrecht, Holland

Sold and distributed in the U.S.A., Canada and Mexico
by D. Reidel Publishing Company, Inc.
306 Dartmouth Street, Boston,
Mass. 02116, U.S.A.

Printed in The Netherlands by D. Reidel, Dordrecht

CONTENTS

PART IV. SEMANTIC INFORMATION

PREFACE

Under the title 'Information, Inference and Decision' this volume in the Theory and Decision Library presents some papers on issues from the borderland of statistical inference philosophy and epistemology, written by statisticians and decision theorists who belonged or are allied to the former Saarbrücken school of statistical decision theory.

In the first part I make an attempt to outline an objective theory of inductive behaviour, on the basis of R. A. Fisher's statistical inference philosophy, on the one hand, and R. Carnap's inductive logic, on the other. A special problem arising in the context of the new theory, viz., the problem of vagueness of concepts (in particular in the social sciences) is treated separately by H. Skala and myself. B. Leiner has contributed some biographical and bibliographical notes on the objective theory of inductive behaviour.

Part II is concerned with inference philosophy. D. A. S. Fraser, the founder of structural inference theory, characterizes and compares some inference philosophies, and discusses his own and the arguments of the critics of his structural theory. In my opinion, Fraser's structural inference theory is suited to complete Fisher's inference philosophy in some essential points, if not to replace it. An interesting task for future research work is to establish the connection between Fraser's theory and Carnap's ideas in the framework of an objective theory of inductive behaviour.

A problem which has undeservedly been neglected in statistics, is the logic of significance. New aspects of this logic are discussed by J. G. Kalbfleisch and D. A. Sprott, mainly by the Poisson distribution.

Both contributions are important complements to my introductory paper where the inferential instruments 'structural probability' and 'significance test' have not been treated.

Part III presents three contributions on the problems of 'probability, entropy, information, and utility'. H. Schneeweiss begins with an exposition of the notions of probability and utility as dual concepts. Although this exposition is based upon probability-subjectivistic ideas (which I have criticized in my introductory paper) H. Schneeweiss' paper is an interesting complement, so to speak, the subjectivistic correlate of the objective theory of inductive behaviour.

M. Behara here for the first time publishes the results of his investigations of many years on entropy and utility which may be considered as an information-theoretical completion of the objective theory of inductive behaviour.

M. J. Beckmann enlarges the duality of entropy and utility by considering the aspect of gravity, as occurring in particular in modern transportation modelling.

Finally, Part IV is concerned with an important aspect of the objective theory of inductive behaviour: the concept and measurement of semantic information. J. Marschak first establishes the connection between semantic information, on the one hand, and a priori as well as a posteriori probabilities, on the other, with respect to the case that the hypotheses exclude each other. The extension with respect to the case that the hypotheses do not exclude each other will be discussed by him in a volume to be published as No. 4 in this series under the editorship of C. Cherry.

While Marschak's concept of semantic information is based upon decision theory, H. Skala's approach to the determination of this concept is undertaken from a quite different point, viz., from the information value of axiomatized theories, as proposed by Belis and Guiasu. The concept of utility, however, is fundamental to both approaches.

I want to thank all authors who contributed to this volume and D. Reidel Publishing Company, for friendly cooperation. Some of the editorial work was carefully done by Mrs Gisela Mschaty.

It is our intention to have further volumes on the same subject matter published in the series Theory and Decision Library. Authors who are interested in this matter and wish to contribute supplementary and critical papers concerned with the objective theory of inductive behaviour are kindly invited to send me their manuscripts.

Heidelberg, July 1973   G. MENGES

PART I

OBJECTIVE THEORY OF INDUCTIVE BEHAVIOUR

GÜNTER MENGES

ELEMENTS OF AN OBJECTIVE THEORY OF INDUCTIVE BEHAVIOUR

1. INTRODUCTION

On the groundwork of R. Carnap's works on inductive logic (1945, 1953, 1962, 1972), the works by R. A. Fisher on the statistical inference problem (1922, 1925, 1930, 1934, 1935, 1950), and my own contributions to decision theory (1958, 1963, 1966, 1968, 1970, 1973), and quite recently influenced by the fourth volume of W. Stegmüller's Wissenschafts-theorie (theory of knowledge) (1973), I shall try in the following to compile the *elements* of an *objective theory of inductive behaviour*.

What I shall present is not a concise and mature theoretical system, but rather the fundamentals of an objective theory of inductive behaviour 'beyond Popper and Carnap', to be developed in the future.

I call this theory *objective* for four closely related reasons. First reason: It is based upon the concept of objective probability and denies the scientific relevancy of so-called subjective, personal, or personalistic probabilities. Second reason: The epistemological principle of this theory is etiality, which – no matter what one thinks about subjective probability – is the only basis of an objective inductive logic. Third reason: In spite of disagreement in many other points, I share Popper's (1973) view of theory of knowledge as an "objective theory of essentially conjectural nature". Fourth reason: I think it is necessary to draw a sharp-cut line between the theory of statistical inference as a confirma-tion theory, on the one hand, and inductive ways of behaviour based on it, which like the background knowledge are inevitably rather sub-jective, on the other. This borderline can only be drawn from the objective (inferential) side of the whole problem. I call this theory an objective theory of *inductive* behaviour because I believe that the part of inductive logic which is not inferential in the statistical sense is based upon the utility of certain consequences of actions and upon the decision function, and hence reflects a deontically justified rational behaviour, and is not a 'logic' proper like the formal deductive logics. This view is in principle

Günter Menges (ed.), Information, Inference and Decision, 3–49. All Rights Reserved.

congruous with Carnap's late works and is obliged to the "normative theory of inductive reasoning" without being identical with it. My attempt differs from Stegmüller's 4th volume, first, by the intention to follow Carnap's theory as far as possible and, second, by the intention declared above to abandon personalistic probability theory which Stegmüller tried to integrate into his system.

2. DEONTIC RULES AND META-RULES

The concept of decision function which is important in the theory of inductive behaviour I am going to outline is not used in the original sense as proposed by Wald, i.e., not observation-a priori, but observation-a posteriori. The two deontic principles are defined and distinguished from each other in the following way:

We first consider the case of direct choice of a proposition. The inductive behaviour is here directed to the acceptance of a hypothesis.

Let Ω be the space of true hypotheses with the elements θ, and $\tilde{\Omega}$ the space of accepted hypotheses with the elements $\tilde{\theta}$. A utility function u is given which maps the Cartesian product of Ω and $\tilde{\Omega}$ into the real numbers, i.e., $u : \Omega \times \tilde{\Omega} \to \mathbb{R}$. θ is considered as parameter (or parameter vector) of an observable random variable X whose realizations (actual observations) x originate from an event space $\mathfrak{X}$. A density function $f(x; \theta)$, $x \in \mathfrak{X}$, fixed $\theta \in \Omega$, is given on $\mathfrak{X}$; $f(x; \theta)\,dx$ is the probability element.

A. BASIC DEONTIC PRINCIPLES – DIRECT CHOICE OF PROPOSITION

observation – a priori (without empirical evidence)	observation – a posteriori (with empirical evidence)

1. Utility expectation

| (1a) $U(\tilde{\theta}) = \displaystyle\int_{\Omega} u(\theta, \tilde{\theta})\,\lambda(\theta)\,d\theta$

 where
 $\lambda(\theta) =$ a priori distribution | (1b) $U(\tilde{\theta} \mid x) = \displaystyle\int_{\Omega} u(\theta, \tilde{\theta})\,\Phi(\theta \mid x)\,d\theta$

 where
 $\Phi(\theta \mid x) =$ inference measure, e.g., fiducial density |

2. Bernoulli rules

classical Bernoulli rule	*observation-optimal Bernoulli rule*
Accept $\tilde{\theta}_0 \in \tilde{\Omega}$ for which (2a) $U(\tilde{\theta}_0) = \sup\limits_{\tilde{\theta} \in \tilde{\Omega}} U(\tilde{\theta})$	Accept $\tilde{\theta}^* \in \tilde{\Omega}$ for which (2b) $U(\tilde{\theta}^* \mid x) = \sup\limits_{\tilde{\theta} \in \tilde{\Omega}} U(\tilde{\theta} \mid x)$

A decision function δ is a mapping of the observation space $\mathfrak{X}$ into the space $\tilde{\Omega}$ of accepted hypotheses, viz.,

$$\delta : \mathfrak{X} \to \tilde{\Omega}.$$

The space of δ is D, the set of admissible (deterministic) decision functions. If the inductive behaviour is not directed to the immediate choice of a proposition, but to the choice of a decision function, i.e., an 'if – then-rule' of the kind: 'If x is observed, then choose $\tilde{\theta}$', then the deontic scheme A reduces to the following one:

B. BASIC DEONTIC PRINCIPLES – CHOICE OF A DECISION FUNCTION

observation – a priori (without empirical evidence)	observation – a posteriori (with empirical evidence)

1. Utility expectation

$$(3) \quad U(\delta, \theta) = \int_{\mathfrak{x}} u(\tilde{\theta}_{\delta(x)}, \theta) f(x; \theta) \, \mathrm{d}x$$

where $\tilde{\theta}_{\delta(x)}$ is the proposition chosen according to the decision function δ and the observation x.

2. Wald optimality rules

(4a) *Bayes criterion*	(4b) *Minimax criterion*
Choose $\delta_0 \in D$ for which	Choose $\delta^* \in D$ for which
$\displaystyle \int_\Omega U(\delta_0, \theta) \lambda(\theta) \, \mathrm{d}\theta$	$\displaystyle \inf_{\theta \in \Omega} U(\delta^*, \theta)$
$\displaystyle = \sup_{\delta \in D} \int_\Omega U(\delta, \theta) \lambda(\theta) \, \mathrm{d}\theta$	$\displaystyle = \sup_{\delta \in D} \inf_{\theta \in \Omega} U(\delta, \theta)$

3. Acceptance rules

Put the observed x into the decision function δ_0, accept $\tilde{\theta}_a = \delta_0(x)$.	Put the observed x into the decision function δ^*, accept $\tilde{\theta}_b = \delta^*(x)$.

With the exception of the observation-optimal Bernoulli rule, which is new (Menges and Diehl, 1969), the deontic rules listed above correspond to the basic types of strong decision criteria most frequently used in statistical decision theory (Menges, 1963, 1964).

The list can be continued by admitting modifications of these basic types (Hurwicz, 1951; Niehans, 1948; Savage, 1951; Hodges-Lehmann,

1952; Menges, 1963; Schneeweiß, 1964), by including weak criteria, and by considering the so-called collective decision rules. In fact, statistical decision theory provides a rich collection of deontic rules.

In order to enable a reasonable selection from this stock, it is recommendable to set up deontic meta-rules. And if the concept of expected utility is considered as fundamental, then from the standpoint of an objective theory of inductive behaviour, in particular of the etiality principle, the following three deontic meta-rules appear to be reasonable and important.

1st meta-rule: Expected utility is a conditional expected value dependent on the observation, i.e., given a utility function, the expected utility is different for different observations (for different empirical evidence). This meta-rule is important as a manifestation of the deontic rules' dependence on empirical evidence.

2nd meta-rule: Expected utility is based upon a confirmation measure. This meta-rule which is closely connected with the first one is important in order to manifest the deontic rules' dependence on the degree of confirmation of the respective hypothesis.

3rd meta-rule: The hypothesis accepted in the light of a deontic rule is independent of the a priori knowledge in terms of the a priori distribution over the hypothesis space, in any case insofar as this a priori knowledge is not objective. (Under certain circumstances, however, it depends on a certain background knowledge, e.g., the background knowledge expressed in the form of the density function over the observation space.) This meta-rule is important in order to guarantee the independence of inductive behaviour on subjective prejudice or dubious a priori knowledge.

Only one of the above-mentioned basic types of deontic rules complies with all three meta-rules, namely just the rule ((1b), (2b)), called the observation-optimal Bernoulli-rule. It is therefore more than any other of the above neo-utilitarian rules suited to play the central role as deontic rule within the framework of an objective theory of inductive behaviour.

This theory is not yet completed, however, it is open for further rules to be included, even for non-neo-utilitarian ones, and particularly for collective decision rules and for ethical principles. The inclusion of collective and ethical principles – with maintenance of the etiality prin-

ciple and the other elements of an objective theory of inductive behaviour – may require an enlargement of the list of meta-rules.

3. PREDECISION ABOUT THE LANGUAGE

The deontic rules and meta-rules presented here already indicate another
meta-theoretical predecision, namely, that on the language used. In this
contribution, preference is given to the richest and yet ontologically
neutral language, viz., the set-theoretical language based upon the
structure concept. One disadvantage of this predecision is obvious: It
implies linguistic departure from Carnap's theory which is formalized
in first-stage predicate logic, and hence renunciation of the lucidity
of the formal language of Carnap's system. Besides, no model theory
does yet exist for set-theoretical languages. This, however, is not too
great a disadvantage, since we are dealing only with empirical models
which are based upon the structure concept and are empirically interpreted through structural data (Leinfellner, 1965). While the pure
structure is defined axiomatically, through a structure-oriented set
theory in the sense of Bourbaki, its empirical interpretation requires
special consideration of individual structural data which are relevant
to the decision maker (cp. especially Section 5).

The disadvantage mentioned above is made up for by the advantage
of general applicability. The customary mathematical symbols and
operators can be applied more easily. And besides, we may draw upon
infinitesimal calculus and measure theory only with respect to the
theoretical nub.

The departure from Carnap's strict predicate-logical language appears
also necessary in order to be able to establish the connection between
Carnap and inferential statistics, predominantly in the sense of R. A.
Fisher. What I am trying here is the reconstruction of Carnap's inductive logic in terms of set theory and its connection with the etiality
principle and inferential statistics, on the one hand, and the idea of
decision, on the other.

4. INDUCTIVE LOGIC

While deductive logic traces its history back to the ancient days of

Aristotele, inductive logic is an achievement of the past 4 decades, although, of course, the problem of induction is a very old one. This recent development of inductive logic is inalienably connected with the name of Rudolf Carnap, who was the first to develop a system of inductive logic within the framework of a well-defined language. The most important notions of inductive logic are due to him, and all recent contributions are more or less based on his works. Carnap's logic, on the other hand, is certainly not the only possible, and perhaps not even the most convenient, inductive logic. His view, to which I would subscribe in the essential parts, can be summarized in three theses (e.g., Carnap and Stegmüller, 1959):

(1) Inductive logic is probability logic, i.e., inductive inference is always reasoning by means of probabilities.

(2) Probability (as the basic concept of inductive logic) measures the degree of confirmation of a hypothesis on the basis of given premises, the premises appearing as data. Therefore, all theorems of inductive logic are analytical. To Carnap, probability, as the basic concept of inductive logic, is a purely logical relation between propositions. By our predecision about the language (cp. Section 3) we cannot, of course, take over this strict version. To us, probability, as the basic concept of inductive logic, is a so-called inverse probability (cp. Section 11).

(3) Other probability concepts cannot serve as basic concepts of inductive logic; the concept of subjective probability e.g., is as little useful in this respect as the concept of frequency.

From this fundamental conception some characteristic difficulties arise which will be pointed out later on. One basic difficulty is the following: Although Carnap's inductive logic is neither concerned with the solution of practical problems nor with methodological problems, but with purely logical problems, and although one has not yet succeeded in establishing the link between inductive logic and inferential statistics, this kind of logic is nonetheless to be drawn upon when the degree of confirmation of hypotheses comes to be judged, or rules of statistical inference are to be set up, it is even to be drawn upon as a 'rule of life'.

The fundamental conception of inductive logic in the sense of Carnap may be demonstrated by a little example:

(a) The premise is formed of two data propositions, called e:

'This packet P contains 52 playing cards, 13 of which are hearts' (first data proposition).
'This card X stems from the packet P' (second data proposition).

(b) The hypothesis h:
'X is hearts' (conclusion).

(c) The degree of confirmation c of the hypothesis h, given the premise e, is

$$c(h \mid e) = r = \text{(in the example)} \ \tfrac{13}{52} = \tfrac{1}{4} \ \text{(in a definite language)},$$

upon the condition that no further evidence of the kind e with respect to the hypothesis h is available.

h as well as e are analytical propositions of a definite object language; $c(h \mid e) = r$ is an analytical proposition of a definite meta-language. $r(r \in [0, 1])$ is called the 'quantitative explicative' of the degree of confirmation, i.e., a 'probability$_1$' in the sense of Carnap, namely, an a priori probability$_1$ which, for the sake of symmetry, a priori assigns identically the same probability measure to all non-contradictory propositions of the language system.

The example shows the strong connection between the propositions of inductive logic and their interpretation; to Carnap, inductive logic is semantics. This example also raises a number of questions, e.g., with respect to the nature of the object language, the numerical determination of the probability$_1$, and the incorporation of further evidence of the kind e with respect to h, a.s.o.

Answers to all these questions cannot be provided by the logic itself (neither the inductive nor the deductive logic). These questions must rather be answered by way of meta-decisions (Leinfellner, 1968) or 'prejudgements' (Hasenjäger, 1962) or 'predecisions' (Menges, 1965).

Of all objections against Carnap's system, the 'new riddle of induction' or Goodman's paradox (1955) has been most discussed.

It purports the following: On the one hand, it follows from Carnap's system of axioms that if a predicate F holds for all objects $a_1, \ldots, a_n$ so far considered, then the proposition that F holds also for the next object a_{n+1} is more confirmed than the proposition that F does not hold for a_{n+1}:

(1) $\qquad c\left(F(a_{n+1}) \mid \bigwedge_{i=1}^{n} F(a_i)\right) > c\left(\neg\, F(a_{n+1}) \mid \bigwedge_{i=1}^{n} F(a_i)\right).$

On the other hand, Goodman has shown that for every predicate $F(x)$, there exists a predicate $F'(x)$ such that

$\qquad F(a_i) = F'(a_i) \quad$ for all $\quad i \leqslant n$

(2) $\qquad F(a_i) = \neg\, F'(a_i) \quad$ for all $\quad i > n, \quad$ for any $\quad n \geqslant 1.$

Hence

(3) $\qquad c\left(F(a_{n+1}) \mid \bigwedge_{i=1}^{n} F(a_i)\right) = c\left(\neg F'(a_{n+1}) \mid \bigwedge_{i=1}^{n} F'(a_i)\right)$

$\qquad\qquad > c\left(\neg F(a_{n+1}) \mid \bigwedge_{i=1}^{n} F(a_i)\right) = c\left(F'(a_{n+1}) \mid \bigwedge_{i=1}^{n} F'(a_i)\right).$

According to (1), however, it holds that

(4) $\qquad c\left(F'(a_{n+1}) \mid \bigwedge_{i=1}^{n} F'(a_i)\right) > c\left(\neg F'(a_{n+1}) \mid \bigwedge_{i=1}^{n} F'(a_i)\right).$

Consequently, the conclusions (3) and (4) are contradictory with respect to Carnap's system.

Goodman's paradox disappears when the a_i may be considered as independent repetitions of the same experiment and if (1) holds only for predicates whose propositions $F(a_i)$ relate to exchangeable events. If $F(a_i)$ and $F'(a_i)$ are exchangeable in this sense, then (3) and (4) are no longer contradictory. This was recently shown by Kutschera (1972, I, pp. 140ff); cp. also Hempel (1960).

In the following we shall obtain exactly this exchangeability condition, by the etiality principle, and we shall thus evade Goodman's paradox within our system.

5. INDUCTIVE AND DEDUCTIVE LOGIC

By deductive logic we understand determined systems of formal languages, principally in the form of propositional logic, syllogistics, and predicate logic. Deductive logic is aptly compared to an EDP-plant where the symbols are transformed according to certain rules, in-dependently of the meaning which these symbols have.

Inductive logic cannot be subordinated to deductive logic, but de-ductive logic, on the other hand, is prerequisite to inductive logic. The latter is developed from the former – according to Carnap – "by addition of the confirmation function c". Carnap goes so far as to interpret deductive logic as "L-semantics" where the L placed ahead means that the respective concept or proposition holds for purely logical reasons. L-semantics is the meaning of a proposition by purely deductive-logical reasons.

The effectivity problem applies to the objective theory of inductive behaviour presented here as well as to Carnap's system, i.e., to semantics as well as to L-semantics (deductive logic) in the sense of Carnap, namely, for none of them there exists an effective procedure [1]. However, the prob-lem of verification due to this lack is quite differently put according as an L-implication $e \supset h$ itself or the proof of an L-implication $b(e \supset h)$ is to be checked.

	L-implication	proof of the L-implication
deductive logic	$e \supset h$ not effective	$b(e \supset h)$ practically effective in the object language
inductive logic	$c(h \mid e) = r$ not effective	$b(c(h \mid e) = r)$ practically effective in the meta-language

This means in particular that the truth of $b(c(h \mid e) = r)$ can at best be checked by means of a meta-language, and that the verification is not rigorously, but only 'practically' [2] or scientifically effective. I think it has been important to mention this in order to show that in this respect there is no difference between Carnap's theory and ours.

The only difference is with $b(e \supset h)$, which in our theory is effective not in the object language, but only in the meta-language (practically), as a consequence of the different language systems (Section 3).

For the rest, inductive logic generally proceeds similarly to deductive logic. There is no difference, in particular, in the proof procedure (proofs of inductive logic are equally made deductively). The deductive relations of deducibility and of incompatibility of propositions in inductive logic are the two limit cases of probability$_1$ (inverse probability, respectively):

$$\text{deducibility:} \quad c(h \mid e) = 1$$
$$\text{incompatibility:} \quad c(h \mid e) = 0.$$

Practical and methodological applications of inductive logic are equally analogous to those of deductive logic, with one important exception: While in deductive logic, we can deduce the truth of h from the truth of e, we cannot deduce anything in inductive logic, from the truth of e; in particular, the truth of e neither influences the confirmation function nor the 'inverse probability' in the sense of statistical inference.

An important difference between our system and that of Carnap is the fact that we make explicit use of the utility concept, as a fundamental concept of our system (Section 2), and that we take account of deontically justified behaviour.

The language system of logic is comparable to a town with different kinds of streets (major roads, one-way streets, dead-end streets, a.s.o.), where deductive logic determines which streets with which properties are admitted for different kinds of traffic. In this example, inductive logic is comparable to the additional judgment on the question whether a given distance covered by some vehicle has been allowed (and if so, to which degree). Logic alone, however, cannot make any statement where to go in a given case, or whether it is reasonable or useful to take a definite way. It cannot even indicate where definite ways begin and where they end. All these questions can only be decided upon by an objective theory of inductive *behaviour*. Nevertheless, inductive logic is not useless (not even when the language system, as is frequently the case with inductive problems, represents a colloquial meta-language).

Carnap and Stegmüller (1959, p. 95) see a theoretical and a practical worth in spite of this. The theoretical worth is seen with respect to the foundation of statistics[3], and the practical worth with respect to statistical decision theory.[4] I believe that this is putting the cart before the horse. I shall in the following try to maintain and to justify my reverse thesis that inductive logic and with it deductive logic, are but aids for rational decision-finding; and thus subordinate themselves to inductive behaviour.

6. INDUCTIVE LOGIC AND PROBABILITY

Besides the concept of probability$_1$ (W_1), as the 'quantitative explicative' of the degree of confirmation, Carnap distinguishes the concept of probability$_2$ (W_2). The object of W_1 is a relation between the hypothesis and empirical data. W_1 is a measure of the degree to which the empirical data substantiate or confirm the hypothesis or make it more plausible. W_2, on the other hand, is a 'physical' property of empirical objects; the consequence or symptom of this property is relative frequency. W_2 (contrary to W_1) is physically interpretable and verifiable, e.g., by experiments. The frequency concept of probability (Reichenbach and v.Mises) is insofar related to W_2. However, W_2 is of no use as a basis for inductive logic. It is quite analogous for a theory of inductive behaviour.

Two other statements by Carnap find my full support:

(1) The axiomatization of the (objective as well as subjective) probability concept does not add anything to the explication of probability.[5]

(2) Real validity of probability statements cannot be established by inductive logic.[6]

Although in many essential points I share Carnap's view, I wish to make some additional remarks which, I believe[7], can help to overcome some of the deficiencies of Carnap's conception.

In my view, the concept of probability is in four different ways the object of scientific recognition:

(a)   by an epistemological foundation by which the real validity of synthetic probability statements (statements in the sense of Carnap's probability$_2$) is established (Section 7),

(b)   by axiomatizations of the probability concept, which in spite of their ontological neutrality (Kolmogoroff, 1933) are indispensable for the mathematical treatment of probability theory (Section 8),

(c)   by the definition and numerical determination of probability$_2$ in the sense of Carnap (Section 9),

(d)   as 'numerical explicative of the degree of confirmation' (probability$_1$ in the sense of Carnap) or as 'inverse probability' or inference measure (Sections 10 and 11).

7. The etiality principle

I recently made an attempt to outline the necessity of epistemological foundation of probability and the role which the etiality principle (Hartwig, 1956) plays in it (Menges, 1970), hence the following suggestions may suffice here: The etiality principle should be 'obligatory' – by analogy with causality in deterministic processes – i.e., it should be taken as the transcendental prerequisite of our conception of reality in order to enable a well-ordered experience even in those cases where the causality principle fails, due to the complexity of the causal relationships and the indetermined, but stochastic, sequence of cause and effect.

Etiality is the principle which links *general causes* with a set of possible effects, i.e., a general cause does not, like the 'causa', produce a unique consequence with certainty, but possible consequences with definite weights, e.g., probabilities (cp. the contribution by Menges and Skala in this volume, in particular Sections 2 and 3).

I shall illustrate some of my ideas concerning the etiality principle by an example.

Until a few years ago I possessed a Fiat 2300 whose old age weakness consisted in frequent starting failures. Very often curious and pitiful contemporaries assembled around my car. A type *A* of spectators, I call them the pure practicians, began without much ceremony to give the car a swing. In most cases they were successful, i.e., the motor started up. A type *B* of spectators, I call them the subjective theorists, gave advice based upon hypotheses which they believed to be true, e.g., to charge the battery, or to dry the distributor, a.s.o. Sometimes their advice was a success, frequently not. After I spent a lot of money in vain for the removal of presumed defects, some day a mechanic (type *C*) in a small repair shop, after listening to my story, had a new hypothesis and found out that the starter pinion was broken. He replaced it, and I had no longer a starting problem.

What does the example tell us? First, the practical man of type *A* solves a given problem by action (giving the car a swing). Of course, he has some vague idea on the inherent etiality mechanism, but his endeavour is not directed to its recognition, i.e., he does not want to find out the causes ('truth'), but he wants performance and optimal behaviour ('usefulness'). This duality between the recognition of truth and usefulness will be discussed below (see Sections 12 to 14).

Second, the practical man of type *B* solves a problem by setting up plausible hypotheses, i.e., hypotheses which in the past often led to performance and optimal behaviour, without empirically verifying them. He dries the distributor and charges the battery, and the success will often prove him to be right. This type corresponds to the modern decision theorist who has largely abandoned the classical scientific principle 'knowledge of the cause→action' and replaced it by the principle of immediate action. To him, epistemological foundation of probability appears dispensable. In the long run, however, his behaviour (same as type *A*'s behaviour) becomes more and more unrational, and that the more quickly the more people act like him. If all people acted according to this principle, civilization would soon end up in blind actionism.

In the long run the decision theorist is bound to follow the classical scientist's example, namely, try to recognize the (etial) causes. Etial recognition, however, is penetration into the objective matter and relationships.

Type *C* sets up hypotheses on actual circumstances and judges them in the light of objective findings. He tries to list the possible effects of an etial complex and to attach weights (probabilities) to them. The etial complex, 'distributor is wet' has a possible consequence 'motor does not start up' with high probability. However, as the consequence 'motor does not start up' because of 'distributor being wet', in spite of correspondingly high inverse probability, has been frequently disproved by empirical evidence, he will introduce another etial complex, which has not yet been empirically disproved, and will found a quite new hypothesis upon it. This is an intuitive, creative, subjective approach, i.e., the mechanic had to activate his intuition and fantasy in order to come to an altogether new hypothesis (starter pinion is broken). He found the hypothesis physically (a priori) confirmed, i.e., the starter pinion was actually broken. The physical a priori confirmation of the hypothesis was not sufficient, after all, as it could be that the broken starter pinion was not or not the only etial cause of the motor's failure to start up. Therefore, after replacing the starter pinion he made the motor some dozens of times start up, then let it cool down, and repeated the experiment a few times. Apart from two or three times (presumably (!) due to an excess of gas in the motor after so many starts) the motor did every time start up. Thus the hypothesis 'broken starter pinion was the cause (more exactly: an essential cause) of non-starting' was empirically confirmed.

The etiality principle preserves scientific recognition especially in those cases where the deterministic borderland case of the 'causal principle' fails. It allows to weaken the pure causality idea without recurring to mere ('blind') chance as trivial explanation.

Etiality is a fundamental concept within the theory here presented. In the sense of the considerations in Section 3, it is only be etiality that we may speak of structures, because only etiality links phenomena (objects) to ordered systems.

The etiality principle allows to interpret the world as a network of logically and empirically possible relationships. In a given case we do not isolate an individual cause, as in the case of strict causality, but a complex of causes with a plurality of logically and empirically possible effects which fall true more or less 'easily'. This 'easiness' of realization of a certain effect is characterized by an indicator (weight, predictor, or probability – in the classical sense). The verification of the etial sequence and the confirmation of the indicator is in principle feasible by experiments. In this particular point, etiality is related to causality where the verification of a sequence is equally possible by experiments.

In the following I shall try to formalize the idea of etiality in accordance with Carnap.

Assuming that

(1)   the range of individuals consists of countably many objects: I (Ind), with

(2) n modalities: $I(\mathfrak{I})=n$,

(3)   each of which is decomposed into a family of attributes: $I(F^m)$ enumerating the attributes for every $m \in I(\mathfrak{I})$

the following definitions may be given:

1st definition: In accordance with Carnap, a model component of the family F^m is understood to be a mapping assigning one and only one attribute index from the mth attribute family to each individual index. Z^m denotes the class of all model components of F^m.

2nd definition: By a model $Z \in \mathfrak{Z}$ we mean an n-tuple of model components.

Roughly speaking, a model is the description of a possible etial environment, when (1), (2), and (3) are given. Sometimes it may be necessary to work with 'vague' descriptions of the etial environment. (Cp. the contribution by Menges and Skala in this volume.)

3rd definition: An etial complex $\mathfrak{K}$ fixes (1), (2), and (3), and hence Z. $\mathfrak{K}$ thus associates (1), (2), and (3) with a 'well-defined' class of causes. The property of being well-defined is certainly not to be understood in the sense that all individual causes can be listed and specified. The class of causes is rather an idealized construction.

Looking for an indicator of the 'easiness' of realization of possible environments we find probability to be a particularly convenient instrument. We therefore choose Z as the set of elementary events. Looking for a convenient field or σ-field respectively, over Z, we find a quite natural solution which Carnap had in mind when defining the concept of probability with respect to all propositions which themselves are considered as sets of models.

4th definition:

(a) For every triplet $\langle m, i, j \rangle$, $m \in I(\mathfrak{F})$, $i \in I(\mathrm{Ind})$, $j = I(F^m)$, the atomic proposition $P_j^m a_i$ is defined as follows:

$$P_j^m a_i = \{Z \in \mathfrak{Z} : Z(m, i) = j\}.$$

$Z(m, i) = j$ is to denote the fact that the jth attribute from the mth attribute family is associated with the ith individual.

(b) The class of propositions $\mathfrak{C}_{m, i}^{at}$ belonging to the pair $\langle m, i \rangle$ is defined as follows:

$$\mathfrak{C}_{m, i}^{at} = \{P_j^m a_i : j \in I(F^m)\}.$$

(c) The class of all atomic propositions $\mathfrak{C}^{at}$ is defined by

$$\mathfrak{C}^{at} = \bigcup \{\mathfrak{C}_{m, i}^{at} : i \in I(\mathrm{Ind}), m \in I(\mathfrak{F})\}.$$

As a convenient field or σ-field, respectively, over $\mathfrak{Z}$ we may take the field or σ-field, respectively, generated by $\mathfrak{C}^{at}$. Carnap, as is well-known, identified the class of molecular propositions or propositions, respectively, with the field or σ-field, respectively, over $\mathfrak{Z}$ generated by $\mathfrak{C}^{at}$.

If, in the light of empirical evidence, we can additionally indicate a linear ordering on the elements of the σ-field or field, respectively, then the indicator problem consists in specifying a probability measure which also represents the given linear ordering. (On the indicator problem, cf. Villegas (1964), Scott (1964), and the contribution by H. J. Skala in this volume.) $a \succ b$ then denotes the fact that we have sufficient reasons to consider the (molecular) proposition a 'more probable' than b.

8. AXIOMATIZATIONS

If we consider the weighting and predictor system in the framework of etiality as probability system in the classical sense and follow Kolmogoroff's (1933) axiomatic construction, then the triplet $(\Re, \mathfrak{S}, \mathfrak{M}_\mathfrak{S})$ is the 'event space' under consideration. Every element of $\mathfrak{S}$ is a (random) event in the classical sense with respect to $\Re$. We can identify the sample space Z with $\Re$, $\mathfrak{S}$ denoting a field or σ-field, respectively, and $\mathfrak{M}_\mathfrak{S}$ denoting a measure on it. A probability measure $\mathfrak{M}_\mathfrak{S}$ is then a mapping

$$\mathfrak{M}_\mathfrak{S} : \mathfrak{S} \to \mathbb{R}$$

with the properties
(1) From $A, B \in \mathfrak{S}$ with $A \cap B = \emptyset$ follows

$$\mathfrak{M}_\mathfrak{S}(A \cap B) = \mathfrak{M}_\mathfrak{S}(A) + \mathfrak{M}_\mathfrak{S}(B).$$

(2) For any $A \in \mathfrak{S}$ it holds that $\mathfrak{M}_\mathfrak{S}(A) \leqslant 1$.
(3) $\mathfrak{M}_\mathfrak{S}(\mathfrak{Z}) = 1$.
However, this does not much profit us.

One has come to realize that the largely accepted axiomatic construction of probability theory, as proposed by Kolmogoroff, is sufficient only for the a priori concept of probability (Section 9), conditionally sufficient for so-called direct conclusion, and not sufficient at all for statistical inference. I cannot enter into the complex problems here involved, but I wish to give expression to the opinion that a sufficient treatment of predictor problems is feasible only in the framework of a multi-valued logic, i.e., an infinite-valued language of the first order admitting of exact treatment of the vague concepts (Menges and Skala, 1974) $\mathfrak{S}$ and $\Re$, or also likelihood and fiducial density, and of constructions like confirmation functions and confirmation logic. By analogy with the deduction rules of classical logic, we would then have to set up the corresponding inductive rules such that it became possible to formulate non-deterministic (stochastic) theories in a corresponding system of axioms, and finally to interpret them, i.e., to establish the relationship with reality through a model. The customary probability concept and its logic would be limit cases of the generalizations, namely the limit case of direct conclusion (inclusive of prediction) in the light of known probability distribution in terms of a two-valued logic of the a priori concept (see Lukasiewicz, Tarski, 1930; Rosser, Turquette, 1952). This task must not be confounded with the epistemological foundation (etiality principle), nor with the definition and numerical determination of probability. This task is a purely formal-language or model-theoretical, respectively, ontologically neutral one, even though it is closely related with the task of finding an appropriate confirmation logic (Section 11).

9. DEFINITION AND NUMERICAL DETERMINATION OF PROBABILITY

Probability as a synthetic judgment, i.e., in the sense of Carnap's probability$_2$ can be defined in three different ways, corresponding to the method of numerical determination. There are three ways:

(i)   objectively a priori,

(ii) objectively a posteriori,

(iii) subjectively.

Concerning (i): We are dealing here with the (objective) a priori assignment of probabilities to events:

$$\mathfrak{M}_{\mathfrak{S}}(A), \quad A \in \mathfrak{S}.$$

This method has nothing to do with probability$_1$ in the sense of Carnap, although it is easily confounded with it. Probability$_1$ in the sense of Carnap or the 'presumptive probabilities' in the sense of Meinong (1915) are purely logical relations of possibility. "Throwing a coin, heads or tails can be up. The W_1 that heads is up is $\frac{1}{2}$." This proposition is analytical, it has nothing to do with reality, its confirmation by experiments is neither possible nor necessary. It is quite different for the objective a priori determination of probability$_2$:

$\mathfrak{R} = $ "This special coin – let us call it Heinrich – has been physically checked whether it is 'practically ideal', i.e., whether its mass is evenly distributed, whether it is not loaded, etc." It has been made sure that these properties of the coin Heinrich do not change in the course of the experiment. A.s.o., a.s.o. The coin Heinrich is arbitrarily thrown into the air, turns around some times a.s.o. There are two possible state descriptions (models), namely 'heads' (Z_1) and 'tails' (Z_2). The etiality proposition is: The probability of Z_1, $\mathfrak{M}_{\mathfrak{S}}(Z_1)=0.5$. This proposition is synthetic. It refers to the here and now considered coin Heinrich. The verification of the proposition by experiments is at any time possible.

Concerning (ii): This matter is somewhat more complicated. A fourth constituent is joined to $(\mathfrak{R}, \mathfrak{S}, \mathfrak{M}_{\mathfrak{S}})$: The statistical mass M of realizations of a certain event $A \in \mathfrak{S}$.

For every unit from M, it is checked in the form of which event it occurred. Suppose that $m(A)$ units of M occurred in the form of A. Then the objective a posteriori probability of A with respect to $(\mathfrak{R}, \mathfrak{S}, \mathfrak{M})$ is defined as

$$\mathfrak{M}_{\mathfrak{S}}(A \mid (\mathfrak{R}, \mathfrak{S}; M)) = \frac{m(A)}{m(M)}$$

or, by the limit definition by Richard v. Mises (1951),

$$\mathfrak{M}_{\mathfrak{S}}(A \mid (\mathfrak{R}, \mathfrak{S}; M)) = \lim_{k \to \infty} \mathfrak{M}_{\mathfrak{S}}(A \mid (\mathfrak{R}, \mathfrak{S}; M_k)),$$

where M_k is the mass of the first k realizations.

For probabilities of this type, Kolmogoroff's system of axioms is not sufficient. Although transitivity and conditionality hold for these probabilities; independence, however, does not (Menges, 1972, pp. 96f).

The method (ii) of determination of a posteriori probabilities is the classical statistical approach of inferring probabilities by experiments (observations). A coin, for example, is thrown $10\,000$ times. If 5316 times heads is up, then we can specify $\mathfrak{M}_{\mathfrak{S}}$ (heads) $=0.53$. Probability is thus defined as relative frequency or its limit in the case of an infinite number of experiments (v.Mises).

Concerning (iii): This method derives probability from the opinion, the feeling, the intuition, or the belief of a human individual. Hence we are not concerned with probabilities $\mathfrak{M}_{\mathfrak{S}}$ as such, but with functions $\pi_i(\mathfrak{M}_{\mathfrak{S}})$ of the individual i of probabilities.

In the paper (Menges, 1970), the three definitions and corresponding methods outlined above have been discussed and compared with each other. In this paper, all I want is to give a short characterization and clarification of the relationship with respect to W_1 and to the epistemo-logical and formal-language foundation. My critique is therefore con-fined to the following items:

    (a) incompatibility with the etiality principle,

    (b) limited interpersonal communicability,

    (c) influence of emotional and intellectual factors,

    (d) incapability of human individuals of distinguishing between probabilities which lie closely together,

    (e) incompatibility of human individuals of measuring their own 'dispositional belief' without technical help.

Moreover, I wish to add three remarks which are important for what follows.

1st remark: The sequence (i), (ii), and (iii) is at the same time an order of scientific foundation of the three concepts of probability, i.e., the objective a priori determination, as far as it is based upon the principle of sufficient reason (cf. remark 2) finds the clearest and logically least contestable justification. The classical instruments of probability theory, especially independence, without any restriction fit probabilities which are objective a priori in nature. 'Second-best' is the a posteriori concept which, like the a priori concept, is in conformity with the etiality principle, which also a large part of the probability theory based upon the classical Kolmogoroff-system of axioms does fit, and which – again like the a priori concept, but unlike probability$_1$ and subjective probabilities – is in principle verifiable by experiments. The a posteriori concept, however, is of less 'dignity', since, for example, the independence form-ulas do not fit it and since – more than the a priori concept – it depends upon so-called meta-hypotheses. The least scientific dignity, namely, none at all is due to the subjective or personal probability concept (Menges, 1970). The attempts of axiomatization [8] of subjective probability so far undertaken, which unquestionably are of a high mathematical standard, do not add anything to the real validity of probabilities and they are altogether unfruitful with respect to their epistemological foundation.

2nd remark: It makes a fundamental difference with respect to the further evolution of the theory here proposed whether in the numerical explication of the a priori concept $\mathfrak{M}_{\mathfrak{S}}(A \mid \mathfrak{R}, \mathfrak{S})$, the events have the identical probability (Laplace rule or numerical determination according to the principle of insufficient reason) or whether the numerical determination is such that the events have a 'just part' each in the whole probability mass 1 (Cournot rule or numerical determination according to the principle of sufficient reason).

3rd remark: Probability subjectivism is often denoted as Bayesianism. This employment of the name of Bayes may originate from three genuine or presumptive doctrines of Rev. Thomas Bayes, namely,

    (1) the subjective probability concept of Bayes,
    (2) the role of the a priori distribution in the Bayesian system,
    (3) the Bayesian theorem.

All three arguments do not appear to be sound, i.e., Bayes was not a Bayesian.

Concerning (1): As I attempted to show in the paper (Menges, 1967a) by the original work of Bayes (1763, 1958), he did not possess a subjective probability concept. The subjectivistic interpretation of the Bayesian idea is due to Laplace (1812).

Concerning (2): Of course, the a priori distribution plays a considerable role both in Bayesian probability theory and in probability subjectivism. However, as the strict probability subjectivists equally require a subjective interpretation of a posteriori distributions, there is no specific reason for calling the subjectivists Bayesians.

Concerning (3): The Bayesian theorem which transforms a priori distributions into a posteriori distributions might justify the utilization of the name of Bayes as far as the a priori distribution is subjectively generated and as far as the 'Bayesians' agree with the general postulate of a transformation of a subjective a priori distribution into an a posteriori distribution. However, since the Bayesian theorem is equally applicable to a priori distributions and since the above postulate is not accepted by many subjectivists, there is no reason even here to call the subjectivists Bayesians.

10. Notion and types of uncertainty

Before we come to the most difficult part of the problem of probability, probability$_1$ in the sense of Carnap, the concept of uncertainty needs some clarification. What is uncertain in our context, is the outcome of the realization of an event caused by the etial complex $\mathfrak{K}$. Uncertainty is also a characteristic of the relationship between an individual and its etial environment. Let the etial environment be described by pairwise disjoint states $\theta_1, \theta_2, ..., \theta_m$, which fill a space Ω. If the true state $\theta \in \Omega$ is unknown to the individual, he acts under uncertainty. We speak of total uncertainty if not even the etial weights (e.g., probabilities) are known with which the several states come true. We speak of partial uncertainty or risk if known etial weights, e.g., probabilities $p_1, ..., p_m$, are assigned to the states θ_j $(j = 1, 2, ..., m)$. The θ_j are produced by disjoint decomposition of the subject concept and can certainly be understood as realizations of a discrete random variable, but it is more profitable for the solution of complicated problems, if the θ_j are interpreted as distribution parameters of a probability distribution or density function on the space Ω. In the sequel we consider but density functions of the kind $f(x; \theta \mid \mathfrak{R}, \mathfrak{S})$, or briefly,

$$f(x; \theta_j) \quad j = 1, ..., m,$$

where the x are realizations of the events from $\mathfrak{S}$.

Another complication one must put up with, as it makes the uncertainty model more elastic with respect to applications, is the following: The θ_j are not necessarily to be considered as fixed quantities but, though still distribution parameters, as realizations of a random variable (of a higher order) which itself obeys a distribution law described by a density function

$$h(\theta; \lambda),$$

where λ is the distribution parameter of this density function. We denote $h(\theta; \lambda)$ as a priori distribution of the generalized uncertainty model. Thus, the true θ is in all cases unknown. This uncertainty can have three different reasons:

(1) Pure randomness: θ is a random variable with a priori distribution $h(\theta; \lambda)$. Although the latter is known we do not know which value $h(\theta; \lambda)$ will assume or has assumed.

(2) Lack of a priori knowledge I: The true θ is constant, but unknown.

(3) Lack of a priori knowledge II: As in the case of (1), θ is a random variable, but the a priori distribution $h(\theta; \lambda)$ is unknown; i.e., the randomness is covered by the lack of a priori knowledge on $h(\theta; \lambda)$.

As example, take again throwing a coin. In the case of uncertainty

(1) one knows the a priori distribution of throwing of the coin, viz., the binomial distribution, but one does not know in advance which side of the coin will be up. This is the situation of uncertainty considered in classical probability calculus. A physical or biological law guarantees the stability of the a priori distribution. What is uncertain, is only the actual expression which nature is going to bring about.

In the case of uncertainty (2), the coin has already been thrown. θ is a fixed quantity now, but it is unknown. It does not matter in that respect what kind of a priori law $h(\theta; \lambda)$ we are concerned with. The task of inference is to estimate the unknown true parameter θ in the light of empirical observations. As compared to case (1), this case involves a stronger form of uncertainty. The strongest form at all is involved in the uncertainty case (3), which is frequent in social sciences. Suppose a box contains several coins, some of which are arbitrarily taken and thrown. We do not know which coins have been thrown nor which will be the outcome of the throws.

11. CONFIRMATION LOGIC AND INFERENCE MEASURE

We have now made all preparations for treating the most difficult part of the problem of probability, viz., probability$_1$ in the sense of Carnap, that is, the numerical explicative of the confirmation function. This construction has met with considerable criticism, in particular from Stegmüller (1973C). His criticism is mainly directed "...against Carnap's notion of partial logical implication, and the difficulties which result from setting this notion equal to that of inductive confirmation,...". Stegmüller tries to show "...that a new approach, which starts from rational decision theory, makes any recourse to the contestable notion of partial logical conclusion unnecessary." (p. 389)

The statistical device which is best suited by its logical structure to preserve Carnap's confirmation logic and to introduce it into statistics is the likelihood function by R. A. Fisher. I share this view of the prominent role of the likelihood function for statistical confirmation logic – though differently motivated – with W. Stegmüller. However, at the same time he overestimates the differences between the Fisherian likelihood function and the confirmation logic based on it, on the one hand, and Carnap's confirmation function and the confirmation logic based on it, on the other. He finds three essential differences (Stegmüller, 1973D, pp. 15ff, esp. p. 25):

(1) Utilization of the concept of statistical data in the ... wider sense including theoretical background knowledge, in terms of accepted statistical meta-hypotheses, into the data framework.

(2) Exclusive consideration of classes of rival hypotheses, but never of isolated hypotheses.

(3) Choice of a merely comparative concept as starting point. This concept may not be described by the phrase "is more probable than", since it has not the formal structure of a probability. (p. 25)

One important difference has not been mentioned by Stegmüller: the problem of evidence. In the confirmation function, the data statement contains all evidence which is relevant for the hypothesis; in the inference measures of statistics, it includes only the findings of the respective observation.

It is true that the confirmation function by Carnap aims at non-comparative ('absolute') confirmation of hypotheses, while the inference measures of statistics (namely, standardized likelihood function, Bayesian a posteriori distribution, fiducial density function) are directed to the comparative ('relative') confirmation of hypotheses. Moreover, unlike the confirmation functions, the inference measures do not refer to a formal language, e.g., predicate logic or an axiomatized set theory, but they hold in principle universally. This general advantage is paralleled by certain shortcomings which I shall discuss individually later on.

But it is not true that the inference measures considered have not the formal structure of probabilities. Only the likelihood function, as long as it is not standardized [9], as a point function is not a fully additive measure, and hence is not a probability. However, the other measures (Bayesian a posteriori distribution, fiducial density function, and standardized likelihood function) can actually be interpreted as probabilities$_1$ in the sense of Carnap.

Of particular interest is the objection under (1) that the theoretical background knowledge is not included in the statistical data. Where this is not the case, it is by negligence. In fact, the density function $f(x; \theta)$ or, written as probability element,

$$(*) \qquad f(x; \theta) \, dx, \quad x \in \mathfrak{S}, \theta \in \Omega,$$

is to be interpreted as probability or probability function, respectively, like probability$_2$, i.e., together with the etial structure $\mathfrak{R}$, the field or σ-field $\mathfrak{S}$, and the measure function $\mathfrak{M}_{\mathfrak{S}}$. We therefore write the probability element in the following form:

$$(**) \qquad f(x; \theta \mid (\mathfrak{R}, \mathfrak{S})) \, dx.$$

This version is to be interpreted as follows: $(**)$ gives the probability of the realization $x \in \mathfrak{S}$, in terms of the etial structure $\mathfrak{R}$, where the realizations $x \in \mathfrak{S}$ fall true according to the density function dependent on the parameter θ.

$(*)$ reduces to a likelihood function, x (after the observation) adopting a fixed numerical value. We therefore write the likelihood function as

$$f^*(\theta \mid x; (\mathfrak{R}, \mathfrak{S})),$$

where besides x, the data statement proper, the terms $\theta, f^*, \mathfrak{S}$, and $\mathfrak{R}$ express the theoretic-statistical background knowledge.

This is to be remembered in all the following considerations, even if, for the sake of simplicity, we write the likelihood function as $f^*(\theta \mid x)$.

The likelihood function is predestined for the special role as statistical confirmation measure, in particular by its linkage to the background knowledge $(\theta, f^*, \mathfrak{R}, \mathfrak{S})$. Besides this, it has numerous helpful properties (besides the shortcoming of being a point function), which have been investigated by Diehl and Sprott (1965) and Sprott (1965).

R. A. Fisher (1922, 1925, 1934, 1946, 1956) always emphasized the likelihood function as an important inference measure because, if there is no background knowledge on the a priori probabilities available or acceptable, the *only* known relationship between the data statement x and the existing background knowledge (f, $\mathfrak{R}$, and $\mathfrak{S}$) is just the likelihood function.

As an example, consider the following situation (cp. Sprott, 1965, p. 99): With $\mathfrak{R}$ and $\mathfrak{S}$, the density functions $f_i(x_i; \theta \mid \mathfrak{R}, \mathfrak{S})$ of the observations $x_1, \ldots, x_n$, are known in particular

$$\bigwedge_{i=1}^{n} f_i(x_i; \theta) = \theta \exp(-x_i \theta).$$

Given independence between the x_i (another piece of background knowledge), the joint density function of the observational vector $x=(x_1, x_2, \ldots, x_n)$ is

$$f(x; \theta)=\theta^n \exp \left(-\theta \sum_{i=1}^{n} x_i\right).$$

Given the hypothesis θ_0, the probability of the observation (sample) is proportional to $\theta_0^n \exp(-\theta_0 X)$; $(X=\sum_{i=1}^{n} x_i)$, and given an alternative hypothesis θ_1, it is proportional to $\theta_1^n \exp(-\theta_1 X)$. A comparative measure is provided by the likelihood ratio

$$R(\theta_0/\theta_1)=f^*(\theta_0 \mid x)/f^*(\theta_1 \mid x)$$
$$R(\theta_0/\theta_1)=(\theta_0/\theta_1)^n \exp(-X(\theta_0-\theta_1)),$$

which indicates *how much more plausible, in the light of the observation, the hypothesis θ_0 is, as against θ_1.* Assume, e.g., $n=1$, $x=1$, and hence $X=1$, $\theta_0=3$, $\theta_1=8$, then

$$R(\theta_0/\theta_1)=(\tfrac{3}{8})^1 \exp(-1(3-8))=\tfrac{3}{8} \exp(5)=55.655,$$

i.e., the observation $x=1$ is about 56 times more probable (frequentist interpretation) under the hypothesis θ_0 than under the hypothesis θ_1, and correspondingly, in the light of the observation x, the hypothesis θ_0 is about 56 times more plausible and consequently about 56 times more confirmed than the hypothesis θ_1 (confirmation measure).

The difference between these two interpretations (frequency versus confirmation measure, and correspondingly, $f(x; \theta)$ versus $f(\theta^* \mid x)$) can be illustrated geometrically as follows:

Let $\mathfrak{S}$ be the sample space of x, and Ω the parameter space of θ, then $f(x; \theta)$ is defined over the real product space $\mathfrak{S} \times \Omega$. For fixed $\theta \in \Omega$, $f(x; \theta)$ is a ˘density function (probability distribution, respectively) over $\mathfrak{S}$.

Before the observation, i.e., when $x \in \mathfrak{S}$ is still unknown, the density function $f(x; \theta_0)$ belonging to the hypothesis θ_0 is obtained by intersecting the plane (or hyperplane, respectively) $\theta=\theta_0$ in the product space $\mathfrak{S} \times \Omega \times \mathbb{R}$ ($\mathbb{R}=$set of real numbers) with the graph of $f(x; \theta)$ and projecting the intersection graph on $\mathfrak{S} \times \mathbb{R}$. The projection is $f(x; \theta_0)$ over $\mathfrak{S}$.

After the observation x_0, i.e., when $x_0 \in \mathfrak{S}$ is known and θ has the logical status of a random variable, the plane (or hyperplane, respectively) $x = x_0$ is intersecting the $f(x; \theta)$ mountain, and the intersection graph is projected on $\Omega \times \mathbb{R}$. The projection is now the likelihood function $f^*(\theta \mid x_0)$ over Ω.

Hence, the main advantages of the likelihood function as a confirmation measure are

universality of application,

frequentist interpretability,

unique linkage to the etial and other background knowledge.

Moreover, its qualification as confirmation measure can be justified by the following four properties:

A_1 *(implication axiom):* From $\theta_1 \Vdash \theta_2$ $(\theta_1, \theta_2 \in \Omega)$ follows

$$f^*(\theta_1 \mid x) \leqslant f^*(\theta_2 \mid x),[10]$$

i.e., for a hypothesis θ_1 which is not stronger than θ_2, the likelihood is at most as large as for θ_2.

A_2 *(conjunction axiom):* From $x \Vdash \theta_2$ follows:

$$f^*(\theta_1 \mid x) \leqslant f^*((\theta_1 \wedge \theta_2) \mid x); \quad \theta_1, \theta_2 \in \Omega,$$

i.e., the likelihood is not reduced, if the hypothesis θ_1 is $\wedge$-linked with a hypothesis θ_2 which occurs simultaneously with x.

A_3 *(transitivity axiom):* From $f^*(\theta_1 \mid x_1) \leqslant f^*(\theta_2 \mid x_2)$ and $f^*(\theta_2 \mid x_2)$ $\leqslant f^*(\theta_3 \mid x_3)$, with $\theta_1, \theta_2, \theta_3 \in \Omega$ and $x_1, x_2, x_3 \in \mathfrak{S}$, follows:

$$f^*(\theta_1 \mid x_1) \leqslant f^*(\theta_3 \mid x_3).$$

This axiom is self-evident.

A_4 *(maximum axiom):* For all $\theta \in \Omega$ and all $x \in \mathfrak{S}$ and an arbitrarily chosen $\theta^* \in \Omega$,

$$f^*(\theta \mid x) \leqslant f^*(\theta^* \mid \theta^*)$$

holds, i.e., the likelihood of a hypothesis confirming itself is a 'maximum', more exactly, never smaller than the likelihood for any other hypothesis, given any observation.

However important and universal the likelihood function may be as a confirmation measure, it is not the only statistical instrument by which hypotheses can be evaluated. Other instruments, which we shall now consider and associate with the uncertainty situations of Section 10, are the Bayesian a posteriori distribution and Fisher's fiducial density.

Structural probability as proposed by Fraser [11] is not further investigated here.

The strongest inference philosophy, namely, Bayesian method of determination of a posteriori probabilities, fits the weakest uncertainty situation, namely case (1) (cp. Section 10):

$$\pi(\theta \mid x) = \frac{f(x;\theta)*g(\theta;\lambda)}{\displaystyle\int_{\Omega} f(x;\theta)*g(\theta;\lambda)\, d\theta}, \quad \theta \in \Omega.$$

The function $f(x;\theta)$ is here no longer a density function in the usual sense, since x is fixed, namely, an observed quantity, and θ is unknown, but a likelihood function. $\pi(\theta \mid x)$ is the Bayesian a posteriori distribution. It differs from a confirmation function in the sense of Carnap with respect to the following four properties:

First, it is not explicitly related to a definite formal object language. This shortcoming, however, is easily removed.

Second, it is primarily a comparative measure, i.e., $\pi(\theta \mid x)$ is to be understood comparatively:

From $\pi(\theta_1 \mid x) > \pi(\theta_2 \mid x)$; with $\theta_1, \theta_2 \in \Omega$, it follows that the hypothesis θ_1 under the data statement x is *more* confirmed than the hypothesis θ_2 under the data statement x, while Carnap's c-function is devised as an absolute measure of confirmation. This property is no deficiency, after all, since probabilities of the kind $\pi(\theta \mid x)$ are fully additive measures, i.e., $\pi(\theta \mid x)$ is a set function, and hence absolute (non-comparative) confirmations are altogether possible. Kolmogoroff's system of axioms in principle fits $\pi(\theta \mid x)$.

Third, the presumably most important difference, however, is the one that in the c-function $c(h \mid e)$ the data statement e shall include *all evidence*. This total evidence principle is certainly not given with the statistical measures of inference.

The practical shortcoming of the determination of probabilities of the kind $\pi(\theta \mid x)$ is the fact that besides the background knowledge on the functional form of $f(x;\theta)$, we need background knowledge in terms of the a priori distribution $g(\theta;\lambda)$. For the practically frequent case that this background knowledge does not exist, Fisher (1930) has proposed the *fiducial method* which is independent of background knowledge of this kind.

On the basis of an observation sample $x \in \mathfrak{S}$, which is transformed into a fixed statistic $T = T(x)$, and in the light of background knowledge on the joint distribution function $F(x, \theta \mid \mathfrak{R}, \mathfrak{S})$, a distribution over Ω is to be found where again (as in the case of the likelihood function) θ is considered to have the logical status of a random variable. The fiducial distribution is obtained in the following way:

Between the parameter space Ω and the event space $\mathfrak{S}$ there is a relationship in terms of the joint distribution function $F(T, \theta)$.

$F(T, \theta \mid \mathfrak{R}, \mathfrak{S})$ must satisfy the following conditions:

(1) T is sufficient with respect to θ.
(2) T and θ are continuous over the same range of values (the discrete case is thus excluded).
(3)   A pivotal quantity exists and is monotone in T and θ.
(4) F is an isotone function of T and decreasing function of θ.

Upon these assumptions we can write the total differential which, according to (2) does exist:

$$dF(T, \theta) = \frac{\partial F(T, \theta)}{\partial T}\, dT + \frac{\partial F(T, \theta)}{\partial \theta}\, d\theta.$$

This total differential admits of frequency interpretation as well as of an interpretation as confirmation measure.

Before the observation, θ is constant and hence $d\theta = 0$; consequently

$$dF(T, \theta) = \frac{\partial F(T, \theta)}{\partial T}\, dT.$$

This term is the frequentist part, indicating the probability density of T, given the hypothesis θ, e.g., for $\theta_0 : dF(T, \theta) = (\partial F(T, \theta_0)/\partial T)\, dT$.

After the observation of x, T is constant and hence $dT = 0$; consequently

$$dF(T, \theta) = \frac{\partial F(T, \theta)}{\partial \theta}\, d\theta.$$

The term $D(\theta \mid T, \mathfrak{R}, \mathfrak{S})$ or shortly, $D(\theta \mid T) = (\partial F(T, \theta)/\partial \theta)\, d\theta$ is what Fisher called fiducial density. It is a measure of the plausibility of a hypothesis $\theta_0 = \theta$ in the light of the observation x and the background knowledge $\mathfrak{K}$, $\mathfrak{S}$, and F.

Note: If a sufficient statistic $T = T(x)$ does not exist, it may nonetheless be possible to find the fiducial density of θ. Let S, T be statistics with the property

$$f(x; \theta) = f_1(S, T; \theta) f_2(x \mid S, T),$$

and let the marginal distribution of the statistic T be independent of θ, then

$$f_1(S, T; \theta) = g_1(S; \theta \mid T) g_2(T),$$

and we can apply the fiducial method to the joint distribution function $G(S; \theta \mid T)$ belonging to $g_1(S; \theta \mid T)$. T is in this context called an ancillary statistic.

In the preceding example (Sprott, 1965, pp. 102f) a sufficient statistic $T = \sum_{i=1}^{n} x_i$ exists, and we determine the distribution of T as

$$f(T; \theta) = \frac{1}{(n-1)!} T^{n-1} \theta^n \exp(-T\theta),$$

and the fiducial density, via the joint distribution function $F(T, \theta)$, as

$$D(\theta \mid T) = f(\theta; T) \, d\theta = \frac{1}{(n-1)!} T^n \theta^{n-1} \exp(-T\theta) \, d\theta.$$

It is a stronger (and particularly a fully additive) measure than the likelihood function $f^*(\theta \mid x)$. For instance, given $n = 1$ and $T = 1$, and the hypothesis $\theta_1 = \theta \in [8, \infty)$, we obtain

$$D(\theta_0 \mid 1) = \exp(-8) = 3.3546 \times 10^{-4}.$$

$D(\theta_0 \mid 1) = 3.3546 \times 10^{-4}$ signifies that the hypothesis $\theta_1 = \theta \in [8, \infty)$ has the fiducial probability, i.e., confirmation, 3.3546×10^{-4} while in terms of the likelihood function we can only say (Sprott, 1965, p. 103) that values of θ in the interval $[8, \infty)$ have a relative likelihood of less than 0.0073.

Nevertheless there have been numerous objections (e.g., Tukey, 1957; Lindley, 1958 and Dempster, 1963) against this method, and examples have been presented where the fiducial method leads to paradoxical results. Some objections have been weakened by Sprott (1965) and Sprott and Kalbfleisch (1967). Without entering into the details of this discussion it must be said here that the exact conditions for the existence of a fiducial density and the absence of paradoxes are not yet known. Nevertheless it is reasonable to utilize the fiducial method in all cases where the a priori distribution over the hypothesis space Ω is not objectively known, but where a fiducial density exists (and the fiducial method does not lead to paradoxical results), since the fiducial density function as a set function admits of comparative and absolute confirmation of hypotheses. The relationship of fiducial density to Carnap's c-function is in principle the same as that of the Bayesian a posteriori distribution, with the only exception that, on the one hand, the background knowledge may be weaker, namely, need not include knowledge of $g(\theta; \lambda)$; on the other hand, the fiducial procedure is less universal, due to its linkage especially to sufficient transformations and continuous types of distribution. The axioms of the fiducial method which will be presented in the following in a somewhat modified version, as compared with Hacking's (1965) and Stegmüller's presentation (1973D, pp. 258ff), show the strong analogy with the axioms of probability$_1$ of Carnap; $\sim_L$ denotes logical equivalence.

A. Axioms of Fiducial Densities

(Instead of $D(\theta \mid T; \Re, \mathfrak{S})$ we shortly write $D(\theta \mid T)$.)

(F_1) *Axiom of the equivalence of observations:* From

$$T_1 \sim_L T_2 \text{ follows } D(\theta \mid T_1) = D(\theta \mid T_2),$$

i.e., the fiducial density of θ is the same, no matter whether T_1 or T_2 is the observation. Carnap's axiom K_1 reads correspondingly.

(F_2) *Axiom of the equivalence of hypotheses:* From

$$\theta_1 \sim_L \theta_2 \text{ follows } D(\theta_1 \mid T) = D(\theta_2 \mid T),$$

i.e., the fiducial density for θ_1 and θ_2 is the same, given the observation (Carnap's axiom K_2).

(F_3) *General multiplication axiom or axiom of incompatibility:* From

$T \wedge (\theta_1 \wedge \theta_2)$ being logically false, i.e., if θ_1 and θ_2 are logically incompatible with respect to T, it follows that

$$D(\theta_1 \wedge \theta_2 \mid T) = D(\theta_2 \mid T) \cdot D(\theta_1 \mid T \wedge \theta_2)$$

(Carnap's axiom K_3).

(F_4) *Special addition axiom:* From $T_1 \wedge (\theta_1 \wedge \theta_2)$ being logically false, it follows that

$$D(\theta_1 \vee \theta_2 \mid T) = D(\theta_1 \mid T) + D(\theta_2 \mid T)$$

(Carnap's axiom K_4).

(F_5) *Standardization axiom:* From $T \Vdash \theta$ follows

$$D(\theta \mid T) = 1$$

(Carnap's axiom K_5).

While there is no analogy with Carnap's axiom K_6 [12] in the fiducial system of axioms, we need, on the other hand, two additional axioms, which give the fiducial density a frequency interpretation.

(F_6) *Frequency axiom:* If $\partial F(T, \theta)/\partial T = f(T, \theta)$ (with $F(T; \theta) = \int_\Omega D(\theta \mid T)$ $d\theta$) exists, then, for given $T = T(x)$, $x \in \mathfrak{S}$, $f(T; \theta)$ has the properties of a likelihood function. This opens out a frequency interpretation of fiducial density, a prospect which was emphasized by Fisher already.

This interpretation implies another property:

(F_7) *Axiom of irrelevancy:* Let $x_1, x_2 \in \mathfrak{S}$ be two samples, and $T_1 = T(x_1)$ and $T_2 = T(x_2)$ their sufficient statistics; then from $f(T_1 \wedge T_2; \theta)$ $= f(T_1; \theta)$, it follows exactly $D(\theta \mid T_1) = D(\theta \mid T_1 \wedge T_2)$. That is, if an additional sample is irrelevant for the fiducial density, then and only then the fiducial density remains unaltered by an additional sample. (For a somewhat more rigorous and more formal-linguistic version of this axiom, cp. Stegmüller (1973D, p. 266).)

The corresponding system of axioms for Bayesian a posteriori probabilities is completely analogous with respect to (F_1) to (F_5):

B. Axioms on Bayesian a posteriori Probabilities

(B_1) From $x_1 \sim_L x_2$ it follows $\pi(\theta \mid x_1) = \pi(\theta \mid x_2)$.

(B_2) From $\theta_1 \sim_L \theta_2$ it follows $\pi(\theta_1 \mid x) = \pi(\theta_2 \mid x)$.

(B_3) If $(x \wedge (\theta_1 \wedge \theta_2))$ is logically false, then $\pi(\theta_1 \wedge \theta_2 \mid x)$
           $= \pi(\theta_2 \mid x) \cdot \pi(\theta_1 \mid x \wedge \theta_2)$.

(B_4) If $(x \wedge (\theta_1 \wedge \theta_2))$ is logically false, then $\pi(\theta_1 \vee \theta_2 \mid x)$
           $= \pi(\theta_1 \mid x) + \pi(\theta_2 \mid x)$.

(B_5) From $x \Vdash \theta$ it follows $\pi(\theta \mid x) = 1$.

The axioms (F_6) and (F_7), however, are to be reinterpreted in the following way:

(B_6) If $f(x; \theta) = k(\pi(\theta \mid x)/g(\theta; \lambda))$, where $k = \int_\Omega f(x; \theta) g(\theta; \lambda) \, d\theta$,
           does exist, then, for given x, $f(x; \theta)$ has the properties of a
           likelihood function.

(B_7) From x_1, $x_2 \in \mathfrak{S}$ and $f(x_1 \wedge x_2; \theta) = f(x_1; \theta)$ it follows
           exactly $\pi(\theta \mid x_1) = \pi(\theta \mid x_1 \wedge x_2)$.

These axioms (B_1) to (B_7) hold equally for the likelihood function itself, with one modification. To see this, multiply the likelihood function $f^*(x; \theta)$ by a constant $k(x)$, dependent on the observation x, so that

$$\int_\Omega k(x) f^*(x; \theta) \, d\theta = 1.$$

The product

$$L(\theta \mid x) = k(x) f^*(x; \theta)$$

is the standardized likelihood function; it can be interpreted as Bayesian probability function, with the equal distribution as a priori distribution. The standardized likelihood function interpreted in this way satisfies the axioms (B_1) to (B_7), in particular the standardization (B_5).

12. MAXIMUM LIKELIHOOD AS ACCEPTANCE RULE ON THE BASIS OF A LOSS FUNCTION

Our considerations have been an outline of the objective part of the induction problem. The result of the objective-statistical investigation has been an inference measure of the form $\Phi(\theta \mid x)$, $\theta \in \Omega$, $x \in \mathfrak{S}$. $\Phi(\theta \mid x)$ is to represent either a standardized likelihood function, or a Bayesian a posteriori distribution, or a fiducial density. $\Phi(\theta \mid x)$ confirms hypotheses θ in the light of observations. However, $\Phi(\theta \mid x)$ alone cannot yet lead to the *acceptance* of a definite hypothesis. We therefore need a criterion like, e.g., the maximum likelihood criterion. In fact, this criterion is the most used one in statistics. In our context it requires the acceptance of the hypothesis θ^* for which the likelihood is a supremum.

$$f^*(\theta^* \mid x) = \sup_{\theta \in \Omega} f^*(\theta \mid x).$$

The underlying idea is that this criterion implies an objective behaviour which does without a loss function. This idea, however, is false, i.e., the maximum likelihood is equally based upon a loss function, as was supposed by Blackwell and Girshick (1954), and by Diehl and Sprott (1965), and as was proved for the one-parameter case by Drygas and Menges (1971).

We introduce a loss measure $L(A, \hat{\theta})$, which can be interpreted as the mean loss to be suffered if the true hypothesis lies in the set $A \subset \Omega$, and $\hat{\theta}$ is the accepted hypothesis.

To see how $L(A, \hat{\theta})$ must be chosen, we will first consider the discrete case, where $\int_A g(\theta, \hat{\theta})\, d\theta$ becomes

$$L(A, \hat{\theta}) = c_2 v(A) + (c_1 - c_2)\, X_A(\hat{\theta}),$$

and where

$$g(\theta, \hat{\theta}) = \begin{cases} c_2 & \text{for} \quad \theta \neq \hat{\theta} \\ c_1 & \text{for} \quad \theta = \hat{\theta} \end{cases} \quad (\text{with } c_1 < c_2)$$

is a loss function of the usual type; $v(A)$ denotes the number of elements in A, and $X_A(\hat{\theta})$ is the indicator-function of the set A at the point $\hat{\theta}$, i.e.,

$$X_A(\hat{\theta}) = \begin{cases} 1 & \text{for} \quad \theta = \hat{\theta} \\ 0 & \text{for} \quad \theta \neq \hat{\theta}. \end{cases}$$

Evidently, $g(\theta, \hat{\theta})$ can also be written in the form

$$g(\theta, \hat{\theta}) = c_2 + (c_1 - c_2)\, \delta_{\theta, \hat{\theta}},$$

where

$$\delta_{\theta,\hat{\theta}} = \begin{cases} 1 & \text{for} \quad \theta = \hat{\theta} \\ 0 & \text{for} \quad \theta \neq \hat{\theta}, \end{cases}$$

that is the Kronecker-symbol.

Now $L(A, \hat{\theta})$ can be generalized straightforward to the continuous case, for if we let $\delta(x) = \delta_{x,0}$, we have either

$$L(A, \hat{\theta}) = c_2 \nu(A) + (c_1 - c_2) X_A(\hat{\theta})$$

or, if $\nu(A) = \int_A f(\theta) \, d\theta$,

$$g(\theta, \hat{\theta}) = c_2 f(\theta) + (c_1 - c_2) \delta(\theta - \hat{\theta}).$$

This loss function is a Schwartz-distribution – the first term being a usual function, the second term a multiple of a δ-function (δ-distribution).

Our loss function is a generalized version of Marschak's 'loss function of the scientist' (1972; see also his contribution in this volume). In the finite discrete case considered by Marschak, the 'scientist's loss function' can be expressed in the following way (if n hypotheses are considered):

$$[g(\theta_i, \hat{\theta}_j)] = \begin{bmatrix} 0 & 1 & 1 & \dots & 1 \\ 1 & 0 & 1 & \dots & 1 \\ \vdots & & & & \vdots \\ 1 & 1 & 1 & \dots & 0 \end{bmatrix}_{(n)} \quad i, j = 1, \dots, n,$$

i.e., the scientist, according to Marschak, evaluates the loss of $\theta_i = \hat{\theta}_j$ ($i, j = 1, \dots, n$) by 0, all other losses $g(\theta_i, \hat{\theta}_j)$ with $\theta_i \neq \hat{\theta}_j$ ($i, j = 1, \dots, n$) by a constant c which, for the sake of simplicity, is set equal to 1.

Using the above generalized loss measure we get the acceptance risk $\bar{r}$ of the hypothesis $\hat{\theta}$, given the empirical evidence x, by

$$\bar{r}(\hat{\theta} \mid x) = \int_\Omega f^*(\theta \mid x) L(d\theta, \hat{\theta}) = c_2 \int_\Omega f^*(\theta \mid x) f(\theta) \, d\theta +$$

$$+ (c_1 - c_2) \int X_{d\theta}(\hat{\theta}) f^*(\theta \mid x)$$

$$= c_2 \int_\Omega f^*(\theta \mid x) f(\theta) \, d\theta + (c_1 - c_2) f^*(\hat{\theta} \mid x),$$

where $f^*(\theta \mid x)$ is the likelihood function, given the observation x.

The first term is independent of $\hat{\theta}$ and, in view of $(c_1 - c_2) < 0$, the second term is minimized if $f^*(\hat{\theta} \mid x)$ is maximized, i.e., if $\hat{\theta}$ has the maximum likelihood property.

By the following considerations it will become clear that our loss measure is a reasonable and meaningful one. For $\theta_0 \neq \hat{\theta}$, we have

$$L(\{\theta_0\}, \hat{\theta}) = c_2 \int_{\{\theta_0\}} f(\theta)\, d\theta = 0$$

$$L(\{\hat{\theta}\}, \hat{\theta}) = (c_1 - c_2) < 0.$$

It is a desirable property for the loss to be small, if the true hypothesis lies in the neighbourhood of the accepted hypothesis, and to be great, if it does not. Therefore, we assume that

$$\sup_{\theta,\, \theta' \in \Omega} |f(\theta) - f(\theta')| \leqslant \frac{|c_1 - c_2|}{2},$$

i.e., that the maximal variation of $f(\theta)$ is at most equal to $(c_2 - c_1)/2$. If this condition is met, we have, by the above assumption, for $\varepsilon > 0$,

$$L(|\theta - \hat{\theta}| \leqslant \varepsilon, \hat{\theta}) - L(|\theta - \theta_0| \leqslant \varepsilon, \hat{\theta}) =$$
$$= \varepsilon [f(\hat{\theta}) - f(\theta_0)] + (c_1 - c_2) + 0(\varepsilon) \leqslant 0,$$

provided that $|\theta_0 - \hat{\theta}| > \varepsilon$.

In $g(\theta, \hat{\theta})$ there appears a δ-distribution, which can always be approximated by ordinary functions. It should also be noted that maximum-likelihood-estimates are always specified only up to a limited number of decimals.

Theorem: If the hypothesis space Ω is one-dimensional, and the maximum likelihood hypothesis $\tilde{\theta}$ is obtained from the maximum likelihood equation $df^*(\theta \mid x)/d\theta = 0$, then, for any $\varepsilon > 0$, there exists a loss function $g_\varepsilon(\theta, \hat{\theta})$, with the property that the optimal hypothesis $\hat{\theta}$ with respect to this loss function is such that

$$|\hat{\theta} - \tilde{\theta}| \leqslant \varepsilon.$$

(For a proof, see Drygas and Menges (1971), pp. 10ff.) This theorem shows two important properties:

(1)   The hypotheses accepted in the light of the maximum likelihood rule are implicitly based upon a definite loss function.

(2)   This loss function is a generalization of the 'scientist's loss function' in the sense of Marschak.

13. Fiducial acceptance rules

Actually a hypothesis can only be accepted decision-theoretically in the light of a given inference function, i.e., if based upon a utility or loss function. This may be shown by the example of fiducial density.

Let $\hat{\Omega}$ denote the space of the hypotheses to be accepted, and Ω the space of the true hypotheses, then the loss function g maps the cartesian product $\hat{\Omega} \times \Omega$ into the real numbers.

The acceptance risk $r(\hat{\theta} \mid T)$ to be suffered if the hypothesis $\hat{\theta}$ is accepted, on the basis of the observation T and the fiducial density $D(\theta \mid T; \Re, \Im)$, is the conditional expectation

$$r(\hat{\theta} \mid T) = \int_{\Omega} g(\hat{\theta}, \theta)\, D(\theta \mid T)\, d\theta.$$

This fiducial acceptance risk function has a certain similarity with the customary risk function of statistical decision theory, but it determines the risk conditionally, i.e., conditionally upon the data statement T. By application of the observation-optimal Bernoulli rule of statistical decision theory (cp. Section 2, where the deontic rule ((1b), (2b)) was given preference over the other rules) we accept the hypothesis $\hat{\theta}^*$ for which the conditional fiducial acceptance risk is the greatest lower bound:

$$r(\hat{\theta}^* \mid T) = \inf_{\hat{\theta} \in \hat{\Omega}} r(\hat{\theta} \mid T).$$

Of course, this acceptance principle is only applicable in case of the uncertainty type (2) (Section 10). In case of the uncertainty type (3) where θ is a random variable with unknown a priori distribution $h(\theta; \lambda)$, the acceptance rule can work in two different ways.

Rule 1: We construct an α-fiducial region in the space Γ of the a priori distribution so that the unknown a priori distribution with (large) fiducial probability, e.g., $\alpha = 0.95$, lies in the subspace $\Gamma^* \subset \Gamma$. We may now center all considerations on this subspace Γ^*, since (in the light of the observation T) it is very unlikely for the true a priori distribution λ to lie outside of Γ^*. To this subspace Γ^* we can now reasonably apply the minimax criterion:

Accept the hypothesis $\hat{\theta}^* \in \hat{\Omega}$ for which

$$\sup_{\lambda \in \Gamma^*} \int_{\Omega} g(\hat{\theta}^*; \theta)\, D(\theta \mid T)\, \mathrm{d}\theta =$$

$$= \inf_{\hat{\theta} \in \hat{\Omega}} \sup_{\lambda \in \Gamma^*} \int_{\Omega} g(\hat{\theta}, \theta)\, D(\theta \mid T)\, \mathrm{d}\theta.$$

If one fears the possibility of a very unfavorable a priori distribution outside of Γ^* one may, before applying the acceptance rule 1, a priori exclude all hypotheses $\hat{\theta}$ for which

$$\sup_{\lambda \in \Gamma^*} \int_{\Omega} g(\hat{\theta}, \theta)\, D(\theta \mid T)\, \mathrm{d}\theta > s,$$

where s is an acceptance risk limit which one is determined not to pass beyond.

Rule 2: In order to obtain a distribution over the a priori space Γ, one may combine the known fiducial density $D(\theta \mid T)$ with the unknown a priori distributions $h(\theta; \lambda)$ in the following way:

$$J(\theta; \lambda \mid T) = D(\theta \mid T)\, h(\theta; \lambda) \quad \text{for all} \quad \lambda \in \Gamma.$$

J is a system of joint distributions over the cartesian product space $\Omega \times \Gamma$. By integration over Ω we obtain a distribution independent of θ:

$$V(\lambda \mid T) = \int_{\Omega} D(\theta \mid T)\, h(\theta; \lambda)\, \mathrm{d}\theta,$$

which is combined with a loss function of the kind $G(\hat{\theta}, \lambda)$ so that again we obtain an acceptance risk function:

$$\bar{r}(\hat{\theta} \mid T) = \int_\Gamma G(\hat{\theta}, \lambda) \, V(\lambda \mid T) \, d\lambda =$$

$$= \int_\Gamma \int_\Omega G(\hat{\theta}, \lambda) \, D(\theta \mid T) \, h(\theta; \lambda) \, d\theta \, d\lambda.$$

By analogy with the above function, $\bar{r}(\hat{\theta} \mid T)$ indicates the fiducial conditional acceptance risk upon which, again by application of the Bernoulli principle, it follows the rule:

Accept the hypothesis $\hat{\theta}^{**}$ for which

$$\bar{r}(\hat{\theta}^{**} \mid T) = \inf_{\theta \in \Omega} \bar{r}(\hat{\theta} \mid T).$$

14. SEMANTIC INFORMATION

Finally I want to sketch some consequences resulting from the conceptions so far discussed with respect to the concept of information.

In the framework of Shannon's (Shannon and Weaver, 1949) information theory, the information content h of a signal x_i $(i = 1, 2, ..., n)$ occurring with probability p_i is defined by

$$h(p_i) = \log \frac{1}{p_i} = -\log p_i,$$

where log denotes the dual logarithm. The information content of the whole vector $p = (p_1, p_2, ..., p_n)$ $(\sum_{i=1}^n p_i = 1)$ is characterized by the entropy measure $H(p)$:

$$H(p) = - \sum_{i=1}^n p_i \log p_i.$$

In conformity with the basic conception of information theory, the entropy is at the same time a measure of uncertainty. As is easily proved, the entropy attains its maximum for $p_i = 1/n = \text{const}$.

The following distinction and notation would be exacter (cp. Section 8):

(a)   Information content of Laplacean a priori probability

$$h(\mathfrak{M}_{\mathfrak{S}} \mid \mathfrak{R}) = h(1/n) = \log n = \text{const}, \quad j = 1, \ldots, n.$$

(b)   Information content of Cournot's a priori probability

$$h(\mathfrak{M}_{\mathfrak{S}} \mid \mathfrak{R}) = -\log \mathfrak{M}_{\mathfrak{S}}(A \mid \mathfrak{R}), \quad (A \in \mathfrak{S}).$$

(c)   Information content of a posteriori probability

$$h(\mathfrak{M}_{\mathfrak{S}} \mid \mathfrak{R}) = -\log \mathfrak{M}_{\mathfrak{S}}(A \mid \mathfrak{R}; M), \quad (A \in \mathfrak{S}),$$

or, by the limit definition by v. Mises

$$h(\mathfrak{M}_{\mathfrak{S}} \mid \mathfrak{R}) = -\log \lim_{k \to \infty} \mathfrak{M}_{\mathfrak{S}}(A \mid \mathfrak{R}; M_k), \quad (A \in \mathfrak{S}).$$

This notation is to make evident that the information-technical utilization of probability is equally concerned with three different concepts of probability and equally involves the etial structure $\mathfrak{R}$, events from $\mathfrak{S}$, the measure function $\mathfrak{M}$, and eventually the mass M or M_k, respectively, of realizations.

An important interpretation of information which Carnap and Bar-Hillel (1952, 1953) called *semantic information* is based upon the concept of probability$_1$. This concept is due to the doubt that the technical information concept by Shannon is also suitable as a measure of the meaning or value of information. What Carnap and Bar-Hillel meant by semantic information was transmission of meaningful symbol combinations or sentences to an intelligent receiver. Carnap and later on especially Hintikka (1970, p. 16) presented, as semantic information, a measure of substantial information: cont (*b*). This measure is defined and substantiated as follows: In a two-valued propositional logic (*L*-language in the sense of Carnap), *b* is a proposition composed of $w(b)$ constituents, where $w(b)$ characterizes the 'width of the proposition'; *b* is composed of $w(b)$ constituents $C_1, C_2, \ldots, C_{w(b)}$, connected by the connective 'or': $b = C_1 \vee C_2 \vee \cdots \vee C_{w(b)}$. A constituent is formed by a finite set of individual propositions $A_1, A_2, \ldots, A_k$, connected by the connective 'and'

$$\bigcirc A_1 \wedge \bigcirc A_2 \wedge \cdots \wedge \bigcirc A_k,$$

where $\bigcirc$ denotes 'true' or 'false'. The number of possible constituents is thus 2^k. The measure $\text{cont}(b)$ relates the number of constituents excluded by the proposition b, namely $2^k - w(b)$, to the whole number of possible constituents:

$$\text{cont}(b) = \frac{2^k - w(b)}{2^k}.$$

For reasons of symmetry (indifference principle) one may set $p(b) = = w(b)/2^k$, where $p(b)$ is the probability of the proposition b; hence

$$\text{cont}(b) = 1 - p(b).$$

Here, again, the surprise concept of information is retained: The greater the probability of the proposition b, the less is the surprise when it occurs and the less is its substantial information in the sense of the content measure $\text{cont}(b)$.

Applying this reasoning to probability$_2$, one finds that it fits only the Laplacean a priori concept. It would be completely meaningless to say that a message is the more informative, the lower its a priori probability in the sense of Cournot, or even, the lower its a posteriori probability. A further clarification of this important problem is found in the contribution by Jacob Marschak in this volume.

The considerations in Section 13, however, provide an access to the measurement of semantic information in the framework of acceptance rules (in the sense of the measure Info (Menges, 1972)). Thus, for example, the semantic information of a known a priori distribution λ^* can be measured through

$$\text{Info}(\lambda^*) = \inf_{\hat{\theta} \in \Omega} \sup_{\theta \in \Omega} \int_{\mathfrak{G}} g(\hat{\theta}, \theta) f(x; \theta) \, dx$$

$$- \inf_{\hat{\theta} \in \Omega} \int_{\Omega} g(\hat{\theta}, \theta) h(\theta; \lambda^*) \, d\theta,$$

where the first term on the right-hand side represents the minimaximal acceptance risk in the case of complete ignorance of the a priori distribution, and the second term on the right-hand side, the minimal acceptance risk in the case of exact knowledge of the a priori distribution. The difference between these two terms provides a measure of the reduction of the acceptance risk due to the exact knowledge ('message') of the a priori distribution over the space of hypotheses.

The measure of semantic information Info (λ^*) is presumably of very little practical use, since the 'message' λ^* is hardly ever obtainable, unless subjectively. In practice it may on the contrary often be important to have the information value of the observation, i.e., to determine Info(x) with respect to the a priori distribution $h(\theta; \lambda^*)$, if this is objectively known, or with respect to the most unfavourable a priori distribution from Γ, if the true one is not objectively known. By analogy to the acceptance rules of the preceding paragraph, the semantic information of x, relatively to the a priori distribution, can be characterized as follows:

$$\text{Info}(x \mid \lambda) = \inf_{\hat{\theta} \in \Omega} \int_{\Omega} g(\hat{\theta}, \theta) \, h(\theta; \lambda^*) \, d\theta$$

$$- \inf_{\hat{\theta} \in \Omega} \int_{\Omega} g(\hat{\theta}, \theta) \, D(\theta \mid T) \, d\theta.$$

The second term on the right-hand side of the equation represents the smallest acceptance risk in the light of the (a posteriori) fiducial distribution; the first term, the smallest acceptance risk in terms of the a priori distribution $h(\theta; \lambda^*)$. The difference between them is the reduction (if there is any) of the minimum acceptance risk through the observation x.

The 'absolute' value of the information x is reasonably to be characterized relatively to the risk of the minimax solution (Menges, 1972), as without the observation x (and without objective knowledge of the a priori distribution) there is nothing to be done but to accept the hypothesis whose risk is minimaximal. In pursuance of this idea, the 'absolute' semantic information of x is measured as

$$\text{Info}(x) = \inf_{\hat{\theta} \in \Omega} \sup_{\theta \in \Omega} \int_{\mathfrak{S}} g(\hat{\theta}, \theta) \, f(x; \theta) \, dx \; - \inf_{\hat{\theta} \in \Omega} \int_{\Omega} g(\hat{\theta}, \theta) \, D(\theta \mid T) \, d\theta.$$

Of course, we may also use the standardized likelihood function instead of the fiducial distribution $D(\theta \mid T)$, if $D(\theta \mid T)$ does not exist.

15. SUMMARY

After a short introduction, mainly intended as a justification of the objective theory of inductive behaviour, the classical criteria of statistical decision theory are interpreted as deontic rules and enlarged by a variant, viz., the observation-optimal Bernoulli rule which in the light of three deontic meta-rules proves to be particularly adequate for the objective theory of inductive behaviour. Diverging from Carnap, the theory presented here is not formalized in the language of first-stage predicate logic, but is based on a set-theoretical language founded on the structure concept. This meta-theoretical decision has the advantage of general applicability and the disadvantage of an abandonment of the lucidity of Carnap's formal language. The basic conception of Carnap's inductive logic is then characterized and discussed with respect to the author's own views outlined in the following paragraphs. The relationship between inductive and deductive logic is treated, with special consideration of the problem of effectivity, and the relationship between inductive logic and the probability concept is clarified. In particular, it is asserted that the concept of probability has four different cognitive functions as predictor or indicator in the framework of the epistemological principle of etiality, as an axiomatized concept of probability calculus, as a numerical concept (Carnap's probability$_2$), and as the numerical explicative of the degree of confirmation (Carnap's probability$_1$, inverse probability, inference measure). These four concepts are then discussed individually. The etiality principle is proposed as the transcendental prerequisite upon which our conception of reality is founded in order to enable well-ordered experience even in those cases where the causal principle fails, due to the complexity of the causal relationships and the indeterministic, but stochastic, sequence of cause and effect. The etiality principle is illustrated by an example and formalized. The central concepts of model component, model, etial complex, and atomic proposition are defined. The axiomatization of probability by Kolmogoroff is discussed and criticized in the context of the etiality principle. For an adequate treatment of the etial predictor or indicator problem, recurrence to a multi-valued logic seems indispensable.

As a numerical concept in the sense of probability$_2$, probability is defined in three different ways, as objective a priori concept, as objective a posteriori concept, and as subjective concept. The three corresponding methods of measurement are discussed and the subjective concept is criticized.

The concept of uncertainty is discussed in the context of the etiality principle; three types of statistical uncertainty are distinguished: Pure randomness (the hypothesis is a random variable with known distribution law), lacking a priori knowledge I (the true hypothesis is fixed but unknown), lacking a priori knowledge II (the hypothesis is a random variable with unknown distribution law).

On this basis, the relationship between confirmation logic and inference measure (inverse probability, Carnap's probability$_1$) is exhaustively discussed. We begin with the likelihood function and its role as confirmation measure, which, due to its universality, its linkage to the etial background knowledge, and its frequentist interpretability, deserves special consideration before all other statistical inference measures. Then the Bayesian a posteriori distribution is discussed and evaluated as a confirmation measure. Its shortcoming is the close linkage to the knowledge of the a priori distribution over the hypothesis space. The fiducial distribution does without this a priori knowledge; it also comes to stronger confirmation measures than the likelihood function. For this reason, fiducial theory is axiomatized as confirmation logic and discussed in greater detail. Its rather strong underlying assumptions are set forth which, unfortunately, set narrow limits to the applicability of this theory.

With that, the objective part of the objective theory of inductive behaviour is completed; it is asserted that the acceptance of hypotheses is possible only on the basis of loss or utility functions, respectively. This statement is maintained by the maximum likelihood rule as acceptance rule for hypotheses. It is shown that the maximum likelihood rule is based upon an implicit loss function which is a generalization of the 'scientist's loss function' (in the sense of Marschak). The connection between loss function and the acceptance rule for hypotheses is shown by fiducial acceptance risk functions and fiducial acceptance rules for the different types of uncertainty.

I finally draw some conclusions from the results so far obtained, with respect to the definition and measurement of semantic information.

Incidentally, the linkage of classical information theory by Shannon to the etial structure of problems is shown. The definitions based on the surprise concept of semantic information are criticized. The surprise concept and semantic information are adequate counterparts only with respect to the Laplacean concept of a priori probability (in the sense of Carnap's probability$_2$). I therefore propose a new definition of semantic information following Marschak's concept of information value. This new definition is founded upon the basic concepts of the objective theory of inductive behaviour, in particular upon the hypothesis acceptance risks. As lower bound and point of reference of semantic information, I take the minimaximal acceptance risk which is incurred if no empirical observations are available and if the a priori distribution over the hypothesis space is not objectively known.

16. ACKNOWLEDGEMENTS

I owe many suggestions and critical hints to Professor J. Marschak with whom I discussed the theory presented here in the course of a joint lecture program presented at the University of Heidelberg in summer 1972, and to Professor W. Leinfellner who, in summer 1973, gave me the opportunity to discuss the subject matter further in a joint seminar at Heidelberg University. Very stimulating discussion partners in both seminars were Dr. H. Skala and Dr. B. Leiner who helped in clarifying a number of details, in particular with respect to the etiality principle which was formalized by Dr. Skala. The original German manuscript was translated into English by Mrs. Dipl.-Volksw., Dipl.-Übers.G. Mschaty. I wish to express my warmest thanks to all of them.

University of Heidelberg

NOTES

[1] A procedure is called effective "...when it is based upon rules which uniquely determine the procedure step by step, and when in every application the procedure, with a finite number of steps, leads to a solution". (Carnap and Stegmüller, 1959, p. 70). Effectivity with respect to arithmetic operations is called computability (Menges and Skala, 1973, p. 206).

[2] Practical effectivity (Carnap and Stegmüller, 1959, pp. 74f): We check for every step of the proof whether it is a case of a simple deductive procedure of which we know that it

holds ... and we expect that under normal conditions we shall arrive at a result after a finite number of operations, namely, checks of the individual steps of a given proof. In this sense we can say that we possess a practically effective method.

[3] "Theoretical worth: ... applies especially to such cases of inductive conclusions where the data, the hypothesis, or both, are statistical in nature. Inductive logic, when it is sufficiently developed, will serve as the logical basis for the methods of mathematical statistics." (Carnap and Stegmüller, 1959, p. 94)

[4] "Practical worth: ... It becomes evident that neither empirical sciences alone nor inductive logic alone can serve as a rule of life, but only the interaction of both." (Carnap and Stegmüller, 1959, p. 94)

[5] "... some theorists erroneously (believed) ... to have solved the problem of explication of the probability concept by the construction of a system of axioms of probability without a complementary interpretation of this system. Such an interpretation, however, is indispensable when it comes to explicate the concept." (Carnap and Stegmüller, 1959, p. 20)

[6] "But with respect to the validity, as contrary to the practical value or applicability of a proposition of inductive as well as deductive logic, it is irrelevant whether the data statement is true or not true, and if it is true, whether its truth is known or not known." [*op. cit.*, p. 79]

[7] Cp. Menges (1967, 1970).

[8] Cp. the paper by Schneeweiß in this volume.

[9] In the form $\int_{\Omega} \mathscr{L}(\theta \mid x) C(x) \, d\theta = 1$; cp. Section 12.

[10] $\Vdash$ is an object-language symbol denoting 'occurs simultaneously with' e.g., $a \Vdash b : a$ occurs simultaneously with b.

[11] Cp. the paper by Fraser in this volume.

[12] Its content is that with lacking knowledge on the facts the worth of the confirmation function is nevertheless greater than 0, since it would be unjustifiable to assign the probability$_1$ value 0 to a description of a state (Carnap and Stegmüller, 1958, p. 152).

BIBLIOGRAPHY

Bayes, T., 'An Essay Towards Solving a Problem in the Doctrine of Chances', *The Philosophical Transactions* **53** (1763), 370–480; and *Biometrika* **45** (1958), 296–315.

Blackwell, D. and Girshick, M. A., *Theory of Games and Statistical Decisions*, New York 1954.

Carnap, R., 'On Inductive Logic', *Philosophy of Science* **12** (1945), 72–97.

Carnap, R., 'On the Comparative Concept of Confirmation', *The British Journal for the Philosophy of Science* **3** (1953), 311–318.

Carnap, R., *Logical Foundations of Probability*, Chicago 1962.

Carnap, R., *Induktive Logik und Wahrscheinlichkeit*, Wien 1972.

Carnap, R. and Bar-Hillel, Y., 'An Outline of a Theory of Semantic Information', MIT Technical Report (Electronics), No. 247, 1952.

Carnap, R. and Bar-Hillel, Y., 'Semantic Information', *The British Journal for the Philosophy of Science* **4** (1953), 147–157.

Carnap, R. and Stegmüller, W., *Induktive Logik und Wahrscheinlichkeit*, Wien 1959.

Dempster, A. P., 'On the Difficulties Inherent in Fisher's Fiducial Argument', read at the *International Statistical Institute* in Ottawa, 1963.

Diehl, H. and Sprott, D., 'Die Likelihoodfunktion und ihre Verwendung beim statistischen Schluß', *Statistische Hefte* **6** (1965), 112–134.

Drygas, H. and Menges, G., 'On the Use of Loss Functions in Econometric Estimation Problems', *European Meeting of the Econometric Society*, Barcelona, September 1971.

Fisher, R. A., 'On the Mathematical Foundations of Theoretical Statistics', *Philosophical Transactions of the Royal Society (A)* **222** (1922), 309–368.

Fisher, R. A., 'Theory of Statistical Estimation', *Proceedings of the Cambridge Philosophical Society, Biological Sciences* **22** (1925), 700–725.

Fisher, R. A., 'Two New Properties of Mathematical Likelihood', *Proceedings of the Royal Society (A)* **144** (1934), 285–307.

Fisher, R. A., *The Design of Experiments*, Edinburgh 1935.

Fisher, R. A., *Statistical Methods for Research Workers*, London 1946.

Fisher, R. A., *Statistical Methods for Research Workers*, Edinburgh-London 1950.

Fisher, R. A., *Statistical Methods and Scientific Inference*, Edinburgh 1956.

Goodman, N., *Fact, Fiction and Forecast*, Cambridge, Mass. 1955.

Hacking, I., *Logic of Statistical Inference*, London 1965.

Hartwig, H., 'Naturwissenschaftliche und sozialwissenschaftliche Statistik', *Zeitschrift für die gesamte Staatswissenschaft* **112** (1956), 252–256.

Hasenjäger, G., *Grundbegriffe und Probleme der modernen Logik*, Freiburg-München 1962.

Hempel, C. G., 'Inductive Inconsistencies', *Synthesis* **12** (1960), 439–469.

Hintikka, J., 'On Semantic Information Usage', in *Information and Inference* (ed. by J. Hintikka and P. Suppes), Dordrecht-Holland 1970, pp. 3–27.

Hodges, J. L. and Lehmann, E. L., 'The Use of Previous Experience in Reaching Statistical Decisions', *Ann. Math. Stat.* **23** (1952), 396–407.

Hurwicz, L., 'Optimality Criteria for Decision Making Under Ignorance', Cowles Commission Discussion Paper, Statistics No. 370, 1951.

Kolmogoroff, A. A., *Grundbegriffe der Wahrscheinlichkeitsrechnung*, Berlin 1933.

Kutschera, F. v., *Wissenschaftstheorie I*, München 1972.

Laplace, P. S. de, *Théorie Analytique des Probabilités*, Paris 1812.

Leinfellner, W., *Struktur und Aufbau wissenschaftlicher Theorien*, Wien-Würzburg 1965.

Leinfellner, W., *Einführung in die Erkenntnis- und Wissenschaftstheorie*, Mannheim 1965a.

Leinfellner, W., 'Generalization of Classical Decision Theory', in *Risk and Uncertainty* (ed. by K. Borch and J. Mossin), New York 1968.

Lindley, D. V., 'Fiducial Distribution and Bayes' Theorem', *Journ. of Roy. Stat. Soc.* (B) **20** (1958), 102–107.

Lukasiewicz, J. and Tarski, A., 'Untersuchungen über den Aussagenkalkül', *Comptes Rendus des Séances de la Société des Sciences et des Lettres de Varsovie, Classe III* **23** (1930), 30–50.

Marschak, J., 'Prior and Posterior Probabilities and Semantic Information', *Discussion paper* **22**, Universität Heidelberg, 1972.

Meinong, A. v., *Über Möglichkeit und Wahrscheinlichkeit*, Leipzig 1915.

Menges, G., 'Das Entscheidungsproblem in der Statistik', *Allgemeines Statistisches Archiv* **42** (1958), 101–107.

Menges, G., 'Gedanken zur Frage der Stabilität statistischer Entscheidungen', *Metrika* **6** (1963), 84–94.

Menges, G., 'The Adaptation of Decision Criteria and Application Patterns', *Proc. of the 3rd. International Conf. on Operational Research*, Paris 1964, pp. 585–594.

Menges, G., 'On the Bayesification of the Minimax Principle', *Unternehmensforschung* **10** (1966), 81–91.

Menges, G., 'Über Thomas Bayes (1702–1761) und das Theorem', in *Geschichte und Zukunft. Festschrift zum 75. Geburtstag von A. Hain* (ed. by A. Diemer), Meisenheim am Glan 1967a, pp. 485–498.

Menges, G., 'Fiduzialaussagen in der Ökonometrie', in *Operations Research-Verfahren III* (ed. by R. Henn), Meisenheim am Glan 1967b, pp. 286–298.

Menges, G., 'On Some Open Questions in Statistical Decision Theory', in *Risk and Uncertainty* (ed. by K. Borch and J. Mossin), London 1968, pp. 140–162.

Menges, G., 'On Subjective Probability and Related Problems', *Theory and Decision* 1 (1970), 44–60.

Menges, G., 'Semantische Information und statistische Inferenz', *Biometrische Zeitschrift* 14 (1972), 409–418.

Menges, G., 'Inference and Decision', *Selecta Statistica Canadiana* 1 (1973), 1–14.

Menges, G. and Diehl, H., 'On the Application of Fiducial Probability to Statistical Decisions', *The Proceedings of the Fourth International Conference on Operational Research* (ed. by D. B. Hertz and J. Melese), New York 1969.

Menges, G. and Skala, H., 'On the Problem of Vagueness in the Social Sciences', this volume, pp. 51–61.

Niehans, J., 'Zur Preisbildung bei ungewissen Erwartungen', *Schweizerische Zeitschrift für Volkswirtschaft und Statistik* 84 (1948), 433–456.

Popper, K. R., *Objective Knowledge*, London 1973.

Rosser, J. B. and Turquette, A. R., *Many-Valued Logics*, Amsterdam 1952.

Schneeweiß, H., 'Eine Entscheidungsregel für den Fall partiell bekannter Wahrscheinlichkeiten', *Unternehmensforschung* 8 (1964), 86–95.

Scott, D., 'Measurement Models and Linear Inequalities', *J. Math. Psychology* 1 (1964), 233–247.

Shannon, C. E. and Weaver, W., *The Mathematical Theory of Communication*, Urbana 1949.

Sprott, D., 'Statistical Estimation – Some Approaches and Controversies', *Statistische Hefte* 6 (1965), 97–111.

Sprott, D. and Kalbfleisch, J. G., 'Fiducial Probability', *Statistische Hefte* 8 (1967), 99–109.

Stegmüller, W., 'Conditio irrealis, Disposition, Naturgesetz und Induktion', *Kantstudien* 50 (1958), 363–390.

Stegmüller, W., *Probleme und Resultate der Wissenschaftstheorie und Analytischen Philosophie*, Berlin-Heidelberg 1973.

Stegmüller, W., 'Probleme und Resultate der Wissenschaftstheorie und Analytischen Philosophie', Volume IV: *Personelle und statistische Wahrscheinlichkeit*, Berlin-Heidelberg (Studienausgabe, Teil C) 1973C.

Stegmüller, W., 'Probleme und Resultate der Wissenschaftstheorie und Analytischen Philosophie', Volume IV: *Personelle und statistische Wahrscheinlichkeit*, Berlin-Heidelberg (Studienausgabe, Teil D) 1973D.

Tukey, J. W., 'Some Examples with Fiducial Relevance', *Ann. Math. Stat.* 28 (1957), 687–695.

Villegas, C., 'On Qualitative Probability σ-algebras', *Ann. Math. Stat.* 35 (1964), 1787–1796.

GÜNTER MENGES AND HEINZ J. SKALA

ON THE PROBLEM OF VAGUENESS IN THE SOCIAL SCIENCES

1. INTRODUCTORY REMARKS: VAGUENESS, UNCERTAINTY AND INEXACTNESS

Vagueness is neither uncertainty nor inexactness, though there are some connections, in particular in the social sciences. *Mors certa, hora incerta* the Romans said. What they meant to say was that the hour of death was *uncertain*. In another respect, too, namely in measurement, the 'hora' was rather 'incerta' in the sense of 'inexact'. The hora was one twelfth of the day, yet, its length varied. The horae were announced by slaves, not by clocks, which did not exist then. The slaves knew what time it was by the length of the shadow cast by the sun, or by the 'clepshydra', the water-clock which measured time by means of a given quantity of water slowly dripping through it, or just by their sense of time.

The fixing of time especially in advance was imperfect and inaccurate, and yet the turn from uncertainty to certainty, that is, the moment of death, was fixed when it occurred, however inaccurate measurement may have been.

Even though, however, uncertainty cannot be identified with exactness, the determination of the range of uncertainty by way of observation is to a certain degree dependent on the exactitude of measurement. When death has occurred, 'the hour' is no longer incerta, but perhaps the minute, the second, etc.

One should think that uncertainty could be reduced and finally overcome by more and more exact measurement. This is true within certain limits only, as can be shown by the example of the hour of death. The definition of the hour of death as the point of passing on is (presumably) right, but inexact. The indication of the second of death is certainly more accurate, but (with high probability) 'false'.

It is probably 'false' for two reasons:

The first is indicated by Heisenberg's uncertainty principle which

Günter Menges (ed.), Information, Inference and Decision, 51–61. All Rights Reserved.

originally with respect to physics says that simultaneous measurement of corresponding determinants of a particle, e.g. place and speed, can never be absolutely determined. The exacter the determination of location, the more inexact is necessarily the determination of speed, and vice versa. This principle holds similarly in other branches of science, e.g. in econometrics (Menges, 1963), it has been modified to a principle of disturbing the systems by the very act of observing them, and it has been generalized to the principle that rational science may be fundamentally limited in its ability to predict and explain nature. Heisenberg recently argued against the construction of bigger nuclear fission plants because of his doubt that more can be learned of the subnuclear by means of bigger plants. Some physicists believe that at least one can arrive at the comprehension of irreducible probability distributions, a view that was passionately rejected by Einstein ("I cannot believe that God plays dice with the universe" is a well-known remark by him). We will return to the problem of probability later (Section 2).

The second reason is *vagueness* of the notions and concepts themselves. Even a notion like death, which at first glance seems to be definite (not vague), is at least with respect to its temporal definition a vague notion, because some organs of the body and within the different organs, some cells or categories of cells are still at life when others have already mortified. Such conceptual vagueness cannot be resolved by improved measurement; and the often recommended probability principle cannot furnish but partial, we might as well say, pseudo-solution (see Section 2).

It seems therefore, that probability is linked more with the concept of uncertainty, not with the concepts of exactness of measurement and vagueness of concepts.

Uncertainty can be characterized as the entire absence of knowledge on probability distributions over a set of states (total uncertainty) or as the state of knowledge *before* the experiment (individual uncertainty), i.e., when the *outcome* of the stochastic experiment is uncertain. Exactness of measurement, on the other hand, is a matter of instruments, and vagueness is a conceptual property.

Vagueness might be described as the insuperable discrepancy between the 'model concept', i.e., the merely formal (logical) expression-form of concepts, on the one hand, and their semantics, i.e., their empirical meaning, what 'is meant' by them, on the other.

2. VAGUENESS AND PROBABILITY

Obviously there is a great temptation to solve the problem of vagueness by the concept of probability. Vice versa this attempt cannot be really successful because of irreducible probability is the expression of *uncertainty* only in those cases where a sequence of events is not strictly deterministic, i.e., where one cause may have more than one effect.

In deterministic view the cause is 'predictor' of the effect. If A occurs, B necessarily follows, i.e., if A occurs, the occurrence of B is *predictable*. If, e.g., – to quote the classical example by Mill (1872, II, p. 84ff) – a bird is put into a pot filled with carbondioxide, the bird's death is the necessary consequence. We can foretell its death (as a consequence of its being put into carbondioxide atmosphere). There remains a bit of 'uncertainty', however: May be the frightened bird has died from a heart attack. If we have such doubts we shall repeat the experiment a second and third time, etc. Every time death occurs. Now we are quite sure and rely on the inevitability of the sequence. Sometimes we are mistaken with that sort of induction. It may be that in reality some ten or twenty or hundred birds died from a heart attack while we are putting them into the acid. However, since by our knowledge of the respiratory organs of birds and of the physiological properties of carbondioxide we can *explain* the bird's death, and the results of the experiments *coincide* with that knowledge, we consider it as incontestable that putting a bird (any bird) into carbondioxide kills it.

But what if we shoot with a gun at a bird? In case we hit its heart or brain, death will be the inevitable consequence. If we miss it, death – due to that cause – does not occur. If we hit its lungs, death may occur or may not.

The shot at the bird is a stochastic experiment $\mathfrak{L}$; it may have several possible consequences: the bird may be dead, or seriously injured, or lightly injured, or not injured at all.

When the effect has appeared, the sequence is susceptible of causal interpretation. Yet, we do not know beforehand which effect the shot at the bird will have. The stochastic experiment $\mathfrak{L}$ has several possible outcomes or consequences: $B_1, B_2, \ldots$, The occurrence of a definite consequence is no longer certain, but uncertain, though *probable* up to a certain degree. We attribute probabilities $p_1, p_2, \ldots (\sum p_i = 1)$ to the possible consequences. The vector $(p_1, p_2, \ldots)$ is called the 'distribution law' or (more technically) the probability distribution of the stochastic experiment $\mathfrak{L}$ (see also Menges' paper in this book, Section 7 about etiality).

Obviously, the assignment of probabilities to the possible outcomes of the stochastic experiment does in principle not depend on the exactness or vagueness of the definition of the outcome. In particular, we cannot rate the vagueness of the outcome by some probability measure.

Nevertheless, there is an indirect connection between vagueness and probability which, thanks to the additivity-axiom of probability, can at least help to solve the problem of vagueness partly.

The stochastic experiment in our example may have the following outcomes and probabilities:

$$\begin{array}{ll}
B_1 = \text{altogether unhurt} & p_1 = 0.4 \\
B_2 = \text{slightly wounded} & p_2 = 0.25 \\
B_3 = \text{heavily injured} & p_3 = 0.1 \\
B_4 = \text{severely injured} & p_4 = 0.05 \\
B_5 = \text{dead} & \underline{p_5 = 0.2} \\
& \sum p_i = 1
\end{array}$$

B_1 and B_5 characterize (fairly) exact concepts, other than the possible outcomes B_2, B_3, B_4. It may be possible to define B_2 as 'though wounded, still capable of flying and living' (in this case, by the way, the vagueness is overcome operationally, by means of a concept, of which, in our view, one could make full use in practical life). The concepts B_3 and B_4 are markedly vague. Their vagueness cannot be overcome unless we drop the disjunction between them and define

$$B^* = B_3 \vee B_4 \quad \text{with} \quad p^* = p_3 + p_4 (= 0.15).$$

This possibility is due to the fact that an event space like $\{B_1, B_2, \ldots, B_5\}$ is exhaustive and complete, its elements disjoint, and correspondingly the probabilities are additive.

This relationship between vagueness and probability accounts for the hope that the fuzzy sets in the sense of Zadeh (1965) can lead to partial solutions of the problem of vagueness.

3. CONCEPTS IN NATURAL AND SOCIAL SCIENCES AND THE PROBLEM OF ADEQUATION

The problem of vagueness exists in natural and social sciences, but it appears more seriously in the social sciences. As Rickert (1913, pp. 30ff) and his school has shown, concepts arise from "...the certainty that no further investigation of the respective individual object will compel us to multiply the elements of the concept at will." (p. 52) For the concept in natural sciences this certainty flows from the fact that "...any combination of elements to a concept is based upon the assumption that the elements combined either are connected by the necessity of natural laws, i.e., by all means and universally, or at least form the pre-stage to such concepts which express a relationship by natural law."

In social sciences, concepts are formed quite differently. Their general validity, according to Rickert ensues from their common relationship to *values* (Rickert, 1913, pp. 333ff).

A concept like foreign trade is not to be found in nature, contrary to a concept like horse; in any case we cannot, like in the case of 'horse' describe the law by definition (e.g., 'perissodactyl with callosities') and, whenever we meet a specimen in the realms of nature, uniquely identify whether it belongs to the species and hence fulfills the definition of a set or a concept or not.

In the field of social sciences one must rather pull down the natural barriers between things and thrust the 'real' into new 'artificial' units. Their common feature in the sense of Rickert are certain abstract ideas, which the researcher himself presets, or 'values', which are given to him.[1]

As, however, only those things are observable and measurable which empirically exist, social sciences face a peculiar adequation problem (Menges, 1972, pp. 40ff; cp. also Hartwig, 1956, p. 261). We cannot enter into the details of this problem here, since treated elsewhere, but let us indicate an inevitable consequence of this peculiarity. Social science concepts, due to the specific concept formation process, are in principle vaguer than natural science concepts. To that extent the problem of vagueness is particularly important in the social sciences and it is necessary to draw upon suitable formalized theories.

In setting up formalized theories in social sciences we have three possibilities:

(a) to fall back on classical logic and set theory, having in mind that a very strong idealization has been made and therefore it is hardly to be expected that this theory describes reality. One may also call people not acting according to the theory irrational. But what to do if living organisms are not involved? Are there irrational instruments and so on?

(b) to use probabilistic concepts (see Section 2),

(c) to accept vague concepts as inherent property of social sciences and try to modify set theory (many-valued sets) or rather the underlying logic in order to be able to handle vague concepts appropriately.

Possibility (c) was mentioned by Rosser and Turquette (1952, p. 109) and has been advocated especially by Zadeh (1965) and Goguen (1967) who introduced the notions of a 'fuzzy set' and an 'L-fuzzy set' respectively. It is our opinion that in the field of social sciences many concepts are inherently vague ones (e.g. the concept of a poor man). This is reflected in a natural language by statements of the sort 'X is a rather poor man'. The usual procedure in setting up formalized theories is to eliminate (or reduce) vagueness in order to make classical logic applicable. This is mostly done by more or less arbitrary auxiliary definitions which can be understood as idealizations (e.g. to define X as poor if he earns less than Y). It is widely accepted that the reason why formalized theories in social sciences are often so sterile is due to the fact that they are patterned after the natural sciences where classical logic was fruitfully applied.[2] Therefore in our opinion the main problem in the social sciences is not how to avoid vagueness but rather how to treat and formalize it in a satisfactory manner. The next few lines are devoted to this problem.

A. *Multi-Valued Logic*

If one is interested in a formal language to handle vague concepts the most natural way is to start with a multi-valued logic, e.g., an infinite-valued first order language L on which set theory can be based. The primitive symbols of L would be:

(1) variables $x_1, x_2, \ldots$;
(2) connectives $\neg$ (not), $\wedge$ (and);
(3) the quantifier $\exists$;
(4) predicate symbols $\in$, $=$.

The formulas of L are built from atomic formulas in the usual way. Instead of the classical truth values {true, false} one may introduce more general value sets, e.g. the closed real interval $T = [0, 1]$ and define the functions $\neg$, $\wedge$, $\vee$, $\rightarrow$, $\leftrightarrow$ as follows:

$$\neg x = 1 - x$$
$$x \wedge y = \min(x, y)$$
$$x \vee y = \max(x, y)$$
$$x \rightarrow y = \min(1, 1 - x + y)$$
$$x \leftrightarrow y = 1 - |x - y|$$

for all x, y in T. (This interpretation is due to Lukasiewicz and Tarski (1930).) Moreover the functions $\exists$ and $\forall$ are immediate generalizations of their two-valued counterparts defined as

$$\exists X = \sup X \quad \text{and} \quad \forall X = \inf X$$

for all non-empty subsets of T (see Belluce, 1964; Chang, 1958 and Chang and Keisler, 1966).

Of all the conceivable languages of the just mentioned type such ones deserve special interest for which the truth value set forms a complete Boolean algebra and thus allows us to set up Boolean valued set theory. We shall not go here into the precise definition of the universe U and the predicates $\in$ and $=$ over U but rather restrict ourselves to some informal remarks (for details see Scott, 1967 and Rosser, 1969).

Let us denote by $[\![a = b]\!]$ and $[\![a \in b]\!]$ the Boolean values of $a = b$ and $a \in b$ respectively and assume that for each a and b in the universe U the Boolean values of $a = b$ and $a \in b$ have been specified. For formulas ϕ, ψ without variables it is then possible to determine the Boolean values inductively as follows:

$$[\![\neg \phi]\!] = [\![\phi]\!]'$$
$$[\![\phi \wedge \psi]\!] = [\![\phi]\!] \& [\![\psi]\!].$$

($'$ and $\&$ denote here the complement and the conjunction in the Boolean algebra.)

Let $\phi(x)$ be a formula with no free variable except x, then we have

$$[\![\exists x (\phi(x))]\!] = \sup_{a \in U} [\![\phi(a)]\!].$$

By using the definitions of $\phi \vee \psi$, $\phi \rightarrow \psi$, $\phi \leftrightarrow \psi$ and $\forall x(\phi(x))$ the above list is easily completed.

Now let us look at the concept of class membership. If a is a member of b then we usually say $a \in b$ is valid. This can also be expressed by means of a characteristic function f with respect to b. Identifying 1 with truth and 0 with false we write

$$f(x)=1 \quad \text{if} \quad x \in b$$
$$f(x)=0 \quad \text{if} \quad \neg x \in b$$

and say that $a \in b$ takes the value $f(a)$. Now the generalization to a Boolean valued logic is immediate. A (non-classical or Boolean) set will now be a function f with values in a Boolean algebra and we put

$$[\![a \in f]\!] = f(a).$$

This was essentially the idea of Zadeh (1965) and Goguen (1967) who introduced the notions of a fuzzy set and an L-fuzzy set, respectively as mentioned above. Let us now shortly discuss the theory of fuzzy sets which was developed by Zadeh within some unspecified naive set theory.

B. *Fuzzy Sets*

Let X be a set. Zadeh (1965) characterized a *fuzzy set* A in X by a membership (characteristic) function $f_A(x)$ which associates a real number in the interval $[0, 1]$, the 'grade of membership'[3] of x in A, with each element in X. If A is an ordinary set, then $f_A(x)$ takes only the values 1 or 0 (ordinary characteristic function) according as the element x belongs to A or not. (Sets with two-valued characteristic functions will be referred to as sets (in the usual sense).)

Example: Let X denote the reals. A fuzzy set A of real numbers is the set of numbers which are much greater than 0. A may be characterized[4], for example, by $\ldots f_A(2)=0 \ldots f_A(5)=0.01 \ldots f_A(20)=0.7 \ldots f_A(1000)=1$, or graphically:

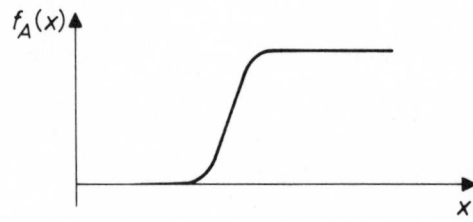

We now can define the extensions of the classical set operations.

(1)   We call a fuzzy set A empty if its membership function is identically zero on X, i.e., $f_A(x)=0$ for all $x \in X$.

(2) $A = B$ if $f_A(x)=f_B(x)$ for all $x \in X$.

(3)   The complement A' of a fuzzy set A is characterized by $f_{A'}(x)=1-f_A(x)$ for all $x \in X$.

(4) $A \subseteq B$ if $f_A(x) \leqslant f_B(x)$ for all $x \in X$.

(5) $C = A \cup B$ if $f_C(x)=\max[f_A(x), f_B(x)]$ for all $x \in X$.

(6) $C = A \cap B$ if $f_C(x)=\min[f_A(x), f_B(x)]$ for all $x \in X$.

One can easily prove (Zadeh, 1965) that the fuzzy sets on X form a distributive lattice with a 0 and a 1. Thus, for example, the following basic identities hold:

$$(A \cup B)' = A' \cap B'$$
$$(A \cap B)' = A' \cup B'$$
De Morgan's laws.

$$C \cap (A \cup B) = (C \cap A) \cup (C \cap B)$$
$$C \cup (A \cap B) = (C \cup A) \cap (C \cup B)$$
Distributive laws

Also the ordinary notion of convexity which plays an important role in optimization problems has a natural 'fuzzy' counterpart. Let us restrict ourselves to fuzzy sets in the Euklidean n-space E^n.

DEFINITION: A fuzzy set A in E^n is convex if the sets $\Gamma_\alpha = \{x : f_A(x) \geq_\alpha\}$ are convex for all $\alpha \in [0, 1]$.

Zadeh (1965) proved an analogue to the classical separation theorem (for any disjoint convex sets A and B there exists a separating hyperplane).

An n-ary fuzzy relation on X is simply a fuzzy set in X^n. Especially interesting are fuzzy orderings, the counterparts of ordinary relations which play an important role in economic theory. For example, we introduce the corresponding weakenings of the ordinary equivalence relation and the linear ordering.

Let R be a binary fuzzy relation on X (fuzzy set in X^2). R is called fuzzy equivalence relation if for all $x, y, z \in X$:

(1) $f_R(x, x)=1$ (reflexivity)

(2) $f_R(x, y)=f_R(y, x)$ (symmetry)

(3) $f_R(x, z) \geq \max_y \{\min[f_R(x, y), f_R(y, z)]\}$.

$(f_R(x, y)$ is to be interpreted as grade of membership of the ordered pair (x, y) in R).

A fuzzy linear ordering is a binary fuzzy relation R which is reflexive, transitive, antisymmetric (i.e. $f_R(x, y) > 0$ and $x \neq y$ implies $f_R(y, x) = 0$) and connected (i.e., $x \neq y$ implies $f_R(x, y) > 0$ or $f_R(y, x) > 0$).

In probability theory, an event is an exactly specified collection of points in a sample space. If the event is a fuzzy set (cannot be precisely defined), then it is still possible to define the concepts of probability theory (Zadeh, 1968).

Generalizations of the concept of a fuzzy set are possible. One can allow the membership function (characteristic function) to take values in a partially ordered set, for example. In order to obtain interesting results, however, the partially ordered set should have more structure, e.g., be at least a lattice.

Let us close our discussion with some remarks.

The concept of a Boolean set was used as a 'negative' device by Scott (1967) in order to prove the independence of the continuum hypotheses. In our opinion, Boolean valued models of the reals may provide an appropriate structure to state representation theorems for fuzzy structures, e.g., the existence of utility functions on fuzzy preference orderings. (Analogy: Nonstandard models of the reals proved to be useful when the Archimedean property does not hold. For this see Skala (1970, 1973) and the paper of Skala in this volume.) Possibly also languages with fuzzy value sets may prove useful in some contexts.

University of Heidelberg

NOTES

[1] Carnap's remarks (Carnap and Stegmüller, 1958, pp. 12ff) on the explication of concepts apply to natural science concepts only: "A scientific concept is the more pregnant the more it can contribute to the formulation of general laws, and this means, the more, in the light of observed facts, it can be related to other concepts."

[2] In this connection it should be mentioned that also considerations on the foundation of quantum mechanics indicated that classical logic is not appropriate (see e.g. Birkhoff and von Neumann, 1936). The main reasons for this are the uncertainty principle and the noncommutativity of physical observations on an subatomic scale.

[3] $f_A(x)$ may be thought of as the truth-value of the proposition '$x \in A$'.

[4] The characterization of A may either be subjective or by convention.

BIBLIOGRAPHY

Belluce, L. P., 'Further Results on Infinite Valued Predicate Logic', *Journal of Symbolic Logic* **29** (1964), 69–78.

Birkhoff, G. and von Neumann, J., 'On the Logic of Quantum Mechanics', *Annals of Mathematics* **37** (1936), 823–843.

Carnap, R. and Stegmüller, W., *Induktive Logik und Wahrscheinlichkeit*, Wien 1958.

Chang, C. C., 'Algebraic Analysis of Many Valued Logics', *Transactions of the American Mathematical Society* **88** (1958), 467–490.

Chang, C. C. and Keisler, H. J., *Continuous Model Theory*, Princeton 1966.

Goguen, J. A., '*L*-Fuzzy Sets', *Journal of Mathematical Analysis and Applications* **23** (1967), 145–174.

Hartwig, H., 'Naturwissenschaftliche und sozialwissenschaftliche Statistik', *Zeitschrift für die gesamte Staatswissenschaft* **112** (1956), 252–266.

Lukasiewicz, J. and Tarski, A., 'Untersuchungen über den Aussagenkalkül', *Comptes Rendus des Séances de la Société des Sciences et des Lettres de Varsovie, Classe III* **23** (1930), 30–50.

Menges, G., 'Three Essays in Econometrics', *Statistische Hefte* **4** (1963), 1–37.

Menges, G., *Grundriß der Statistik*. Teil I: 'Theorie', 2nd ed., Opladen 1972.

Mill, J. St., *System der deduktiven und induktiven Logik, eine Darstellung der Grundsätze der Beweislehre und der Methoden wissenschaftlicher Forschung*, Leipzig 1872.

Rosser, J. B., *Simplified Independence Proofs*, New York and London 1969.

Rosser, J. B. and Turquette, A. R., *Many-Valued Logics*, Amsterdam 1952.

Rickert, H., *Die Grenzen der naturwissenschaftlichen Begriffsbildung*, Tübingen 1913.

Scott, D., 'A Proof of the Independence of the Continuum Hypothesis', *Mathematical Systems Theory* **1** (1967), 89–111.

Skala, H. J., 'An Application of Model Theory to the Theory of Measurement', *2nd International Game Theory Workshop*, Berkeley 1970.

Skala, H. J., 'Über einige Grundprobleme der Nutzentheorie – Nichtarchimedische Nutzentheorie', Habilitation-Thesis, Heidelberg 1973.

Zadeh, L. H., 'Fuzzy Sets', *Information and Control* **8** (1965), 338–353.

BERND LEINER

NOTES ON ETIALITY,
THE ADAPTATION CRITERION,
AND THE 'INFERENCE-DECISION' PROBLEM

Some Biographical and Bibliographical Notes
about Menges and His School

1. A SHORT BIOGRAPHICAL NOTE

In 1958 Günter Menges was appointed Professor of Statistics and Econometrics to the Saar University at Saarbrücken. Such was his scientific activity and influence on colleagues, assistants and students there that one can speak of the Saarbrücken school of statistical decision theory.

In numerous publications on the development and applicability of statistical decision theory Menges propagated his decision-theoretical results and principles in the German-speaking area. Internationally, he represented and interpreted the Saarbrücken school on the occasion of some reports on congresses and during his guest-professorships and visits at several universities in North-America. Menges pleads for the universal applicability of statistical decision theory. His views have been further propagated and discussed by his scholars, to mention only a few ones: Hans Schneeweiss (Professor of Statistics at München), Martin Rutsch (Professor of Statistics at Karlsruhe), who both habilitated under his guidance at Saarbrücken, Minaketan Behara (Associate Professor at the Dept. of Mathematics at Hamilton), who graduated at Saarbrücken, Heinz J. Skala, who habilitated under his guidance at Heidelberg, and Helmut Diehl, Luxembourg, who graduated at Saarbrücken – all well-known decision-theorists.

The Saarbrücken school of statistical decision theory around Professor Menges not only attracted many scholars, but also derived itself great benefits from some guest-professorships and visits of outstanding statisticians. During the summer 1965 David A. Sprott (Waterloo) stayed at Saarbrücken; Henri Theil (Chicago), Gideon Rosenbluth (Vancouver), Erwin Baumgarten, Washington, among others reported there. In 1971 Menges followed an appointment to the University of Heidelberg where, again, he became the centre and promoter of decision-

Günter Menges (ed.), Information, Inference and Decision, 63–73. All Rights Reserved.
Copyright © 1974 by D. Reidel Publishing Company, Dordrecht-Holland.

theoretical work, with reports of John E. Walsh, Grace Kelleher (Dallas), Herman Wold (Uppsala), and guest-professorships, by invitation of Menges, of Jacob Marschak (Los Angeles) and Minaketan Behara during summer 1972, and Werner Leinfellner (Lincoln) during summer 1973.

As editor of Statistische Hefte, International Journal for Theoretical and Applied Statistics, Günter Menges made a broad circle of theorists and empiricists in statistics familiar with the aims and problems of statistical decision theory.

To facilitate the access to modern decision theory Menges edited a bibliography, together with the author, in 1968.

2. ETIALITY AND SUBJECTIVE PROBABILITIES

In the following I shall try to summarize the main parts of the writings of Günter Menges on the philosophical and practical aspects of statistical decision theory. Where the publications are written in German, the quotations are translated by the author.

Already in his article 'Das Entscheidungsproblem in der Statistik' (The Decision Problem in Statistics) (1958), Menges was deeply engaged in considerations on the borders and promises of decision theory in statistics. At that time already he searched a connection between classical deontic principles of the continental European school of statistics, on the one hand, and modern decision-theoretic criteria on the other. The article nevertheless reveals a certain scepticism (1958, p. 105ff):

It may be that the problems of hypothesis testing, parameter estimation, confidence statistics, and even the technical organizational decisions in the sense of Zizek may become the object of Wald's theory but some domains of statistics including, in particular, the logical decisions in the sense of Zizek, will continue to arise – to use an expression of Hegel – out of the effort of the concept.

In spite of this scepticism, Menges has always striven for a widening of the field of application of statistical decision theory, but not to the detriment of scientific objectivity of statistics. That is why the epistemological foundation both of classical and modern decision-theoretical methods has been accorded priority in all his work. In his habilitation thesis (1959) at Frankfurt University on 'Stichproben aus endlichen Gesamtheiten: Theorie und Technik' (Theory and Technique of Sampling

Finite Populations), he presented an epistemological justification of R. A. Fisher's philosophy of scientific inference in terms of a modification of the etiality principle proposed by Hartwig in 1956. The etiality principle (1959, p. 49) implies the following statement:

Natural relationships can be recognized in two different ways, according as to certain real conditions a definite real consequence can be associated or not. In case that a unique real consequence is attached to certain real conditions, this consequence is thought to be based upon the principle of causality. To quote to the classical example by John Stuart Mill, if we put a bird into carbonic acid and see that it dies, there remains a bit of uncertainty that we may have squeezed it to death, but we can with great confidence assume that the carbonic acid was the cause of the bird's death. At any time we can convince ourselves of the rightness of this causal result by repeating the experiment under equal conditions.

However, in case that *no* unique real consequence can be assigned to certain real conditions, ... we can no longer speak of a causal consequence, and therefore it was only consequent that Hartwig replaced the dubious position of the 'law of large numbers' or of 'Cournot's bridge' by the '*etiality principle*' in analogy to the causal principle. For, if no unique real consequence can be assigned to certain real conditions, we must of course put the 'possible' consequences with their respective probabilities under some principle, and we will put them under the principle of *general conditions* and 'possible' consequences. In the same way as in the case of causality a change of the conditions changes the unique real consequences, in the case of etiality, a change of the general conditions changes the possible real consequences and their probabilities.

With respect to the Fisherian approach this means, first of all, that – if we may be sure that the general conditions are constant – we may, with the same right as we recur to causal inference in the case of constant conditions, recur to probability inference in the case of general conditions. And in the same way as an experiment under the same conditions at any time provides a verification of causal inference, we can at any time make an experiment under the same general conditions in order to verify our probability-inference.

Consistently applying the etiality principle in statistics, Menges was bound to adopt a strict counter-position against probability subjectivism. His scientific creed on that issue is expressed in his papers (1965) and (1970); it is summarized in the latter as follows (pp. 55f):

(1) Axiomatization of subjective probability (as such; B.L.) is nonsensical and useless.

(2) Axiomatization of (objective; B.L.) probability is sufficient for probability calculus and for the stochastic parts of decision theory.

(3) Beside the axiomatization of probability, that of utility (let us say, in the sense of von Neumann-Morgenstern) is legitimate. It plays a part in judging of decision-making behavior.

(4) Subjective probability, together with the principle of insufficient reason, expresses the relationship of logical possibility (Meinong: Vermutungswahrscheinlichkeit).

(5) The three classical 'positions' (objective a priori, objective a posteriori, subjective) characterize different methods of numerical specification of probabilities.

(6) Subjective probability as 'degree of dispositional belief' is a surrogate for numerical a priori or a posteriori specification of probability.

(7) Probability as component of a statement on matters of fact is the expression of the relationship of ontological possibility.

(8) Relationships of ontological possibility are founded upon the etiality principle which connects complexes of causes with 'laws of distribution', or, mathematically speaking, distribution functions.

For decision theory, ... the following consequences ensue: The process of decision-making, as a rule, relies upon a measure of utility, on the one hand, and a statement on probability, on the other. For the acquisition and utilization of probability statements we need that calculus of probabilities which, for its part, rests on (e.g. Kolmogoroff's) axioms. Moreover, probability must be numerically specified – a problem of statistics. Such measurement can be a priori, a posteriori, or (at last need) subjective. The (objective) real validity of the probability statement is warranted by the etiality principle. For the acquisition and utilization of the utility measure we need utility theory which, for its part, rests on (von Neumann-Morgenstern's) axioms. The utility measure must be numerically specified (i.e., measured in reality). This measurement can also be a priori, a posteriori, or subjective; it is again a statistical problem.

3. FUNDAMENTAL PROBLEMS AND THEIR SOLUTION

Menges, out of his epistemological scepticism with respect to the practical applicability of statistical decision theory, formulated a number of fundamental problems not without indicating possible ways to their solution.

The first fundamental problem was the stability problem (Menges, 1963a; Menges and Behara, 1963). The stability problem is met by considering time-dependent constituents and setting up time-dependent decision criteria (1963b). Menges also developed decision criteria which take not only the stability problem but also different information levels of decision makers into account (1964, 1963b). A detailed motivation is found in (1963b, p. 164f):

The criteria of optimal decisions under uncertainty considered so far belong to three basic types:

(1) The Bayes type, covering the Bayes criterion itself and the Bernoulli-Laplace criterion,

(2) the minimax type, covering the criteria by Wald, Niehans and Savage, and Hurwicz,

(3) the mixed type, a combination of the two preceding types, covering the Hodges-Lehmann criterion.

Of course, one could also take other properties and arrange the criteria into other classes. The above classification, however, is probably of greatest practical worth since it refers to the degree of uncertainty or the extent of knowledge about reality. The Bayes type implies knowledge of the a-priori distribution or substitutes it by the principle of insufficient reason (the Bernoulli-Laplace variant). The minimax type starts from complete ignorance of the states of reality.

The degree of uncertainty, however, has certainly more than these two expressions; and therefore Hodges and Lehmann proposed a criterion that takes any possible degrees of uncertainty into account. This concept can be considerably generalized by consideration of first, different degrees of uncertainty (as Hodges and Lehmann propose) and of definite ranges of uncertainty, second, different *degrees* and *orders* of instability of the states of reality; for the latter will hardly ever be constant over an arbitrary period of time, and third, different kinds of alteration of the states of reality and – simultaneously – different ways of influencing reality; for instability does certainly not only refer to the states of reality but to their whole interaction with the decision-making itself.

Such a generalization, besides its immediate purpose of providing an adaptable criterion, admits of a detailed analysis of the decision situation even in complex cases.

Actually the traditional decision criteria (with the exception of the Hodges-Lehmann criterion) fit but some idealized or 'pure' types of situations exactly, realistic decision problems are more or less adequately treated. Mechanical application of these somehow prefabricated criteria is in almost all cases a violation of reality. Decision theory is certainly not exhausted with some ready-made recipes, but it represents a new method for the solution of practical problems by mathematical tools. In order to transform this idea of flexibility into a criterion we shall provide the classical Wald criterion with a quite general, so to say, 'empty' structure, which is accessible to further information and thus can more easily (or at all) adapt the criterion to the numerous special problems.

In terms of this basic idea Menges developed a new class of adaptable deontic criteria which he called adaptation criteria. In this context two new fundamental problems arose, viz., the problem of meta-decisions or predecisions (1965a, 1967f) and that of the 'Bayesification of the Minimax Principle' (1966a). The wider range of problems called for a more general principle which was found in terms of the accommodation principle (1967f). A survey on the whole theory so far developed is found in (1967b, 1968a and 1968b).

As the new theory puzzled many statisticians, economists, and sociologists, Menges wrote some popular articles (1967b and 1967c (where the connection between the decision problem and the inference problem already appears), 1968a, 1968b). Mengesian scepticism with respect to the applicability of decision theory culminated in his report to the International Economic Association (1968c).

4. THE ACCOMMODATION PRINCIPLE

The positive epoch then following was based upon the accommodation principle developed in 1967 (1967f), which implies the following statements:

(1) Every decision-theoretical model M is to be divided into an 'objective' (inferential, probabilistic) part M_1 and a 'subjective' (deontic, utilitaristic) part M_2.

(2) The discrepancy between the part M_1 and the empiric situation should objectively be as small as possible.

(3) The part M_2 must be specified by choosing the constituents (problem of predecisions) and the decision criterion (adaptation criterion) such that in the light of the 'objective' part M_1, on the one hand, and decision-maker's objectives and preferences, on the other hand, it allows of optimal behavior.

Menges formalized the accommodation principle to some degree, but he admitted that an exact algorithmic form could only be obtained in a limited number of cases. This fact, however, does not reduce its fundamental signification with respect to the logic of decision-making based on it.

5. INFERENCE AND DECISION

In recent works Menges sharply separates the inference part from the decision part proper, but on the other hand he demonstrates the dualism, if not dialectics, of these two parts within the framework of an objective theory of inductive behavior.

This point became a central one in his work since by his basic epistemological conception (etiality principle) Menges considers the subjectivistic approach to decision theory as a wrong way. The conclusions from this basic epistemological conception and the accommodation principle are drawn very clearly in the article (1969).

Menges' first report on the 'inference-decision' problem with respect to fiducial inference was delivered at the 4th International Conference on Operations Research in Cambridge, Mass. (Menges and Diehl, 1966b). A generalization with respect to likelihood inference was presented by Menges and Diehl at the 6th Prague Conference on Information Theory, Statistical Decision Functions and Random Processes in 1971. On this occasion the notion of observation-optimality was introduced and utilized for the solution of decision problems. In the introduction to this paper the authors state:

Two main approaches for the solution of decision problems under uncertainty have so far been advocated and applied: The Wald type of the determination of optimal decision functions or strategies (information-a-priori) and the Bernoulli type of the determination of optimal actions with the help of an a-posteriori distribution on the basis of Bayes theorem (information-a-posteriori). The second approach, while more reasonable, is often not applicable because of lacking a-priori knowledge. The authors hold that two possible solutions can compensate this disadvantage: fiducial and likelihood optimality, i.e., the determination of optimal actions with the help of either a fiducial density or a likelihood function.

Menges' work on the 'inference-decision' problem found its preliminary settlement in his inaugural lecture at the University of Heidelberg on June 16, 1971. Let me quote two passages from this lecture (Menges, 1973a):

I wish to outline the relationship between inference and decision, which in principle retains Fisher's inference conception, but allows for the two modifications stated above.

Consider a given decision problem. It is formalized by indicating the decision alternatives, called actions, which fill an action space, and the possible states, i.e., the phenomena which are relevant to the outcome of the decision but are not controlled by the decision maker. The possible states fill a space whose elements are considered as probability measure of a random variable, called state variable .... The values of the state variables measured have no inferential meaning whatever in this model; they only serve as arguments of the decision function; that is, as the if-component in the if-then-rule; if x is observed, then choose the action a. If the density over the state space – which is usually called *prior* or *a priori distribution*, I call it *distribution law of the states* – is known, that is, if it is known *how probably* the individual states occur, the expected value of the utility functional can be determined ....

If this distribution law is objectively known *a priori*, then, as long as the utility function exists and is known, no further problem arise; in particular, no inference problems.

If the distribution law of the states is not objectively known *a priori*, then there are three possibilities:

The first possibility, an *as-if* philosophy, was shown by Abraham Wald....

The American decision statisticians have found another way out. They make use of subjective probabilities. (1973a, p. 6f).

As a third way out there remains only the inference which is and remains to be the proper and genuine method of overcoming uncertainty.

To give a more precise definition than above: The task of inference is to provide a probability measure over the state space by means of measurements or observations. I call this measure over the state space, after the experiment or the observation has been made, *the inference measure*. In the cancer example the inference measure, for a given experiment matrix, i.e., objectively a posteriori – indicates the probability for a smoker to contract pulmonary cancer.

I find only three precedures within statistics to determine such an inference measure:

(1) The Bayesian method of determining the *a posteriori* distribution, when an *a priori* distribution exists and is at least approximately known.

(2) Fisher's fiducial method, when the so-called fiducial density over the state space exists and can be specified.

(3) Fraser's structural method, when a so-called structural probability for the state space exists and can be specified....

The likelihood method does provide a measure on the parameter space, but no fully additive one, i.e., none which possesses the properties of probabilities....

With the construction of a measure of inference, the inferential and hence the proper task of statistics is done. What follows are estimations, tests, and forecasts, that is, solutions of decision problems. (1973a, p. 9f.)

The problem of point estimation of parameters is taken as an example to illustrate his theses. The lecture was concluded with the following statements.

What we need is a principle connecting general causes with distribution laws, i.e., a principle like the *etiality principle* proposed by Hartwig.

For such an epistemological justification we must then have a language, i.e., a logic within which we must find a set of induction rules by analogy with its deduction rules. Rudolf Carnap attempted to construct such an inductive logic which included the inference problem.

The weakness of his statements is due to the fact that his logic is syntactically too meagre, i.e., that it is too poor in its means of expression as to be capable of adequately representing the inevitable vagueness of statistical statements.

One can altogether doubt if the customary two-valued logical systems are adequate languages for the inference problem. Here we would prefer a multivalued logic by which concepts like vagueness could be formulated. In particular, one could think of a set theory where the ε-relation can take more than two values.

After the logic has been fixed, theories can be formulated in a system of axioms, for example. A theory, however, only tells us how to manipulate the symbols in order to obtain syntactically correct sequences of symbols, similar to a data processing system where the meaning of the individual signs is not known. The *reference to reality* is finally established by interpreting the theory, i.e., by a model. This only allows us to find out whether a theory fits an empirical problem.

The more statements of a theory and the more frequently those statements fit empirical problems – every empirical case being a possible model of the theory – the '*better verified*' this theory is.

On the long way from the epistemological principle to the empirical verification of a theory, one must make – decisions, yet, on this level, no statistical, but *cognitive decisions*, and that with the help of *epistemological utility functions*. Cognitive decisions form the basis of inference, and inference is the basis for statistical decisions. (1973a, p. 13f.)

This passage, together with the paper (1972c) on inference and semantic information defined on a decision-theoretical basis, indicates the objective theory of inductive behavior presented in this volume.

University of Heidelberg

BIBLIOGRAPHY

The following bibliography is merely a selection from Günter Menges' and his former and present collaborators' publications on statistical decision theory.

Bott, D., 'Allgemeine und historische Betrachtungen zum Entscheidungsbegriff', *Statistische Hefte* **3** (1962), 1–38.

Diehl, H., 'Modell und Methoden zur Vorausrechnung von Rinderprozessen', Ph. D. thesis, Saarbrücken 1970.

Diehl, H. and Louwes, S. L., 'Zur Optimierung von Informationsprogrammen bei statistischen Entscheidungen', *Statistische Hefte* **9** (1968), 176–188.

Diehl, H. and Sprott, D. A., 'Die Likelihoodfunktion und ihre Verwendung beim statistischen Schluß', *Statistische Hefte* **6** (1965), 112–134.

Louwes, S. L., Diehl, H., and Menges, G., 'A Decision Model for the Determination of Optimal Statistical Programmes', Discussion papers of the University of Heidelberg, Nr. 29, Heidelberg 1973.

Menges, G., 'Das Entscheidungsproblem in der Statistik', *Allgemeines Statistisches Archiv* **42** (1958), 101–107.

Menges, G., *Stichproben aus endlichen Gesamtheiten: Theorie und Technik. Ein Beitrag zur Methodenlehre der Statistik*, Frankfurt a. M. 1959.

Menges, G., 'Gedanken zur Frage der Stabilität statistischer Entscheidungen', *Metrika* **6** (1963a), 84–94.

Menges, G., 'Kriterien optimaler Entscheidungen unter Ungewißheit', *Statistische Hefte* **4** (1963b), 151–171.

Menges, G., 'The Adaptation of Decision Criteria and Application Patterns', in *Proceedings of the International Federation of Operational Research Societies-Congress*, Oslo 1963, Paris 1964, pp. 585–594.

Menges, G., 'Vorentscheidungen', in *Operations Research Verfahren II* (ed. by R. Henn), Meisenheim am Glan, 1965a, pp. 24–40.

Menges, G., 'Über Wahrscheinlichkeitsinterpretationen', *Statistische Hefte* **6** (1965b), 81–96.

Menges, G., 'On the "Bayesification" of the Minimax Principle', *Unternehmensforschung* **10** (1966a), 81–91.

Menges, G., 'The Suitability of the General Decision Model for Operational Applications in the Social Sciences', in *Operational Research and the Social Sciences*, (ed. by J. R. Lawrence), London-New York-Sydney-Toronto-Wellington, 1966, pp. 565–577.

Menges, G., 'A Note on Games, Decisions and the Social Sciences', in *Chance and Change. Proceedings of a Seminar on Decision Theory, March 10, 1967*, University of British Columbia, Vancouver, 1967a, pp. 15–21.

Menges, G., 'Probleme des statistischen Entscheidungsmodells (mit einem Beispiel aus der Fischerei)', *Statistische Praxis* **22** (1967b), 485–488 and 539–541.

Menges, G., 'Die Überwindung der Ungewißheit', in *Wissenschaft und Praxis*, Festschrift zum zwanzigjährigen Bestehen des Westdeutschen Verlages, Köln-Opladen 1967c, pp. 357–387.

Menges, G., 'Fiduzialaussagen in der Ökonometrie', in *Operations Research-Verfahren III* (ed. by R. Henn), Meisenheim am Glan, 1967d, pp. 286–298.

Menges, G., 'Über Thomas Bayes (1702–1761) und das Theorem', in *Geschichte und Zukunft*, Festschrift zum 75. Geburtstag von A. Hain (ed. by A. Diemer), Meisenheim am Glan, 1967e, pp. 485–498.

Menges, G., 'Über ein Akkomodationsprinzip in der statistischen Entscheidungstheorie', in *Abhandlungen der Deutschen Akademie der Wissenschaften zu Berlin*, Berlin 1967f, Heft 4, pp. 101–110.

Menges, G., 'Entscheidungstheorie und Wirtschaftspolitik', *Der Volkswirt* **22** (1968a), Heft 12, 31–33.

Menges, G., 'Entscheidungen unter Risiko und Ungewißheit', in *Entscheidung und Information. Einführung in moderne Entscheidungskalküle und elektronische Informationssysteme* (ed. by G. Menges), Frankfurt-Berlin, 1968b, pp. 9–35.

Menges, G., 'On Some Open Questions in Statistical Decision Theory', in *Risk and Uncertainty* (ed. by K. Borch and J. Mossin), London-Melbourne-Toronto, 1968c, pp. 140–162.

Menges, G., 'Statistische Entscheidungstheorie', in *Beiträge zur Unternehmensforschung. Gegenwärtiger Stand und Entwicklungstendenzen* (ed. by G. Menges), Würzburg-Wien 1969, pp. 61–101.

Menges, G., 'On Subjective Probability and Related Problems', *Theory and Decision* 1 (1970), 40–60.

Menges, G., 'Some Decision- and Information-Theoretical Considerations About the Econometric Problems of Specification and Identification', *Statistische Hefte* **12** (1971), 22–31.

Menges, G., 'Entscheidungsmodelle in den Wirtschaftswissenschaften', in *Systemtheorie. Forschung und Information; Schriftenreihe der RIAS-Funkuniversität* (ed. by R. Kurzrock), Colloquium Verlag, Berlin, 1972a, pp. 132–140.

Menges, G., 'Measuring Social Utility and the Substitution Axiom', in *Operations Research Verfahren XIV* (ed. by W. Krelle), Meisenheim am Glan, 1972b.

Menges, G., 'Semantische Information und statistische Inferenz', *Biometrische Zeitschrift* **14** (1972c) Heft 6, 409–418.

Menges, G., 'Inference and Decision', *Selecta Statistica Canadiana* 1 (1973a), 1–14.

Menges, G., *Economic Decision Making – Basic Concepts and Models*, Harlow 1973b; German edition: *Grundmodelle wirtschaftlicher Entscheidungen*. First edition: Köln-Opladen 1969; second edition: Köln-Opladen 1974.

Menges, G. and Behara, M., 'Das Bayes'sche Risiko bei sequentiellen Stichprobenentscheidungen', *Statistische Hefte* 3 (1962a), 39–61.

Menges, G. and Behara, M., 'Einige grundsätzliche Betrachtungen über prozessuale Entscheidungen unter Ungewißheit', *Zeitschrift für handelswissenschaftliche Forschung* 14 (1962b), 483–494.

Menges, G. and Behara, M., 'On Decision Criteria under Various Degrees of Stability', *Journal of the Indian Statistical Association* 1 (1963), 185–196.

Menges, G. and Diehl, H., 'Über die operationelle Eignung von Entscheidungsmodellen', *Statistische Hefte* 7 (1966a), 30–41.

Menges, G. and Diehl, H., 'On the Application of Fiducial Probability to Statistical Decisions', in *Proceedings of the Fourth International Conference on Operational Research* (ed. by D. B. Hertz and S. Melese), New York-London-Sydney-Toronto, 1966b, pp. 82–91.

Menges, G. and Diehl, H., 'Entwicklung eines allgemeinen dynamischen Entscheidungsmodells', *Statistische Hefte* **8** (1967), 173–182.

Menges, G. and Leiner, B., *Bibliography of Statistical Decision Theory 1950–1967*; German title: *Bibliographie zur statistischen Entscheidungstheorie 1950–1967*, Köln-Opladen 1968.

Menges, G. and Rutsch, M., 'Bemerkungen zum Substitutionsaxiom des Bernoullinutzens', *Statistische Hefte* 10 (1969), 314–315.

Menges, G. and Skala, H. J., 'Main Concepts of Game- and Decision Theory', Discussion papers of the University of Heidelberg, No. 17, Heidelberg 1971.

Rutsch, M., 'Über Rationalitätskriterien für Wahlhandlungen', *Weltwirtschaftliches Archiv* **92** (1964), 396–404.

Rutsch, M., 'Über Modelle und Strukturen der Entscheidungstheorie', thesis for the habilitation, Saarbrücken 1970.

Schneeweiß, H., 'Einige Experimente mit Entscheidungsspielen', *Statistische Hefte* **3** (1962), 62–78.

Schneeweiß, H., 'Nutzenaxiomatik und Theorie des Messens', *Statistische Hefte* **4** (1963), 178–220.

Schneeweiß, H., 'Eine Entscheidungsregel für den Fall partiell bekannter Wahrscheinlichkeiten', *Unternehmensforschung* **8** (1964), 86–95.

Schneeweiß, H., 'Konsequenzen des Bernoulli-Prinzips für die Präferenzstruktur von Normalverteilungen', *Unternehmensforschung* **9** (1965a), 238–249.

Schneeweiß, H., 'Lagerhaltung bei beschränkter Information', in *Operations Research-Verfahren II* (ed. by R. Henn), Meisenheim am Glan, 1965b, pp. 41–64.

Schneeweiß, H., 'Bemerkungen zur lexikographischen Ordnung', in *Operations Research-Verfahren IV* (ed. by R. Henn), Meisenheim am Glan, 1966a, pp. 336–352.

Schneeweiß, H., 'Das Grundmodell der Entscheidungstheorie', *Statistische Hefte* **7** (1966b), 125–137.

Schneeweiß, H., 'Minimax-Lösung eines einfachen Lagermodells, wenn nur Mittelwert und Streuung der Nachfrageverteilung bekannt sind', *Unternehmensforschung* **10** (1966c), 101–117.

Schneeweiß, H., *Entscheidungskriterien bei Risiko*, Berlin-Heidelberg-New York 1967a.

Schneeweiß, H., 'Theorie der rationalen Entscheidungskriterien bei Ungewißheit', *Industrielle Organisation* **36** (1967b), 501–507.

Skala, H. J., 'Bemerkungen zur Bayes'schen Entscheidungstheorie', *Jahrbücher für Nationalökonomie und Statistik* **183** (1969/1970), 141–149.

Skala, H. J., 'Empirische Bedeutung und Nutzenmessung', *Jahrbücher für Nationalökonomie und Statistik* **184** (1970a), 509–516.

Skala, H. J., 'An Application of Model Theory to the Theory of Measurement', *Second International Game Theory Workshop*, Berkeley 1970b.

Skala, H. J., 'Nichtstandard-Bestätigungsfunktionen', in *Transactions of the Sixth Prague Conference on Information Theory, Statistical Decision Functions and Random Processes*, 1971.

Skala, H. J., 'On the Existence of Nonstandard Utility Functions', Discussion papers of the University of Heidelberg, No. 26, Heidelberg 1972.

Zschocke, D., 'Das Entscheidungsproblem bei Abraham Wald und Richard Bellman', *Statistische Hefte* **3** (1962), 79–98.

Zschocke, D., 'Die Behandlung von Entscheidungsproblemen mit Hilfe dynamischen Programmierens', *Unternehmensforschung* **8** (1964), 101–127.

PART II

PROBLEMS OF INFERENCE

D. A. S. FRASER

COMPARISON OF INFERENCE PHILOSOPHIES

ABSTRACT. The components of some inference philosophies are examined in Sections 1 and 2. Certain difficulties for having probabilities for unknowns with information, with no information, and on the basis of the model are examined in Sections 3, 4 and 5. And the conservative, fiducial and Bayesian theories are compared with structural theory in Sections 6, 7 and 8.

1. COMPARING INFERENCE PROCEDURES

Consider the comparison of various statistical models and inference theories as used in an application. There is of course the system under investigation – some physical biological or social system; the commonly used term experiment will be avoided as it has substantial additional meaning. For the comparison of models and theories it is important to distinguish the various components involved. These components will be labelled I, M, D, A, C for convenience of reference: *I*nformation, *M*odel, *D*ata, *A*ssumptions, *C*onclusions.

Information I. The information concerning the system, its components, their properties, and their interactions. The information typically is available from general theory concerning the system and its components, and from antecedent experience with similar systems or the same system under other conditions.

Model M. To some given degree of description or identification the model is the collection of possible descriptions for the system. In the usual statistical context the information is incomplete and thus allows the various descriptions for the system; and with a correct model some one of the descriptions is the true description – that is, within some reasonable approximation. The model may be the common minimum kind of model M_0 that provides external descriptions for one or several responses; or it may be a more incisive kind of model M_+ that provides descriptions also for various internal variables and their interactions. For example, a piece of electronic equipment might have an M_0 model that describes some output variables and their dependence on input

Günter Menges (ed.), Information, Inference and Decision, 77–98. All Rights Reserved.
Copyright © 1974 by D. Reidel Publishing Company, Dordrecht-Holland.

variables, or more realistically might have an M_+ model that presents the circuit diagram together with the theory for various components and their interactions.

Data D. The realized values in a performance of the system as obtained from the response variables represented in the model.

Assumptions A. The organizing and reduction principles that are used for the mathematical analysis of the *D*ata and the *M*odel. As examples consider: (1) sufficiency, (2) exhaustiveness, (3) restriction to the likelihood function and its model, (4) ancillarity, (5) restriction to tests of a given size, (6) evaluation by means of power functions, (7) restriction to unbiased estimators, (8) valuation by means of variance, (9) restriction to specific decision procedures, (10) adoption of a nonobjective numerical assessment of the elements in M (prior likelihood), (11) adoption of a nonobjective probability assessment of the elements in M (prior probability), (12) pivotal inversion, (13) restriction to the likelihood function alone,.... With an objective prior likelihood or objective prior probability the model could reasonably embrace the prior system that produced the likelihood or probability.

Conclusions C. The output obtained from the analysis of the model M, data D, and assumptions A. As examples consider: (1) significance test, (2) likelihood function, (3) decision concerning the true element (parameter value) in the model M, (4) a confidence or probability interval for the true parameter value, (5) a distribution for a realized value of some system variable, (6) a distribution for the true parameter value,....

Analysis A. The mathematical analysis or deduction from model M, data D, and assumptions A to conclusions C.

These components that arise in the use of models and theories in an application provide the basis for making comparisons. For example: one model may be more extensive than another in the sense that the latter can be deduced from the former; one theory may be weaker than another in the sense that it requires more assumptions or has an assumption with less justification.

2. THE COMPONENTS OF SOME THEORIES

Consider some current statistical theories and the kind of model, assumptions, and conclusions that arise in their application.

The conservative theory of contemporary mathematical statistics collects together a range of approaches associated with the Neyman-Pearson, Cramér-Rao, and Lehmann-Scheffé methods. The theory uses an M_0 model which describes one or several response variables. The assumptions needed depend on the kind of conclusions wanted and include some selection from the Assumptions (1, 2, 5, 6, 7, 8, 9). The possible conclusions then are those numbered (1, 3, 4). This can be summarized as:

$$M_0, D, A(1, 2, 5, 6, 7, 8) \rightarrow C(1, 3, 4).$$

The fiducial theory of statistical inference was promoted by R. A. Fisher. The theory uses an M_0 model; the assumptions include those numbered (1, 2, 4, 12); and the Conclusion (6) is a distribution for the true parameter value. Thus

$$M_0, D, A(1, 2, 4, 12) \rightarrow C(6).$$

The validity of the conclusion $C(6)$ has been questioned by some in the statistical profession; the criticisms tend to focus on the Assumption (12) for pivotal inversion. An interpretation for $C(6)$ under additional assumptions has been proposed in Fraser (1961).

The Bayesian approach to statistical inference has come to prominence in the last decade partly in reaction no doubt to the extremely limited field of success for the conservative methods. The Bayesian theory uses an M_0 model, and one or a spectrum of Assumptions (11). The probability assessment in an Assumption (11) is taken to represent relative feelings, impressions, and shadings from one to another among the possible descriptions that form the model. The conclusion is one or a spectrum of Conclusions (6) giving distributions for the true parameter value. Thus

$$M_0, D, A(11) \rightarrow C(6).$$

The validity of the conclusions $C(6)$ has been questioned by some in the statistical profession; the criticisms tend to focus on whether differential feelings and shadings can be represented by a probability assessment and indeed on whether such a subjective assessment should be included in the inference process.

The structural approach to inference places first emphasis on determining the consequences that follow from the direct analysis of the given structure – the model and data without assumptions. The approach then uses methods from the conservative theory that are consistent with the consequences already determined. For example with a continuous M_0 model it is shown in Fraser (1972a), that

$$M_0, D \to A(3):$$

thus the use of a continuous M_0 model reduces the data D to the observed likelihood function; the subsequent analysis then uses those conservative methods that ordinarily require the sufficiency and exhaustiveness Assumptions (1), (2), and we indicate this as

$$M_0, D \to A(3)+.$$

This aspect of the structural approach thus delineates a range of conservative methods and eliminates the need for the common Assumptions (1, 2).

The structural approach is also concerned with a range of M_+ models – which have more structure for direct analysis. A *probability space model* has a single probability distribution and a class of random variables; in an application the distribution describes the variation objectively identified in the response, and the class of random variables presents the various possibilities for the response some one of which is the actual response variable. The analysis (Fraser, 1968, 1974) of such a model satisfying a closure property gives

$$M_+, D \to C(5)$$

and then

$$M_+, D \to C(1, 2, 4, 5, 6);$$

thus various conservative and other methods are obtained without assumptions for the analysis. Without the closure property, certain difficulties can arise; see Fraser (1973).

A generalized probability space model can be formed as a combination of an M_0 model and an M_+ model as just described. The direct analysis of such a model gives

$$M_+, D \to A(3)$$

concerning the M_0 parameter and thus leads to the conservative methods that are based on likelihood; and for a given value of the preceding parameter the analysis gives

$$M_+, D \to C(1, 2, 4, 5, 6)$$

concerning the remaining parameter. The analysis of these M_+ models has been discussed in Fraser (1966, 1968, 1974).

3. PROBABILITIES ON THE BASIS OF INFORMATION

The Bayesian approach to statistical inference uses an Assumption (11) that presents an assessment of the various possible values for the parameter, an assessment in terms of numbers that obey the rules for probabilities and are called probabilities. The numerical assessment is viewed as representing the investigator's feelings, impressions, and differential shadings from one to another concerning the possible parameter values. Whether such numerical assessments can in any generality represent feelings and impressions concerning unknowns is a serious question – at least if the catholic claims for the Bayesian approach are taken seriously. The usual justification for the probability assessments is by means of axioms for preferences which lead to utility and then to personal probabilities. There would seem to be two direct approaches to the question – examining the validity of the axioms and examining the validity of the probability assessments.

A. Blyth (1972a, b) presents some interesting probability paradoxes which have the effect of denying the general validity of two axioms used in developing utility and personal probability. The paradoxes are of general interest in that they suggest ways in which we should be cautious in our informal thinking about probabilities. And they are of special interest here for the direct way they indicate how the plausibly-presented axioms for personal probability can be invalid in simple contexts. The four Bayesian discussants of the Blyth papers do not seem to come to grips with the paradoxes or their implications for Bayesian theory, and tend to emphasize a reassertion of belief in utility and personal probability. Or as Blyth in part notes in his rejoinder the discussants seem to say "we should take care not to apply (an axiom – and thus the

Bayesian approach) to situations in which it is false...." Which is of
course what Blyth is emphasizing in the original two papers – that
personal probability and the Bayesian approach do not have the universal
generality claimed for them.

B.   Alternatively Fraser (1972a) considers the possibility for personal
probability for the case of a realization from an objectively identified
random system where there is information concerning the realization.
The Bayesian believes he can have probabilities for an unknown on
the basis of feelings and information concerning the unknown. It is
shown in Fraser (1972a) that quite different objective probabilities can
be applicable depending on how the information was generated. This
nonuniqueness then invalidates any general argument from information
concerning an unknown to meaningful probabilities for that unknown.
And in particular it denies the universality of the Bayesian claim.

4. PROBABILITIES ON THE BASIS OF NO INFORMATION

It is fairly common practice among some Bayesians to use a flat or
noninformative prior distribution for the Assumption (11) of a Bayesian
analysis. This envisages an application in which the investigator has
no feelings or information that favour one possible value over another
for the parameter – sometimes referred to as *insufficient* reason for one
value over another.

A.   A statistical model is a set of possible descriptions for the system
under investigation, or more simply it is a set of parameter values –
values that index the possible descriptions for the system. This is of
course in accord with the standard scientific practice of representing an
unknown by a set – or *space*, the set of possible values for the unknown.
   A space by itself is the mathematical description for an unknown
about which we have no information. And to add further mathematical
description is either to say something more or to say something contradictory to that already said.

B.   The Bayesian approach however takes the space as just described
and with no differential feelings or information concerning the values

in the space, the approach argues to a flat or uniform distribution on the space. Of course if a distribution on the space is assumed and if certain transformations on the space are appropriate then a uniform or flat distribution is obtained. This is how the equiprobability assignments are derived by symmetry for the classical games of chance. But mathematically – and scientifically – there is a very large step from a *space* to a *probability space*, and ingredients are needed to make the step – essentially that *there be* a distribution and *there be* invariance under certain transformations.

Perhaps the common consideration of finite spaces has made the step appear deceptively trivial: We do need that there be a distribution – but of course this is implicit within the Bayesian approach. And we then find that the transformations are almost self defining – the group of permutations on the finite space. We thus obtain the uniform distribution as in the classical games of chance.

But with a nonfinite space the step is far from trivial. If the space is countable then the distribution must be improper. And if the space has continuity properties then a special choice of transformations must be made, and further the distribution may need to be improper. For this continuity case different choices of transformations give different flat distributions – thus the flat prior depends in fact on the way we use transformations to express 'no information'.

A space by itself is the mathematical description for an unknown about which we have no information. The occurrence then of improper priors and nonuniqueness provide an after-the-facts warning that the use of a distribution to represent no information is an attempt at over-expression and is logically incorrect.

5. PROBABILITIES ON THE BASIS OF THE MODEL

The preceding section notes that essentially two ingredients are needed to produce a prior distribution representing no information – that there be a distribution, and that there be invariance under certain transformations. The Bayesian approach to inference premises the first of these ingredients; and the second ingredient is taken as an expression of equivalence among various possible values for the unknown being investigated. For the second ingredient it is common practice among some

Bayesians to use properties of the model to obtain transformations that express the equivalence or invariance.

A.   In certain contexts the statistical model may indeed be representing certain physical properties concerning the unknown and its possible values. Transformations that relate to the model could then be expressing properties of the unknown as a physical quantity, and thus have the merits and demerits as discussed in the preceding two sections.

In other contexts there may be different possible investigations with different models and with different transformations. This would lead to different prior distributions as calculated from properties of the model. It follows then that the use of a model as such to determine transformations and a prior is a contradictory procedure in general. We thus have a further after-the facts warning to add to those discussed in the preceding section.

B.   But consider briefly some further more technical problems connected with the use of such transformations in relation to a statistical model. In some familiar contexts the parameter space can be put into one-one correspondence with an invariance group for the model; let $\Omega = \{\theta\} = G$ be the parameter space and the group. If a prior distribution on Ω is to be invariant in the same way that the model is invariant then it must be a left Haar measure $d\mu(\theta)$. Somewhat surprisingly however the Bayesians tend to prefer a right Haar measure $d\nu(\theta)$. This choice runs counter to a direct expression of invariance and has not had convincing justification within the Bayesian framework; for some further comments see Fraser (1972a).

C.   And there are internal problems that can arise with the use of the right (or left) Haar priors. Suppose the group $G = H_2 H_1$ factors as a semidirect product of subgroups H_2 and H_1; correspondingly let $\theta = \beta\alpha$. The right Haar measure then factors as

$$d\nu(\theta) = d\nu_1(\alpha) \cdot \Delta^{-1}(\beta) \, \Delta_2(\beta) \, d\nu_2(\beta)$$

where ν_i, Δ_i are the right Haar, modular function in H_i and Δ is the modular function in G. Now suppose that information becomes available which specifies the value for α. The conditional distribution is then given by

$$\Delta^{-1}(\beta)\, \Delta_2(\beta)\, dv_2(\beta)$$

which is not in general equal to the right Haar measure $dv_2(\beta)$. Thus the use of right Haar priors is internally inconsistent.

D. And there are external problems that can arise with the use of the right Haar prior. Suppose the parameter space is $\Lambda \times \Omega = \{\lambda, \theta\}$ where a copy of Ω is viewed as a fibre over each value of λ. Then a right Haar prior for θ is given by $dv(\theta)$. But just as validly a right Haar prior for θ is given by $k(\lambda)\, dv(\theta)$ for any function k. This additional arbitrariness is often overlooked by proponents of the Bayesian approach.

Some Bayesians have recently shifted away from the general use of flat priors. Perhaps in doing this they are in part sensing some of the preceding technical difficulties.

6. THE CONSERVATIVE AND STRUCTURAL THEORIES

Consider some comparisons between the conservative and the structural theories discussed in Section 2. The *conservative theory* can be represented by

$$M_0,\, D,\, A(1, 2, 5, 6, 7, 8) \rightarrow C(1, 3, 4).$$

And the *structural theory* can be represented by

$$M_+,\, D \rightarrow A(3)+$$

concerning the M_0 parameter and by

$$M_+,\, D \rightarrow C(1, 2, 4, 5, 6)$$

concerning the principal parameter.

A. Consider first an application that admits only an M_0 model. The conservative theory with various assumptions may or may not be able to obtain a solution – that is, a reasonably unequivocal conclusion concerning the parameter value.

The structural theory implies Assumption (3) which in turn implies the sufficiency and exhaustiveness Assumptions (1, 2). This in turn leads to those conservative-theory results that use Assumptions (1) and (2) but *without* those as needed assumptions.

Thus in an application admitting only an M_0 model, the structural theory has the modest effect of restricting the methods to those based on the observed likelihood function together with its model.

B.   Consider briefly the kind of statistical model for which the conservative theory is successful.

For the Cramér-Rao approach generalized to local unbiasedness, success of the method requires the model to be exponential with the number of parameter components equal to the dimension of the parameter.

For completeness as used for minimum variance unbiasedness, success places strong restrictions on the model both in the fixed carrier case and in the variable carrier case but it seems generally true that success is limited to cases in which the likelihood-function statistic has the same dimension as the parameter.

For the likelihood ratio approach to uniformly most powerful tests, success requires the likelihood ratio to be monotone in terms of a real valued function and thus requires the likelihood-function statistic to be one-dimensional.

For the unbiasedness approach to uniform most powerful (unbiased) tests, success of the method seems to require an exponential model with the number of parameter components equal to the dimension of the parameter or in a larger context to require a combination of completeness for certain parameters and monotone likelihood ratio for other parameters; this indicates that the method is effectively restricted to cases in which the likelihood-function statistic has the same dimension as the parameter.

For the invariance approach to obtaining uniformly most powerful (invariant) tests, success is largely restricted to cases where the likelihood statistic has the same dimension as the parameter; the method operates mainly to isolate component statistics for treating component parameters.

The success then of this range of conservative methods effectively requires *the likelihood-function statistic to have the same dimension as the parameter* and typically it requires much more.

Now consider cases in which we have multiple observations on the response. For the case of model with a fixed region of positive density (fixed carrier case) the fixed dimension for the likelihood-function statistic requires *the model to be exponential with the number of parameter components equal to the dimension of the parameter*. Some parallel results occur in the variable carrier case.

Now consider some applications and the kind of model that can satisfy the preceding requirements for success of the conservative methods. For brevity we restrict attention to the fixed carrier case. If the distribution for the response is known except for a location parameter then the model must be either (1) *Normal* or (2) *the logarithm of a gamma variable*. And if the distribution is known except for a location and scale parameter then the model must be *normal*. And for a response having a linear model with or without known scaling then the model must be Normal (or log-gamma in special known scaling cases).

Of course the binomial and the Poisson are amenable to the methods but then they have such exceptional simplicities that they hardly need the theory.

In broad summary then the conservative methods are successful if the distribution form is normal. Such models are of course the examples in the standard statistical texts – but what the texts do not mention is that these models are effectively the only ones for which the theory works.

C.   Now consider an application that admits an M_+ model but without any M_0 parameter. Some simple examples involving location scale and linear models are examined in Fraser (1974) and more general examples in Fraser (1968). All that is needed to justify an M_+ model of the kind mentioned is the objective identification of the variation as presented by its distribution. As indicated in Section 2 we have

$$M_+, D \rightarrow C(1, 2, 4, 5, 6).$$

Thus without any of the conservative theory assumptions we obtain a broader range of conclusions deleting only the decision-theoretic 'conclusions'.

Now consider some applications and a model that is an M_+ model as just described. If the distribution for the response is known except for location, scale, and linear location then the structural analysis yields unique conclusions. This is in sharp contrast with the conservative theory which essentially produces conclusions only for the case of normal variation. For some numerical details see Fraser (1974).

There are of course some of conservative persuasion who might argue that Conclusions (4, 6) could be obtained by an appropriate combination of assumptions including a specific choice of ancillary Assumption (4). True – but so also can a variety of contradictory 'conclusions' in a range of problems. And indeed with that approach, one would need to sort through assumptions to obtain the combination that yields the conclusion deemed desirable by direct analysis within the other theory.

D.　Now consider an application that admits an M_+ model which also has an M_0 parameter. Some examples involving location, scale, and linear models are examined in Fraser (1974) and more general examples in Fraser (1968). As indicated in Section 2 we have

$$M_+, D \to A(3)+$$

concerning the M_0 parameter and we obtain for that parameter all the conservative theory results that build on Assumptions (1, 2). And given the M_0 parameter we have

$$M_+, D \to C(1, 2, 4, 5, 6)$$

concerning the primary parameter.

The examples in Fraser (1974) show how the parameter for the distribution for variation can be given preliminary likelihood analysis, and how distributions relating to the primary parameters can then be derived for any value of the first parameter.

In summary, the structural approach does all that the conservative approach does and in addition it extends the direct analysis of location, scale, and linear location from the *normal case only* to arbitrary distributions for variation. And these more general results are obtained uniquely with fewer assumptions.

7. THE FIDUCIAL AND STRUCTURAL THEORIES

Consider some comparisons between the fiducial and the structural theories discussed in Section 2. The fiducial theory can be represented by

$$M_0, D, A(1, 2, 4, 12) \rightarrow C(6).$$

And the structural theory can be represented by

$$M_+, D \rightarrow A(3) +$$

concerning the M_0 parameter and by

$$M_+, D \rightarrow C(1, 2, 4, 5, 6)$$

concerning the principal parameter.

A. The fiducial theory needs four strong assumptions and leads only to a distribution concerning the true parameter value. The theory is used typically as an adjunct to a spectrum of conservative theory methods.

The structural theory on the other hand leads to and selects a broad range of conservative methods without the need for the common Assumptions (1, 2). And for an M_+ parameter it produces without assumptions a range of conclusions – just one of which is a distribution concerning the true parameter value.

B. A partial comparison can be obtained by considering the range of applications to which both theories can be applied, to which fiducial but not structural can be applied, and to which structural but not fiducial can be applied.

Both theories can be applied to the familiar range of location, scale, and location scale applications. In these applications the fiducial theory requires a specific set of assumptions which are chosen from possible assumptions more for what they lead to than for the objective justifications available. In contrast the structural theory needs only the objective identification of the distribution describing variation – do we know its distribution to some reasonable degree of approximation? For more complex applications involving regression and linear relations the fiducial approach again has problems connected with the assumptions and particularly with the choice of an Assumption (4). In contrast the structural analysis is routine probability-theory analysis.

The applications to which fiducial can be applied and not structural are few if any. The original fiducial example involves the correlation coefficient and it is not directly amenable to the structural approach. The correlation situation however does not arise by itself but typically from some bivariate applications – and the usual forms of the bivariate application *are* amenable to the structural approach.

The applications to which structural can be applied and not fiducial are extensive. An application needs only the objective identification of the distribution for variation – which gives the probability space, and a closure property for the transformations – which justifies the probability analysis.

C. A further comparison can be made by considering the conclusions that follow from each approach – in an application where both approaches are available. The fiducial approach produces a distribution concerning the true value of the parameter. In contrast the structural produces a range of conclusions – objective tests of significance for parameters, likelihood functions, confidence and probability intervals, a distribution describing the realized variation, and indeed a distribution concerning the true value of the parameter. Some of these of course can be obtained by adding conservative methods to the fiducial, but then further assumptions are required that are not needed with the structural approach.

D. The availability and the use of statistical methods depends in part on the amount of promotion and the type of sanctions applied by reviewers and commentators. In this regard it is of interest to consider some of the more detailed reviews of the principal published presentation (Fraser, 1968) of structural methods.

The more detailed reviews of the book, for example Lindley (1969) and Williams (1970), have mostly been by statisticians with strong commitments or involvements with other approaches to inference. In considering a review it is of interest to note what aspects of the method are being observed and commented on, to note whether the observations are correct, and indeed to examine the logic used by the reviewer as he in part is commenting on logic in the book itself.

A frequent comment in reviews concerns ancillary statistics: "Although Fraser does not use the phrase, the concept of an ancillary statistic is basic to the argument..." (Lindley, 1969, p. 456); "He does not use this language but his restriction to orbits is mathematically equivalent to the choice of an ancillary" (Lindley, 1971, p. 12); and other reviews and reviewers. These observations are in fact incorrect as can be seen by examining the components in Section 2, the discussion in Section 6, or the present section, or indeed (Fraser, 1968) itself. The term ancillarity has of course some negative associations and it is certainly conceivable that these could be used inadvertently to support another position. This does not seem possible however for the reviewer cited. The alternative must then be that the reviewer read the material somewhat casually or superficially, or read it with such a commitment to another persuasion that the words and analyses changed their meanings. On the topic ancillarity the necessary change in meaning is substantial: from – a condition that arises on a probability space because of observational information – to – a class of probability distributions and the invariance property of some marginal measure.

In a somewhat different vein a reviewer (Williams, 1970) comments as follows: "I feel if the reduction of the structural model were unique, the accompanying inference theory would long ago have been widely known and advocated. Unfortunately the correspondence between the elements on the orbit of X and elements of G is not always uniquely determined and as a result inferences with two different reduced structural models... can be quite different for the same set of data." And "The ideas behind the reduced structural model were worked out during the 1930's by R. A. Fisher... and by E. J. G. Pitman."

In a reply (Fraser, 1972b) I noted that the reduction was in fact unique, and also commented that the logical consequences of using objective error (a probability space) had unfortunately been neglected by the statistical profession since the early use of explicit error by Gauss and Laplace.

In a rejoinder (Williams, 1972) the reviewer remarked that he had meant something different by *reduction* – not the *reduction* explicitly defined in the book, but the *development* of a model from a response distribution. A very large change of meaning for a single word.

The reviewer then remarked on the *development* of a model suggesting that different structural models can describe the same response distributions. This remark reveals a basic misunderstanding of the nature of a statistical model, the set of possible descriptions at some level of description. For if two models are viewed as contenders then the proper model of course is at least the union of those contenders. The apparent difficulty raised by the remark thus vanishes.

And on the use of objective error and the neglect of its logical consequences since the work of Gauss and Laplace, the reviewer remarks "Dr. Fraser rightly attributes his structural model to Gauss and Laplace...." The change from what was said to what is ascribed is incredible. How can such a misrepresentation be proffered? And why?

E. The reviewer's claim that it has all been worked out by Fisher and Pitman or that it is all attributable to Gauss and Laplace needs some further comments.

The use of symbols corresponding to error may be found in the works of Gauss and Laplace. With observed response values there are then certain logical consequences that follow by classical probability theory: for illustration if you have partial information (can observe 2 hands at bridge) concerning a stochastic realization, then the proper probability description (of the other 2 hands) is given by conditional distribution. There is no indication that this was noted by Gauss and Laplace. Nor was it noted by Fisher or Pitman in their fiducial analyses. Indeed there seems to be no indication that Fisher and Pitman were organizing any fiducial ideas around the notion of objective error.

How then can a claim be made that one theory is a 'reworking' of the other? Certainly in simple contexts the two theories can have formulas in common (although surrounding argument may often be proceeding in opposite directions). A nonempty intersection however is certainly not an equivalence in the way suggested by the claim. In Section 2 we noted the substantial difference in the Assumptions: from many Assumptions for fiducial theory to no Assumptions for the structural theory. And in Section 2 we noted the substantial difference in the Conclusions: from a single Conclusion for fiducial theory to a range of Conclusions for structural theory. Indeed an Assumption for one theory becomes in part a Conclusion for the other. The claim seems somewhat remote from facts.

Certainly a lot of statisticians would have been wasting their time in the 1950's and 1960's if it were all in the error of Gauss and Laplace or just a reworking of Fisher and Pitman. Of course there are evolutionary and historical connections but supposedly the claim is concerned with substance itself. Certainly there are those who examined fiducial in 1950's and 1960's and found it wanting; it could then be possible perhaps to assume that a somewhat related theory was also wanting. Perhaps a significant thing about certain of the review comments is the unfamiliarity with the substance of what was presented in Fraser (1968). Indeed the changes in judgment from review (Williams, 1970) to rejoinder (Williams, 1972) give some indication of the basis for judgment. For in an objective detail the rejoinder cites the "derivative of distributions (for normal regression analysis) woven through 54 pages." The derivation of the basic distribution takes somewhat more than one page; in Fraser (1974) the derivation is presented in less than one page and some 52 pages of general discussion surrounding the model and least squares is replaced by one other page: two pages in total; the reviewer's weaving is thin.

8. THE BAYESIAN AND STRUCTURAL THEORIES

Consider some comparisons between the Bayesian and the structural theories discussed in Section 2. The Bayesian theory can be represented by

$$M_0, D, A(11) \rightarrow C(6).$$

And the structural theory can be represented by

$$M_+, D \rightarrow A(3)+$$

concerning the M_0 parameter and by

$$M_+, D \rightarrow C(1, 2, 4, 5, 6)$$

concerning the principal parameter.

A.   The Bayesian theory needs a strong Assumption (11) that presents a probability distribution concerning the true value of the parameter.

Of course in applications there are occasional instances where the parameter value has been produced by some antecedent system that can be described by a probability space. The investigator would then have rather reasonable justification for introducing an Assumption (11) involving the antecedent probability space; and the analysis would be the standard Bayesian use of the definition of conditional probability. Quite properly however the investigator could record separately the results from the antecedent system and the results (by say conservative or structural approaches) from the current system. Any user would then have the options of combining the results to get an overall result, of comparing the results to determine whether the results are in harmony, or indeed of ignoring the antecedent results if the current results are based on careful design and control of the system under investigation. From this latter point of view, then, the Bayesian method is not a method of inference but rather a procedure for combining probability results when it is deemed appropriate to so combine them.

B.   In the more common instances however the Bayesian Assumption (11) is intended to describe the feelings and impressions of the investigator concerning the value of the parameter.

Historically these feelings and impressions are exactly what experimentation is designed to eliminate. Of course the questions raised and the hypotheses considered may well derive from feelings and impressions but an experimental investigation as developed within the scientific tradition is specifically designed to provide an entirely objective and unbiased assessment of the possibilities under consideration. The use of feelings and impressions as part of an inference approach is thus running directly counter to the scientific method, and cannot then reasonably be considered a respectable part of the scientific method.

C.   Quite apart from whether feelings, impressions and diffuse information can properly be used in statistical inference is the question of whether they can even provide the basis for a probability measure representing possible values for the unknown under investigation. This question concerning probabilities for an unknown has been examined in Section 3 and the conclusion is that probabilities concerning unknowns are not available in general on the basis of information. Indeed it is shown in Fraser (1972a) that rather strict conditions must be fulfilled even for the case of an objective system and partial information. The conclusion then is that feelings and diffuse information *cannot* in general be used for statistical inference.

D.   A related question is whether no information can provide the basis for a probability measure representing possible values for the unknown. This question concerning probability on the basis of no information has been examined in Section 4 and the conclusion is that *no information* does not produce probabilities on the space of possible values for the unknown and thus cannot be used as input to a Bayesian analysis.

E.   Now consider the question of a probability measure for an Assumption (11) chosen on the basis of compatibility with the statistical model. If the measure is presented as representing the absence of information then the arguments in Section 5 are relevant. Not only does such a measure not represent the absence of information but the usage of such a measure involves both internal and external contradictions.

If however a measure for Assumption (11) is presented entirely as a device for statistical analyses then somewhat different questions are involved. For example – how desperate are we to obtain any 'answer' even if it is appropriate to some enlarged process embracing a bypo-thetical prior system. Certainly, if we consider the effectiveness of the conservative methods, then it is clear that we were quite desperate in the late 1950's, a period that marked the beginning of the current period of popularity for the Bayesian approach. Indeed perhaps the need then almost justified the attempted solution.

Thus – do we view the use of Assumption (11) purely as a mechanical means for generating spectrums of statistical methods – to be sub-sequently evaluated in some empirical manner? Certainly any way of generating potentially useful methods is of some value. The question here however is whether Assumption (11) is a necessary of even relevant part of such an activity. The answer is a clear No. For, any posterior distribution from a Bayesian analysis can be obtained by modulating the likelihood with a weight function. Indeed the free use of weight functions as a formal procedure for generating potential methods has the decided advantage that there is little chance that an output will be called a posterior probability and thus mistaken for a probability.

E. The Bayesian theory needs a strong assumption, an assumption that is unjustified as we have seen in the earlier parts of this section; and it leads only to a distribution concerning the true value.

The structural theory however leads to and selects a wide range of conservative methods concerning the M_0 parameter and produces without assumptions a wide range of conclusions concerning the primary parameter – just one of which is a distribution concerning that parameter.

A partial comparison can be made by considering the range of application for the two theories. As we have noted, the Bayesian claims universality; but we have cited at the beginning of this section how this claim is unfounded and indeed contradictory. As we have noted in Section 6 the structural approach selects the likelihood based methods for the M_0 parameter, and produces a wide range of results for the primary parameter. On the other hand the structural approach does have universal application but accepts the limitations that go with the conservative methods in ordinary applications.

F. Some comparison between the two theories can be obtained by considering a review of the structural theory by a deeply committed adherent to the Bayesian persuasion: Lindley (1969).

As the Bayesian approach produces only a distribution for the parameter it is not surprising that the reviewer concentrates on those structural results that have a close connection to the Bayesian posterior, and on how those results might be obtained from the Bayesian posterior.

The reviewer in commenting on the structural distribution for the parameter remarks that it "appears to be true generally that the distribution of θ is obtained by multiplying the likelihood by a function of θ that can be interpreted as a prior density." But then the justification for the distribution in the structural approach is no longer available and is replaced by Assumption (11) using a right Haar prior with all the problems that go with that prior as indicated in Section 5. The remark may have weight as far as the mechanics discussed in part D but not in terms of meaning and justification.

And in commenting on the (marginal) likelihood function for the M_0 parameter the reviewer remarks that "It is the integration of the likelihood with respect to this prior that provides the marginal likelihood available for inferences when the full structural model is not present." In all cases as indicated in Section 5D there is in fact a spectrum of right Haar priors not just a single prior as assumed by the reviewer. Thus the remark has content only if the Bayesian has some means – with justification – for choosing the particular prior that works so as to produce the marginal likelihood. And if this were available it does not cover the more complex cases where the *prior* would need to depend on the (*posterior*) observed response! A disturbing situation at the very least. By contrast the (marginal) likelihood in the structural approach is an ordinary likelihood from the only realization observed.

The Bayesian reviewer also raises the question of two structural models for the same physical response, and with respect to the corresponding conclusions asks 'which is right?' As indicated in Section 7 this indicates a misunderstanding as to the nature of a statistical model. For if two models are judged contenders then the proper model is at least the union of these 'contenders'. The apparent difficulty thus vanishes.

G. As noted earlier the reviewer concentrates on these structural methods that relate closely to the Bayesian posterior. He thus considers Conclusions $C(6)$ and overlooks $C(1, 2, 4, 5)$ except for the reference to (marginal) likelihood and a brief reference to a significance test.

The distribution $C(5)$ does not have a position in the Bayesian framework and it is not surprising perhaps that it was overlooked. The distribution $C(5)$ however is fundamental: it is obtained by a direct application of probability theory without assumptions; and it gives immediately the tests of significance for various reasonable hypotheses – no recourse to hypothesis testing theory.

Perhaps the manner in which structural theory leads into the conservative methods (Fraser, 1968, p. 185) – "the remaining part can be analyzed by methods appropriate to the (M_0) model" – was rather easily overlooked. The structural approach had already examined the normal models of the conservative approach – in fact had examined them with arbitrary error form – and hardly needed to present the conservative method at that stage.

But the reference to the significance test is perhaps the most illuminating concerning present statistics. It suggests that the assessment of an observed value in relationship to a distribution is a complicated thing. It should not be for someone with a background with probability-theory and application. It only becomes complicated to the degree that elementary statistics develops the notion that a hypothesis must be accepted or rejected – rather than assessed.

University of Toronto

BIBLIOGRAPHY

Blyth, C. R., 'On Simpson's Paradox and the Sure-Thing Principle', *Jour. Amer. Statist. Assoc.* **67** (1972a), 364–366.

Blyth, C. R., 'Some Probability Paradoxes in Choice from Among Random Alternatives', *Jour. Amer. Statist. Assoc.* **67** (1972b), 366–373.

Fraser, D. A. S., 'The Fiducial Method and Invariance', *Biometrika* **48** (1961), 261–80.

Fraser, D. A. S., 'Structural Probability and a Generalization', *Biometrika* **53** (1966), 1–9.

Fraser, D. A. S., *The Structure of Inference*, Wiley, New York, 1968.

Fraser, D. A. S., 'Bayes, Likelihood, or Structural', *Annals Math. Statist.* **43** (1972a), 777–790.

Fraser, D. A. S., 'Reply', *Technometrics* **14** (1972b), 809–810.

Fraser, D. A. S., 'Comments on the McGilchrist Paper', *Jour. Amer. Statist. Assoc.* **68** (1973), 97–106.

Fraser, D. A. S., 'Necessary Analysis and Adaptive Inference', *Jour. Amer. Statist. Assoc.* **68** (1974), in press.

Lindley, D. V., 'Review', *Biometrika* **56** (1969), 453–6.

Lindley, D. V., 'Bayesian Statistics', A review, SIAM, Philadelphia, 1971.

Williams, J. S., 'Book Review', *Technometrics* **12** (1970), 709–711.

Williams, J. S., 'Rejoinder', *Technometrics* **14** (1972), 810.

JAMES G. KALBFLEISCH AND D. A. SPROTT

ON THE LOGIC OF TESTS OF SIGNIFICANCE
WITH SPECIAL REFERENCE TO TESTING
THE SIGNIFICANCE OF POISSON-DISTRIBUTED
OBSERVATIONS

ABSTRACT. Some logical aspects of tests of significance are illustrated using the example of equality of means of Poisson-distributed observations. Specifically, in the conventional test for the significance of a difference between two Poisson-distributed observations, the significance level is computed from the conditional distribution given their observed total. However, an unconditional test has greater power and so is sometimes advocated in place of the conditional test. The present paper argues that power considerations are not relevant in choosing between conditional and unconditional tests, and that the conditional test is the appropriate one. The example is extended to include tests of equality of means of two Poisson samples (pointing out an error in a formula that is sometimes used) and also to include tests concerning the ratio of Poisson means. There is a general discussion of significance tests with reference to the above examples.

1. INTRODUCTION

Let X_1 and X_2 be independent Poisson variates with means μ_1 and μ_2. The problem is to test the significance of observed values x_1 and x_2 in relation to the hypothesis $H: \mu_1 = \mu_2 = \mu$ (unspecified). We define

$$T = X_1 + X_2, \qquad U = |X_1 - X_2| / \sqrt{T}$$

and use small letters t, u to denote their observed values. In the conventional two-tail exact test, the significance level is calculated from the conditional distribution of U given that $T = t$,

(1) $$p_t = \Pr(U \geqslant u \mid T = t) = \sum \binom{t}{i} (\tfrac{1}{2})^t,$$

where the sum extends over all i such that $|i - t/2| \geqslant u\sqrt{t/4}$.

An unconditional test can also be based on U. The significance level is then

(2) $$p = \Pr(U \geqslant u) = \sum_{t=0}^{\infty} \Pr(U \geqslant u \mid T = t) \Pr(T = t)$$

$$= \sum_{t=0}^{\infty} p_t \Pr(T = t).$$

Günter Menges (ed.), Information, Inference and Decision, 99–109. All Rights Reserved.

For $\mu \geqslant 2.5$, p is nearly independent of μ, and is well approximated by $2\{1 - \Phi(u)\}$, where Φ is the standardized normal cumulative function (cf. Detre and White, 1970).

It is sometimes argued that the unconditional test (2) is more powerful than the conditional test (1), and is therefore to be preferred. Mantel (1971) points out that this argument must be interpreted cautiously. What it shows is that the unconditional test is preferable for use as a routine signalling device, where many Poisson comparisons are to be made, and one wishes to fix the frequency of a trouble signal when everything is satisfactory. However, it does not follow that the unconditional test is to be preferred when the intention is to test the significance of the difference between x_1 and x_2 in a particular case. We shall argue that for the latter problem of testing significance, the conditional test (1) is appropriate.

Whether (1) or (2) should be used is a question of some theoretical importance, since similar situations involving a comparison of conditional and unconditional tests seem frequently to arise (e.g. contingency tables). It is also of practical importance, because the numerical difference between (1) and (2) can be large. For instance, if $x_1 = 4$ and $x_2 = 0$, the conditional test gives $p_4 = 2(\frac{1}{2})^4 = 0.125$, while (2) gives $p \simeq 2\{1 - \Phi(2)\} = 0.045$. The unconditional test leads to rejection at the 5% level, whereas the conditional test does not lead to rejection at even the 10% level.

2. CONDITIONAL VS. UNCONDITIONAL TESTS

The conditional test (1) will never lead to rejection at the 5% level unless the observed total t exceeds 5. If $\mu_1 + \mu_2$ is small, $\Pr(T \leqslant 5)$ is large, and hence the frequency with which H would be rejected in repeated applications of the conditional test will be substantially less than 5%. Detre and White found that the frequency of rejection in the unconditional test (2) will be much closer to the nominal 5%. This increase in the rejection rate carries with it an automatic increase in the power. Since the unconditional test has the greater power, some might be tempted to prefer it to the conditional test (1).

In this section, we argue that power comparisons are not relevant when the choice is between a conditional test and an unconditional one.

In the first place, the unconditional power of a conditional test can be defined in many different ways. For example, consider the two test statistics $U=|X_1-X_2|/\sqrt{T}$ and $V=|X_1-X_2|$, with observed values u and $v=u\sqrt{t}$. Then, whatever the observed results x_1 and x_2,

$$\Pr(U\geqslant u \mid T=t)=\Pr(V\geqslant v \mid T=t)$$

so that U and V define precisely the same conditional test. However, the unconditional probabilities $\Pr(U\geqslant u)$ and $\Pr(V\geqslant v)$ will in general be different. Hence the unconditional power of the conditional test depends upon whether U or V is taken to be the test statistic. More generally, let V be any function of U and T such that, given T, V is strictly increasing in U. Then U and V will define the same conditional test, but their unconditional powers will be different. There seems to be no good reason for choosing U rather than V as the test statistic for the conditional test, and hence its 'power' is not unambiguously defined.

Even if we ignore this difficulty and agree to base the computations on a particular test statistic U, a strong argument can be made against the use of power to choose between conditional and unconditional tests. In fact, it is easy to find examples, such as the following which is a slight modification of one due to Professor G. A. Barnard, in which the unconditional test is much more powerful, but the conditional test is clearly the appropriate one.

An experiment is undertaken to test the hypothesis $\theta=1$, where θ is the sex ratio for a certain type of animal. Animals are sampled in such a way that they enter the sample independently with a probability not depending upon their sex. Then, if $\theta=1$, the probability of x_1 males in a sample of t animals is $\binom{t}{x_1}(\tfrac{1}{2})^t$, and the two-tail significance level will be given by (1). For instance, if $x_1=59$ males are observed in a sample of $t=100$, we would obtain

$$p_{100}=\Pr(U\geqslant 1.8 \mid T=100)=0.089.$$

The above analysis treats the sample size as constant. However, it may be that the sample size is a random variable T, so that if the experiment were repeated, a different number of animals might be observed. For instance, it may be that the sample size depended upon the approval of a grant application whose chance of success was only 50%, and that in the event of failure, only one animal could have been sampled. We would then have

$$\Pr(T=1)=\Pr(T=100)=\tfrac{1}{2}, \qquad \Pr(U\geqslant 1.8 \mid T=1)=0,$$

and we could obtain the unconditional significance level

$$p=\Pr(U\geqslant 1.8)=\tfrac{1}{2}\Pr(U\geqslant 1.8 \mid T=1)+ \\ +\tfrac{1}{2}\Pr(U\geqslant 1.8 \mid T=100)=\tfrac{1}{2}(0.089).$$

The unconditional test halves the significance level, thereby increasing the frequency of rejection and hence also the power. If we followed customary 'text book' power considerations, we would advocate use of the unconditional test because of its greater power. Nevertheless, a scientist would most certainly wish to use the conditional test to assess the strength of the evidence provided by the data against the hypothesis $\theta=1$.

There is a very general convention in the application of statistical analysis to data, namely: we should compare the result actually obtained with only those others which, so far as possible, have the same precision. In the present case, the sample size t indicates the precision with which the experiment determines θ. An observed sample of 100 should be compared only with other samples of 100; the fact that some future repetition of the experiment might yield a sample of a different size should not alter the significance level of the data actually obtained. For this reason, it is the conditional test (1) which is appropriate.

3. RATIO OF TWO POISSON MEANS

The preceding argument also applies if T has some distribution other than the one selected in the example. The requirement that the observed sample should be compared only with others of the same size implies that inferences about θ should be based on the conditional distribution

$$(3) \qquad \Pr(x_1; \theta \mid T=t)=\binom{t}{x_1}\left(\frac{\theta}{1+\theta}\right)^{x_1}\left(\frac{1}{1+\theta}\right)^{t-x_1}.$$

This conclusion holds whatever the distribution of T, provided only that T itself contains no information (or a negligible amount of information) about the magnitude of θ. (This condition is necessary because such information would be lost in conditioning on T.) In general, T may be said to contain no information about θ if any parameters upon which its distribution depends are functionally independent of θ.

In particular, suppose that in the preceding example the probability of an animal's entering the sample is small, independent of its sex, and proportional to the amount of effort put into collecting the sample. Then T will have a Poisson distribution

$$(4) \qquad \Pr(t:v) = v^t e^{-v}/t!$$

where v is proportional to the amount of effort. It is easy to show that (3) and (4) together imply that X_1 and X_2, the numbers of males and females observed, will be independent Poisson variates with means $\mu_1 = \theta v/(1+\theta)$ and $\mu_2 = v/(1+\theta)$. Since $\theta = \mu_1/\mu_2$, the problem of making inferences about the sex ratio θ is now equivalent to the problem of making inferences about the ratio of two Poisson means, as previously discussed by Cox (1958). Specifically, a test of the hypothesis that the sex ratio is unity, $\theta = 1$, is equivalent to testing the equality of the two Poisson means, $\mu_1 = \mu_2$.

In terms of this example, the question under discussion is whether the considerations of the preceding paragraph justify us in reducing the significance level of 0.089 which we obtained from (1) in Section 2, by averaging over the distribution of T as suggested by power considerations. The answer to this question is no, for the reasons outlined in Section 2. The variate T cannot, by itself, provide any information about the magnitude of θ. However, its observed value t is the effective sample size for inferences about θ. The requirement that the sample size should be held fixed in making inferences about θ implies that inferences about the ratio of two Poisson means should be based on (3), the conditional distribution given $T = t$. In particular, the conditional test (1) should be used for testing the equality of Poisson means ($\theta = 1$).

The same arguments apply to the problem of making inferences about the common ratio of n pairs of Poisson means. Suppose that X_{1i} and X_{2i} are independent Poisson variates with means μ_{1i} and μ_{2i}, where it is assumed that $\mu_{1i} = \theta \mu_{2i} (i = 1, 2, ..., n)$. Let $v_i = \mu_{1i} + \mu_{2i}$ and $T_i = X_{1i} + X_{2i}$. Then $T_1, T_2, ..., T_n$ and $X_1 = \sum X_{1i}$ are jointly sufficient for $v_1, v_2, ..., v_n$ and θ. Furthermore, the distribution of $T_1, T_2, ..., T_n$ depends only on $v_1, v_2, ..., v_n$ which are functionally independent of θ. Consequently

$T_1, T_2, \ldots, T_n$ provide no information about θ, and inferences about θ should be based on the conditional distribution of X_1 given $T_1, T_2, \ldots, T_n$. This is given by (3) with $X_1 = \sum X_{1i}$ and $T = \sum T_i$.

Similar principles apply in the estimation of the 'hit number' h in a dilution series model involving Poisson-distributed observations which arises in virology (Alling, 1971; Kalbfleisch and Sprott, 1974), in a model arising in time dependent Poisson processes (Cox and Lewis, 1969), in contingency tables, and even in classical regression theory.

4. POISSON SAMPLES

Suppose that one has independent samples of sizes n_1 and n_2 from Poisson distributions with means m_1 and m_2, respectively. The sample means and totals will be denoted by $\bar{X}_i$ and $X_i = n_i \bar{X}_i$ ($i = 1, 2$). Then X_1 and X_2 are independent Poisson variates with means $\mu_1 = n_1 m_1$ and $\mu_2 = n_2 m_2$. The hypothesis $m_1 = m_2$ is equivalent to the hypothesis $\mu_1 / \mu_2 = n_1 / n_2$, and the discussion of Section 3 applies. Under the hypothesis $m_1 = m_2$, (3) becomes

$$(5) \qquad \Pr(x_1; \theta = n_1/n_2 \mid T = t) = \binom{t}{x_1} q^{x_1} (1-q)^{t-x_1}$$

where $q = n_1/(n_1 + n_2)$. Whatever test statistic is chosen, the significance level of observed values $\bar{x}_1, \bar{x}_2$ should be calculated from this conditional distribution.

If t is large, the binomial distribution (5) may be approximated by a normal distribution with mean tq and variance $tq(1-q)$, so that

$$(6) \qquad (X_1 - tq)/\sqrt{tq(1-q)} = (\bar{X}_1 - \bar{X}_2)/\sqrt{\frac{\bar{X}_1}{n_2} + \frac{\bar{X}_2}{n_1}}$$

is approximately standardized normal. The approximation is good whenever both tq and $t(1-q)$ are large. However, if either of these terms is small, the approximation should not be used. Instead, the significance level should be obtained by summing the binomial probabilities (5). This may be done quickly and easily on a computer. Indeed, the need for such approximations is now much diminished owing to the availability of high speed computers.

In considering the comparison of Poisson samples it has sometimes been reasoned that the variance of $\bar{X}_1 - \bar{X}_2$ is $m_1/n_1 + m_2/n_2$, which is estimated by $\bar{X}_1/n_1 + \bar{X}_2/n_2$. This results in the use of an approximate test based on taking

$$(7) \qquad (\bar{X}_1 - \bar{X}_2)/\sqrt{\frac{\bar{X}_1}{n_1} + \frac{\bar{X}_2}{n_2}}$$

to be standardized normal. This differs from (6) in that n_1 and n_2 are interchanged in the denominator. If $n_1 \neq n_2$, (6) and (7) may lead to quite different significance levels for the same data, and hence it is important to determine which of them is appropriate.

The arguments put forward in this paper clearly indicate that (6) is appropriate, because it arises from the normal approximation to the conditional distribution (5). The previous line of reasoning in (7) is unsatisfactory because it ignores the fact that, under the hypothesis $m_1 = m_2 = m$, the variance of $\bar{X}_1 - \bar{X}_2$ is $m(1/n_1 + 1/n_2)$. If the common mean m is now estimated from the combined sample by $(X_1 + X_2)/(n_1 + n_2)$, the revised estimate of $\text{var}(\bar{X}_1 - \bar{X}_2)$ will be

$$\frac{X_1 + X_2}{n_1 + n_2}\left(\frac{1}{n_1} + \frac{1}{n_2}\right) = \frac{\bar{X}_1}{n_2} + \frac{\bar{X}_2}{n_1}$$

which leads to (6). The revised estimate gives greater weight to the mean of the larger sample, whereas (7) gives greater weight to the mean of the smaller sample.

5. GENERAL CONSIDERATIONS

The foregoing examples illustrate some general features of tests of significance which are further considered in this section.

The purpose of a test of significance is to measure the strength of the evidence provided by the experimental data *against* an hypothesis. The significance level of the data in relation to the hypothesis is the probability of obtaining an outcome at least as unfavourable to the hypothesis as the one observed. A small significance level can be explained in only two ways: either the hypothesis is true and an event of small probability has occurred, or the hypothesis is false. The smaller the significance level, the greater the reluctance to accept the first explanation and hence the stronger the evidence that the hypothesis is false. A large significance level indicates that, with respect to the particular test used, the data provides no evidence that the hypothesis is false. This does not mean that the data supports the hypothesis, but only that the data and hypothesis are compatible.

A test of significance requires two ingredients for its specification:

(a) a reference set R, and a probability measure on R;

(b) a discrepancy measure (test criterion) D.

The reference set is the set of experimental outcomes to which, for the purpose of the test, the data is considered to belong, and upon which probability statements are based. The discrepancy measure is a real-valued function (random variable) on R, which assigns to each point x in R a real number $D(x)$. The role of the discrepancy measure is to rank the points of R according to the strength of the evidence they would provide against the hypothesis in question. The larger the discrepancy $D(x)$, the stronger the evidence provided by outcome x against the hypothesis. The significance level of the data in relation to the hypothesis is then $P(D \geqslant d \mid R)$, where d is the observed discrepancy and the probability is calculated from the measure defined on R, the hypothesis being assumed true.

The choice of the reference set R depends upon the structure of the problem and the nature of the hypothesis being tested. It frequently happens that, when the appropriate reference set has been selected, there is a natural and obvious choice for the discrepancy measure or test statistic D. In other cases, the choice of D will depend upon what type of departure from the hypothesis is anticipated. *A comparison of two test statistics D_1 and D_2 must be made on the same reference set R if it is to be meaningful.* Two test statistics which produce the same ordering of the points in R will always give equal significance levels on the same data, and hence define completely equivalent tests.

It is important to recognize the two separate ingredients of a test of significance: the population R and the criterion D. The test criterion D does not, of itself, provide any test whatever until the reference set has been specified. In the case of the Poisson means, the two criteria

$$U = |X_1 - X_2| / \sqrt{X_1 + X_2}; \qquad V = (|X_1 - X_2| - 1) / \sqrt{X_1 + X_2}$$

define the same test if one takes the reference set to be conditional on $X_1 + X_2$. However they can lead to different significance levels in the unconditional population of all pairs (x_1, x_2). The primary question is thus the choice of the reference set – whether conditional or unconditional – rather than the choice of the criterion.

6. CHOOSING A REFERENCE SET

When a test is intended for use as a routine signalling device, the reference set will correspond to a series of actual repetitions of the experiment, with the observed data being merely a single realization. No single decision is of particular importance, and there is a well-defined long run within which decision rules can be evaluated. However, as Fisher (1959) has emphasized, the situation is much different when the test is intended to weigh the statistical evidence against an hypothesis. The experiment is then essentially unique, and will not be repeated endlessly. The experiment is imbedded in a *hypothetical* probability model *by the statistician*. The same data can often be imagined to be a member of any number of different hypothetical populations. There is no single well-defined long run within which inferences must be evaluated. As a result, in problems of inference the reference set need not correspond to actual repetitions of the experiment. In fact, the same data set may be regarded as belonging to two or more different reference sets, depending upon what type of information one seeks to obtain from it.

For example, consider an experiment which involves n trials, each of which results in success or failure. The sample space would normally be taken to contain 2^n points corresponding to all possible sequences, and some sequence of, say, x successes and n-x failures would be observed. If one wished to test the independence of successive trials, one would regard x as fixed and consider only the order in which the successes and failures occurred, so that the reference set would contain $\binom{n}{x}$ points. A test of significance might be based on the number of runs of like outcomes, with probabilities being calculated on the assumption that all $\binom{n}{x}$ points in the reference set were equally probable. On the other hand, it may be that independence of successive trials is to be assumed, and that one's aim is to test an hypothesized value of the common probability of success. Then only the number of successes would be considered, the order of their occurrence being ignored. The reference set would contain $n+1$ points whose probabilities were given by a binomial distribution. Thus, depending upon the type of information sought, the data may be regarded as belonging to two different reference sets, both of which are different from the sample space.

The various possible outcomes of an experiment sometimes vary considerably in the amount of information they provide concerning the hypothesis of interest. This is of no consequence in routine signalling situations, where only the long-run average informativeness is important. An outcome of below-average informativeness will be compensated for by one that is above-average at some time in the future. However, this will not be true in problems of inference, where one wishes to interpret the results of the experiment actually performed. If one unluckily obtains an uninformative outcome from which little or nothing can be learned (e.g. a small value of t in (1)), no consolation will be derived from the fact that some future repetition, which may never be performed, could yield a more informative outcome to the experiment.

In problems of inference, the informativeness of the outcome actually observed must be taken into account. The data should be compared only with those outcomes which are of approximately the same informativeness or precision. In a test of significance, the observed outcome is compared with the other points of the reference set R. Therefore, *R should contain only those outcomes which are of approximately the same informativeness or precision as the one observed.*

The experiment described earlier in this section will be quite uninformative about the independence of successive trials if x is near 0 or n, but much more informative is x is near $n/2$. Hence, in testing for independence, the observed sequence should be compared only with those sequences which contain the same number of successes. The reference set in a test for independence of successive trials will be conditional on x, the observed number of successes.

For the comparison of Poisson means, the observed total t is a measure of the experiment's informativeness concerning the ratio of the means.

Hence the reference set for the comparison of the means was taken to be conditional on t.

Similar principles are involved in the analysis of contingency tables and of the 'play the winner' rule (Zelen, 1969), and in many other problems as well. Although results are not always as clear cut as they are for the examples considered here, it seems that a conditional reference set is frequently appropriate (Cox, 1958; Fisher, 1959).

The specification of R raises the subject of ancillary statistics, of which T is an example. The purpose of the ancillary statistic is to specify R. This is an important subject not dealt with in most statistics books; a general discussion of ancillary statistics is however beyond the scope of this paper.

University of Waterloo

BIBLIOGRAPHY

Alling, David W., 'Estimation of Hit Number', *Biometrics* **27** (1971), 605–613.
Cox, D. R., 'Some Problems Connected with Statistical Inference', *Ann. Math. Statist.* **29** (1958), 357–372.
Cox, D. R. and Lewis, P. A. W., *Statistical Analysis of Series of Events*, Methuen, London, 1966, p. 46.
Detre, K. and White, C., 'The Comparison of Two Poisson-Distributed Observations', *Biometrics* **26** (1970), 851–854.
Fisher, R. A., *Statistical Methods and Scientific Inference*, 2nd edition, Hafner, New York, 1959.
Kalbfleisch, J. G. and Sprott, D. A., 'Inferences About Hit Number in a Virological Model', 1974. (To be published in *Biometrics*.)
Mantel, N., 'The Continuity Correction in Comparing Two Poisson-Distributed Observations', *Biometrics* **27** (1971) 747–749.
Zelen, M., 'Play the Winner Rule and the Controlled Clinical Trial', *J. Amer. Statistical Assoc.* **64** (1969), 131–146.

PART III

PROBABILITY, INFORMATION AND UTILITY

HANS SCHNEEWEISS

PROBABILITY AND UTILITY – DUAL CONCEPTS IN DECISION THEORY

1. INTRODUCTION (GAMES OF CHANCE)

In evaluating a risky prospect a decision maker will usually take into account

(a) all the possible gains and losses (i.e. the consequences), that might occur if the prospect were adopted,

(b) the corresponding probabilities of the occurrences of these gains or losses.

One may say that risk-situations are characterized by two dimensions: possible consequences and corresponding probabilities.[1] This is at least true for prospects for which objective probabilities are given and known to the decision maker. As will be seen, this is true even when no such objective probabilities exist.

Consider the simplest case: a gamble where one can win a prize x with probability p or nothing with probability $1-p$. The expected value of this gamble is $x \cdot p$. It can be calculated as the area of a rectangle, and in this way the two dimensions (consequence and probability) can be seen clearly.

In the early days of probability theory it was held that such a game of chance must be judged by its expected value $x \cdot p$. Given two gambles (x_1, p_1) and (x_2, p_2), that which yields the largest expected value should (and normally will) be preferred. More generally, suppose a game of chance allows the realisation of exactly one of, say, n states $s_1, s_2, ..., s_n$, which will occur with probabilities $p_1, p_2, ..., p_n$ $(\sum p_i = 1)$, and with each state s_i an amount x_i is associated that will be obtained if and only if state s_i occurs. Then, according to this view, this game of chance is to be evaluated by its expected value $\sum x_i p_i$.

Therefore if there are two such games a_1 and a_2, differing in the distribution of monetary outcome, that one should be chosen which yields the greatest expected value. In addition, two such games are considered equivalent (the decision maker is indifferent) if and only if

Günter Menges (ed.), Information, Inference and Decision, 113–144. *All Rights Reserved.*
Copyright © 1974 *by D. Reidel Publishing Company, Dordrecht-Holland.*

they yield the same expected value. In symbols:

$$
\begin{array}{cc}
p_1 & p_2 \cdots p_n \\
s_1 & s_2 \cdots s_n
\end{array}
$$

$$
\begin{array}{c}
a_1 \\
a_2
\end{array}
\left|
\begin{array}{c}
x_{11} \quad x_{12} \dots x_{1n} \\
x_{21} \quad x_{22} \dots x_{2n}
\end{array}
\right|
\begin{array}{c}
\rightarrow \sum x_{1i} p_i \\
\rightarrow \sum x_{2i} p_i
\end{array}
$$

(1) $\quad a_1 \gtrsim a_2 \Leftrightarrow \sum_i x_{1i} p_i \geqq \sum_i x_{2i} p_i .$

Here $\gtrsim$ reads 'is preferred to' and $\sim$ reads 'is equivalent (indifferent) to'.

This very simple, and somewhat naive, decision rule treats the two dimensions, consequence and probability, symmetrically. It is not surprising, therefore, that these two concepts and their modifications show many similar properties. Historically they developed along parallel lines. A development of one concept was often mirrored by an analogous, and sometimes independent development of the other.

One may go even further and say that the development of these two concepts of decision theory often showed traits of complementarity. Decision theory could be improved by modifying or enriching either the structure of the consequence space or of the probability space. Both alternatives were tried, and typically a synthesis was eventually found.

It is the purpose of this paper to make these dualities clear. As will be seen, they can be traced back to the axiomatisation of decision theory, where they find their ultimate synthesis. Thus this paper will also discuss, in an elementary way, the essential ideas of an axiomatic system of decision making.

2. SUBJECTIVE ELEMENTS

2.1. *Alternative Decision Criteria*

Very early in the development of probability theory it was recognized that the simple expected value decision rule cannot be applied universally. It suffices to cite the example of an insurance taker.

An insurable risk may be viewed as a game of chance with negative outcomes. Typically, its expected value is less in absolute value than the insurance premium an individual is willing to pay in order to get rid of this risk. This behaviour characterizes risk aversion and can be found in many individuals when they face risky prospects.

One may try to include risk aversion (and similarly the adverse behaviour of risk preference) in the original expected value principle by modifying the consequence or probability of a game of chance.

Daniel Bernoulli (1738) suggested modifying the consequence component of a game of chance by replacing the monetary outcome x by some function $v(x)$, called the utility of x. If this is done, the ordinary expected value $x \cdot p$ of a simple gamble (x, p) will then be replaced by the expected utility value $v(x) \cdot p$, such that if a choice among several gambles is made, that one is chosen which yields the greatest expected utility. This decision principle is called Bernoulli principle.[2] More generally, it takes the form:

$$(2) \qquad a_1 \succsim a_2 \Leftrightarrow \sum_i v(x_{1i})\, p_i \geqq \sum_i v(x_{2i})\, p_i .$$

Indeed, in adopting this principle as a general decision principle, many (but not all) forms of behaviour towards risk can be explained which could not be explained within the framework of the ordinary expected value rule. E.g. risk aversion will follow from the assumption of a concave utility function, and risk preference from a convex utility function.

Figure 1 shows a utility function which could be used to explain both.

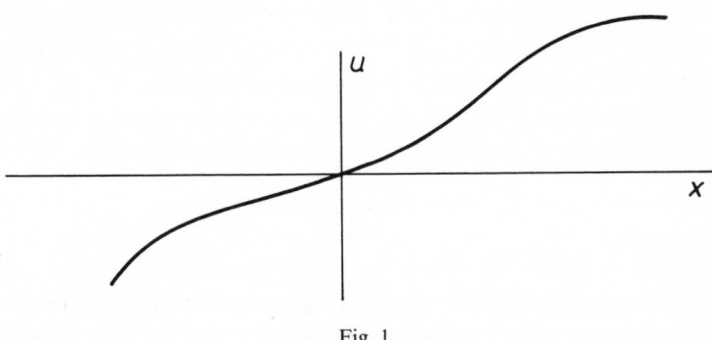

Fig. 1

Alternatively, one can modify the probability component of a game of chance so as to explain the behaviour of an insurance taker and other forms of risk behaviour. Thus an individual may interpret the objective probability p as a personal or subjective probability $\pi(p)$ and evaluate a game of chance by calculating the expected value $x\pi(p)$ instead of *xp*, or more generally:

$$(3) \qquad a_1 \succsim a_2 \Leftrightarrow \sum_i x_{1i} \pi(p_i) \geqq \sum_i x_{2i} \pi(p_i).$$

An experiment conducted by Rosett (1967) gives rise to the conjecture that small (objective) probabilities are overestimated and large (objective) probabilities are underestimated. This already would explain why people buy insurance contracts (risk aversion) as well as lottery tickets (risk preference) (Figure 2).

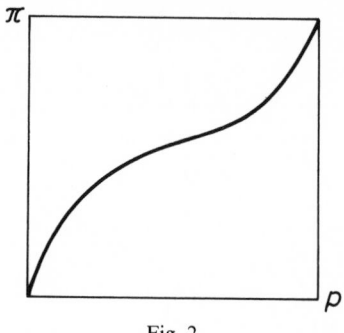

Fig. 2

This principle sometimes is called Bayes Principle (cf. Marschak, 1955), because one may interpret the definition of probability in the famous 1763 article as being essentially of a subjective nature.[3]

Combining these two principles we are led to what is sometimes called the Ramsey Principle (Marschak, 1955; Ramsey, 1951):

$$(4) \qquad a_1 \succsim a_2 \Leftrightarrow \sum_i v(x_{1i}) \pi(p_i) \geqq \sum_i v(x_{2i}) \pi(p_i).$$

The transformations of monetary consequences into utilities and of objective probabilities into subjective probabilities have in common that they replace objective values by subjective (or personal) ones. In so doing, the resulting decision criterion comes closer to the actual decision making process, which is essentially of a subjective nature. And indeed, the new, more flexible decision criteria can describe risk behaviour far better than the classical expected value criterion.

These new subjective concepts, however, are not only modifications of the old objective ones. They can also be used to enlarge the domain of applications. Utility can be attached to any kind of consequence, not necessarily describable by monetary values. Subjective probabilities, on the other hand, may be assigned to any event whose occurrence is unknown (to the decision maker), e.g. to events whose probabilities are unknown, or even to those events to which no frequentist would think of applying the probability concept. Consider e.g. a historical event which for some reason is unknown to an individual. He may be quite able to express his opinion as to whether this event has occurred or not by some (subjective) probability value.

We thus arrive at very general uncertainty situations which may have little resemblance to a game of chance. The previous symbolic description on p. 114 will be replaced by

$$
\begin{array}{c|ccc}
 & s_1 & s_2 \ldots s_n \\
\hline
a_1 & e_{11} & e_{12} \ldots e_{1n} \\
a_2 & e_{21} & e_{22} \ldots e_{2n}
\end{array}
$$

$$
(5) \qquad a_1 \succsim a_2 \Leftrightarrow \sum_i u(e_{1i})\, P(s_i) \geqq \sum_i u(e_{2i})\, P(s_i).
$$

Here $s_1, s_2, \ldots, s_n$ are exhaustive and mutually exclusive descriptions of the possible states of the world where the true state is unknown to the decision maker. $S = \{s\}$, the set of all possible states of the world, is called the 'world' (Savage, 1954).

e_{ji} denotes the consequence of action a_j when s_i is the prevailing state of the world (it is an element of the set of all possible consequences E, the so called 'consequence space'); $u(e_{ji})$ is its utility, and $P(s_i)$ is the (subjective) probability of state s_i. These last two concepts are again the two dimensions of the more general uncertainty situation, and they are now essentially subjective.

(4) is a special case of (5) which applies when (a) a monetary consequence $x = x(e)$ can be assigned to each consequence e, and the utility of e is attached to $x(e)$, i.e. $u(e) = v(x(e))$, and (b) an objective probability $p = p(s)$ can be assigned to each state of the world s, and the subjective probability is attached to $p(s)$, i.e. $P(s) = \pi(p(s))$.

It should be clear that (5) implies a preference ordering on E: If a_e is an action which has consequence e for any state s then $e \succsim f \Leftrightarrow a_e \succsim a_f \Leftrightarrow$
$\Leftrightarrow u(e) \geqq u(f)$ by (5).

From now on the term 'probability' will be used to denote subjective probability, unless otherwise stated. By 'objective probability' we mean the commonly known frequentist concept (disregarding the logical difficulties inherent in its definition as well as in its application).

2.2. Conditioning

Utility and probability, as understood here, are subjective concepts. However, they usually cannot be set up completely arbitrarily but are more or less stringently linked to objective entities, if these are given. E.g. under certain circumstances, utility may be set equal to monetary consequence $x(e)$. If the gains and losses in an uncertainty situation are not too widely spread and if – as is usually the case – the utility function is smooth, so that it does not deviate very much from a linear function, then one can say approximately

$$u(e) \doteq x(e).$$

On the other hand, if one has a long sequence of observations of the occurrence or nonoccurrence of a certain state s and if one (subjectively) believes that these observations were made independently and always under the same conditions, then a rational decision maker will usually assign a probability $P(s)$ to s that will not differ very much from the observed relative frequency of occurrences of s. This relative frequency can be assumed to come close to the objective probability $p(s)$ of s:

$$P(s) \doteq p(s).$$

In these cases, the classical decision criterion (1) may be a good approximation to the more general one (5).

More generally, it is to be expected that experience will alter the preference structure of an individual and therefore his utilities. At the same time, incoming information will change an individual's beliefs about probabilities.

In general, changes in taste and belief due to experience and information are unpredictable as they represent changes of the personality of the individual. One may, however, conceive of a person who at some instant of time considers all such possible changes by means of his then-held utility function and subjective probability distribution. That is to say, future changes in utility and/or probability according to newly gathered experience and/or information may be inferred from the now-existing utility function and/or probability distribution. This inference can be formalized by introducing the concepts of conditional utility and conditional probability. Whereas the latter is well known and is of great importance in probability theory, the former has not received much attention, perhaps because it is comparatively trivial.

In probability theory, we define the conditional probability of an event A (i.e. a subset of the world S) as conditional on the occurrence of an event B by

$$(6) \qquad P(A \mid B) = \frac{P(A \cap B)}{P(B)}.$$

In order to derive a similar concept in utility theory we must enrich the structure of the consequence space by assuming that two consequences e_1 and e_2 may be combined to give rise to the consequence 'e_1 and e_2' (in symbols: $e_1 + e_2$). For example, this possibility of combining consequences is relevant if the e_i are commodity bundles to be consumed or if they are money incomes and if the combining operation $+$ is understood to be vector-addition or scalar addition respectively. Now if a utility function u is given, we may define a conditional utility function given an outcome e_0 by putting

$$(6') \qquad u(e \mid e_0) = u(e + e_0) - u(e_0).$$

The term $-u(e_0)$ is not essential and has been added as a conventional normalization to ensure (e.g. in the case of commodity bundles) that $u(0 \mid e_0) = 0$. It brings out more clearly the formal analogy to conditional probability. $u(e \mid e_0)$ can be understood as the utility of an additional commodity bundle e when the commodity bundle e_0 has already been received (or is certain to be received). To state an example: A glass of milk will have different conditional utilities depending on whether a piece of chocolate will go with it or whether there will be a second glass of milk.

3. ORDINALITY, CARDINALITY, INDEPENDENCE

The concepts of utility and probability may be used as ordinal or as cardinal entities or as concepts endowed with special properties (like independence).

3.1. *Ordinal Concepts*

An ordinal utility function is a mapping $u: E \to R$ of the consequence space to the set of real numbers such that the preference relation on E is mapped into the order relation on R, i.e.:

$$e_1 \mathrel{\underset{\sim}{\succ}} e_2 \Leftrightarrow u(e_1) \geqq u(e_2).$$

Thus, an ordinal utility just reflects the preferences among consequences. In fact, it contains almost the same information as the preference relation, since (cf. Debreu, 1954) under very general conditions a preference ordering can always be represented by an ordinal utility function. Nevertheless, ordinal utility has played an important role in microeconomic theory, since this theory can be based on the ordinal quality of utility only.

The analogous concept of ordinal probability is less popular, and is mainly viewed as a step in an axiomatic approach towards cardinal probability. It is defined by a relation $\succ$ among events which is to be read as 'more probable than' and a corresponding relation $\sim$ to be read as 'as probable as'. The composite relation $\mathrel{\underset{\sim}{\succ}}$, called probability relation, is transitive and reflexive just as the analogous preference relation $\mathrel{\underset{\sim}{\succ}}$ in utility theory.

In addition to this common property, another fundamental property is postulated for ordinal probability. This property has no counterpart in ordinal utility (and thus reflects the relative complexity of probability theory as compared with utility theory): If A, B, C are events and if $A \cap C = B \cap C = \emptyset$, then

$$(7) \qquad A \mathrel{\underset{\sim}{\succ}} B \Leftrightarrow A \cup C \mathrel{\underset{\sim}{\succ}} B \cup C.$$

This postulate is the ordinal analogon of the addition axiom in cardinal probability theory.

Finally, the empty event is a lower bound with respect to the probability relation, and S is an upper bound:

$$\forall A: \emptyset \mathrel{\underset{\sim}{\prec}} A \mathrel{\underset{\sim}{\prec}} S.$$

3.2. *Dominance*

As is obvious from (5), ordinal concepts of utility and/or probability are not sufficient to make decisions in general risk situations. There are, however, many important special cases where knowledge of preference ordering and/or of probability ordering is sufficient to make a rational decision. Such cases are considered in Fishburn's book (1964).

A trivial one is presented by the dominance principle. It has two different forms corresponding to our two 'dimensions' of the decision problem. Consider the simplest case of a gamble with two possible consequences e_1 and e_2, such that e_i will be realized if and only if A_i occurs, where A_1 and A_2 are two disjoint events, and $A_1 \cup A_2 = S$. If the consequences are changed to f_1 and f_2 and if $f_1 \succ e_1$, $f_2 \succsim e_2$, then this new gamble will dominate the former one and will be preferred. In symbols:

$$(8) \qquad \left.\begin{matrix} f_1 \succ e_1 \\ f_2 \succsim e_2 \end{matrix}\right\} \Rightarrow \begin{pmatrix} A_1 & A_2 \\ f_1 & f_2 \end{pmatrix} \succ \begin{pmatrix} A_1 & A_2 \\ e_1 & e_2 \end{pmatrix}.$$

We note that the only information necessary to ascertain dominance are the preference relations among the consequences, i.e. their ordinal utilities. Knowledge of cardinal utilities is not necessary.

Another form of dominance is presented (in its simplest form) by the following situation. Suppose that in the first gamble just considered $e_1 \succ e_2$. If events A_i are replaced by new events B_i with $B_1 \cap B_2 = \emptyset$, $B_1 \cup B_2 = S$, and if $B_1 \succ A_1$ (and therefore $B_2 \prec A_2$) then the new gamble dominates the first one and will be preferred:

$$(9) \qquad \left.\begin{matrix} B_1 \succ A_1 \\ (B_2 \prec A_2) \end{matrix}\right\} \Rightarrow \begin{pmatrix} B_1 & B_2 \\ e_1 & e_2 \end{pmatrix} \succ \begin{pmatrix} A_1 & A_2 \\ e_1 & e_2 \end{pmatrix}.$$

Again in order to ascertain dominance only knowledge of the ordering of events according to ordinal probability is required.

(8) may be called 'dominance in utility', whereas (9) could be termed 'dominance in probability'. These two concepts can be defined more generally for arbitrary probability distributions. Interesting enough, they coincide for continuous probability distributions on the real line (cf. Schneeweiss, 1968).

3.3. Cardinal Concepts

With a cardinal utility function one can not only describe an ordering on the set of consequences but one can also compare (and order) utility differences. It is a useful device in welfare economics and an indispensable instrument in decision theory, if criteria (2) or (5) are used.

By definition, a cardinal utility function is uniquely determined if the zero point on the scale of measurement and the unit of measurement are given. A change in the zero and in the unit of measurement implies a positive linear transformation of the utility function. By contrast, an ordinal utility function may be changed by any arbitrary order preserving transformation.

Cardinal probability is the conventional numerical probability measure (whether objective or subjective) for which Kolmogorov's axioms hold true. If an ordering of events according to the 'more probable than' relation is given, we say that a numerical probability measure agrees with this relation if for all events A, B:

$$A \succsim B \Leftrightarrow P(A) \geqq P(B).$$

Because of $P(\emptyset) = 0$ and because of the normalization rule $P(S) = 1$, the unit of measurement and the zero are fixed. For this reason, linear transformations of probability measures do not occur in probability theory.

3.4. Independent Components

An important additional property sometimes imposed on a utility function, or on a probability measure, is its decomposability into independent components. Suppose the consequence space is the direct product of two sets:

$$E = E^1 \times E^2.$$

That is, any consequence $e \in E$ has two components: $e = (e^1, e^2)$, $e^i \in E^i$, as e.g. a commodity bundle consisting of two different commodities. We say that these components are independent if a utility function u – possibly after some order preserving transformation – can be decomposed into a sum of component utility functions:

(10) $u(e^1, e^2) = u^1(e^1) + u^2(e^2).$

An additive utility function is necessarily cardinal.

Necessary and sufficient conditions for a preference ordering on E to be representable by an additive utility function of two or more components have been investigated (cf. Fishburn, 1970, pp. 42–79, 89–99). An implication of (10) which explains the term 'independence' is:

(11) $(e^1, e^2) \succsim (e^1, f^2) \Leftrightarrow (f^1, e^2) \succsim (f^1, f^2)$.

A preference relation between elements of the second component remains unchanged if the first component is changed, and consequently it is independent of the first component. (A similar statement can be made about the first component.) Modifying the concept of conditional utility, introduced in Section 2.2, in an obvious way, we may also say that the components are independent if the conditional utility of one component does not depend on the specific value of the conditioning component.

The analogy to the well-known independence concept in probability theory is clearly seen: Suppose $S = S^1 \times S^2$ and so any state of the world is decomposable: $s = (s^1, s^2)$. Any probability measure P on S will define marginal probability measures P^i on S^i. They are said to be independent if

(12) $P(s_1, s_2) = P^1(s_1)\, P^2(s_2)$.

This implies (in analogy to (11)):

(13) $(s^1, s^2) \succsim (s^1, t^2) \Leftrightarrow (t^1, s^2) \succsim (t^1, t^2)$.

Again we may express independence with the help of conditional probability: $P(s^2 \mid s^1) = P^2(s^2)$.

In decision theory an additive utility function is of special interest, because its expected value is the sum of the expected values of its components. Suppose in addition, that $S = S_1 \times S_2$ is a direct product of factors corresponding to the factors of $E = E_1 \times E_2$ (i.e. for each action a the consequence function[4] $\varepsilon(a, .): S \to E$ is decomposable into two independent consequence functions $\varepsilon_i(a, .): S_i \to E_i$); then we need only know the marginal distributions of P on S_1 and S_2 in order to be able to evaluate the expected values of the additive components of the utility function. The criterion (5) is much easier to apply in this case.

4. Axiomatic systems: introspective

As a result of great endeavours in the last 30 or 40 years a large number of axiomatic systems have been proposed as foundations of utility and (subjective) probability. They try to reduce these concepts and their laws to a small number of fundamental properties from which all other properties can be derived. The most important objective is to prove the existence of utility and probability as measurable (cardinal) entities. Ideally these fundamental properties (i.e. the axioms) are so chosen that they are regarded as plausible or as self-evident by almost everybody. At the same time, the theoretical foundation of utility and probability by axiomatic systems will indicate methods of measuring these concepts (at least in principle).

We may distinguish between axiomatic systems that base their fundamental concepts (a) on the introspection of an individual or (b) on the observable reactions of an individual when he is forced to make decisions. Both approaches seem to be well suited for their purpose, which is to give foundations for *subjective* concepts, i.e. concepts that refer to an individual.

With the help of introspection one might discover the motives of an individual's utility valuation and of his opinion formation. However, it is not clear how a utility function u and a probability measure P derived from introspection are related to actual decision making. In other words, there is no guarantee that these u and P can be used in a decision rule like (5). The second approach is much better suited for applications in decision theory.

Nevertheless, brief mention of some variants of the first approach seems appropriate here. The most direct approach takes a preference relation among pairs of consequences (e.g. of commodity bundles or of levels of wealth) as a starting point. A relation like

$$(13) \qquad (e_1, e_2) \succ (e_3, e_4)$$

is to be interpreted as follows: The transition from e_2 to e_1 is preferred to the transition of e_4 to e_3. Suppose a utility function u exists such that

$$e_1 \succsim e_2 \Leftrightarrow u(e_1) \geqq u(e_2)$$

$$(13') \qquad (e_1, e_2) \succsim (e_3, e_4) \Leftrightarrow u(e_1) - u(e_2) \geqq u(e_3) - u(e_4).$$

Then we might also say that the above preference relation (13) asserts that the strength of preference of e_1 over e_2 is greater than the strength of preference of e_3 over e_4. In fact, such a utility function (which then is cardinal) exists if certain 'consistency' assumptions on the preference relation (13) are made (cf. e.g. Fishburn, 1970, pp. 80; Alt, 1936). Among these, an independence axiom seems to play an important role, as pointed out by Samuelson (1938).

There are other somewhat indirect methods of deriving a cardinal utility. They replace (13) by some equivalent relation or operation. One example is the midpoint operation (cf. Pfanzagl, 1968, p. 120).

In probability theory perhaps one of the most refined axioms systems based on introspection was developed by Koopman (1940). It is remarkable because it uses the concept of conditional probabilities as a fundamental concept and not just as a definition to be attached to a system of axioms on unconditional probabilities (as in Kolmogorov's system). On the other hand, no new order relation like (13) is introduced. It suffices to start with the ordinal probability concept and to make sure, by an appropriate set of axioms, that (7) holds true (cf. p. 120).

This clearly shows that the formal analogy between the concepts of utility and probability does not go too far. The fundamental reason for this is that the laws of probability are richer than those of utility. (As mentioned earlier there is nothing like (7) in utility theory.)

5. AXIOMATIC SYSTEMS: BEHAVIOURAL

In the other approach, we are most interested in those axiomatic systems that are based on observable decisions under uncertainty and that will ultimately lead to decision criteria like (2) to (5). (Other treatments that are also based on observable choices and that lead to a cardinal utility function – but not to decision criteria (2) to (5) – utilize special situations where independence among components of consequences can be assumed (cf. Section 3.4.).)

5.1. *Axioms for the Bernoulli Principle*

The most famous axioms system has been proposed by v. Neumann and Morgenstern (1947). It assumes a given probability distribution P on S (given objectively) known to the decision maker (and hence

also given subjectively). Its purpose is to state plausible axioms of behaviour in decision situations under risk (with probabilities given) such
that a utility function and criterion (2) may be derived. It is assumed in
this theory that S is so large (in fact, S must be infinite) and P on S is
so 'rich' (it should be atomless) that any probability distribution on E
can be generated by an appropriate assignment of consequences to
states of the world. In fact, any action a gives rise to a random element
in E via the mapping $\varepsilon(a, .): S \rightarrow E$, and hence induces a probability
distribution on E. It is assumed that all possible probability distributions
on E can be generated in this way by choosing an appropriate action a.
For simplicity we also assume that E is finite.

The *first axiom* (ORDER) states that a preference among actions
depends only on the probability distributions generated by these actions
on E and that this preference relation is transitive and complete. Thus,
the problem of ordering actions by a decision criterion like (2) is reduced
to the problem of ordering the set of probability distributions on E.

The *second axiom* (CONTINUITY) states that, given $e_3 \succsim e_2 \succsim e_1$,
then there exists an event A with probability p such that the action a
which results in e_3 whenever A comes true and in e_1 whenever $\bar{A}$ comes
true is indifferent to e_2. Denoting this action (or rather the resulting
probability distribution) by $e_3 p e_1$ we have: $e_2 \sim e_3 p e_1$.

This axiom is the basis for one method of measuring a person's utility
function: If e_1 and e_n are the least and the most preferred consequences
in E, then for any $e_i \in E$ we have $e_n \succsim e_i \succsim e_1$. Hence, by the axiom, there
exists a probability w_i such that $e_i \sim e_n w_i e_1$. This w_i is the utility of e_i
and can be denoted as

$$(14) \qquad w_i =: u(e_i).$$

The *third axiom* (INDEPENDENCE) states that, if in the probability
distribution $W'pW$, with $p > 0$, W' is replaced by a preferred probability
distribution W'' (i.e. $W'' \succ W'$), then $W''pW \succ W'pW$. The same applies
when $\succ$ is replaced by $\sim$. Here W, W' and W'' are probability distributions on E, and the meaning of $W'pW$ is that of a distribution on E which
arises when W' is realized with probability p and W is realized with
probability $1 - p$.

This is the independence axiom which is crucial for the derivation
of the Bernoulli decision principle (2). Without this axiom we could

derive a 'utility function' (with the help of the second axiom) but we would never be sure that it is this utility function which is to be inserted into our expected utility criterion (2). That this can be done is a consequence of the independence axiom.

The proof is simple. If Q is a probability distribution on $E = \{e_1, ..., e_n\}$ with $Q(e_i) = q_i$, we may replace each e_i by the probability mixture $e_n(u(e_i)) e_1$, which is equivalent to e_i. The resulting distribution $\tilde{Q}$ is a probability mixture of e_n and e_1, i.e.: $\tilde{Q} = e_n(\sum u(e_i) q_i) e_1$. By the independence axiom $\tilde{Q} \sim Q$. Now suppose Q' is another probability distribution on E. As before, we can construct an equivalent distribution $\tilde{Q}' = e_n(\sum u(e_i) q_i') e_1 \sim Q'$. Therefore $Q \succsim Q' \Leftrightarrow \tilde{Q} \succsim \tilde{Q}' \Leftrightarrow \sum u(e_i) q_i \geq$ $\geq \sum u(e_i) q_i')$ which is criterion (2) (with x_i replaced by e_i). The last equivalence ($\Leftrightarrow$) follows from the dominance principle (9), which is another consequence of the independence axiom.

The predominant role of the independence axiom in utility theory is elucidated by the famous counter example of Allais (1953). It shows how in certain situations 'rational' persons may behave contrary to the expected utility criterion (2): In fact, persons that behave according to Allais violate the independence axiom.

5.2. Axioms for the Bayes Principle

By analogy, one may try to develop an axiomatic foundation of subjective probability and of the Bayes decision principle (3) by assuming that the utility function is given or, alternatively, that the utility of income x is proportional to x. For simplicity, let us use this latter assumption. We assume that a larger income is preferred to a smaller one. We try to set up three axioms parallel to the previous Neumann-Morgenstern axioms. This time, however, the problem is not to order probability distributions – there are no probabilities given –, but to order the actions themselves, i.e. the rows of a decision matrix. Again, we assume that the set of actions is so rich that any function $S \to E$ can be considered as being induced by some action a via the mapping $\varepsilon(a, .): S \to E$. Here $E = R$, the continuum of real numbers. On the other hand, S may be taken to be finite.

Our *first axiom* (ORDER) states that the preference relation $\succsim$ on the set of actions gives rise to a complete ordering (in particular $\succsim$ is transitive).

The *second axiom* (CONTINUITY) states that, given an event $A \subset S$ and an action a_{Ax} which results in some income x if and only if A obtains, then there exists an income y such that the lottery a_{Ax} is considered to be equivalent to the certain gain y:

$$a_{Ax} \sim y.$$

If $x > 0$ then $y \geqslant 0$. Clearly y is unique.

With this continuity axiom we can 'define' the (subjective) probability of A by

$$(15) \qquad P(A) := \frac{y}{x}.$$

From our next axiom it will follow that this ratio is unique, and so our definition makes sense. Furthermore, the laws of probability will be seen to be satisfied by (15). Also, it will be shown that, with probabilities defined in this way, the Bayes decision criterion (3) is valid.

The *third axiom* (INDEPENDENCE) states that if action a_1 is equivalent to income y_1 and, equally, a_2 is equivalent to y_2 then $a_1 + a_2$ is equivalent to $y_1 + y_2$:

$$(16) \qquad a_1 \sim y_1, \quad a_2 \sim y_2 \Rightarrow a_1 + a_2 \sim y_1 + y_2$$

Here $a_1 + a_2$ is defined as an action that leads to the consequence

$$\varepsilon(a_1 + a_2, s) = \varepsilon(a_1, s) + \varepsilon(a_2, s)$$

for every state $s \in S$.

An immediate consequence of this axiom is the following *Lemma*: If all outcomes of an action a are multiplied by some factor λ, where $\lambda = m/2^n$ with integers m and n, then (denoting the resulting new action by λa) we have

$$(16') \qquad a \sim y \Rightarrow \lambda a \sim \lambda y.$$

By a continuity argument it can be shown that (16') is true for any λ.

Applying (16') to the probability definition (15), we see that $P(A)$ is uniquely defined. Also, $0 \leqslant P(A)$ and $P(S) = 1$, since $a_{Sx} \sim x$.

Finally, (16) implies the additivity of P, for if A and B are two disjoint events, and if $a_{Ax} \sim y_A$, $a_{Bx} \sim y_B$, then

$$a_{(A \cup B)x} = a_{Ax} + a_{Bx} \sim y_A + y_B.$$

Hence

$$P(A \cup B) = \frac{y_A + y_B}{x} = \frac{y_A}{x} + \frac{y_B}{x} = P(A) + P(B).$$

Therefore P, defined by (15), is a (finitely additive) probability measure. (15) is very similar to the original 'definition' of probability in Bayes' famous paper (1763).

Further application of the axioms proves the validity of (3): Suppose a leads to the consequence x_i if s_i obtains:

$$\varepsilon(a, s_i) = x_i, \quad i = 1, 2, \ldots, n.$$

Then a can be decomposed into

$$a = \sum a_{s_i x_i}.$$

By the continuity axiom there exists y_i such that

$$a_{s_i x_i} \sim y_i.$$

By (16) and (15)

$$a \sim \sum y_i = \sum x_i P(s_i).$$

If, now, we want to compare a with another action a' with $\varepsilon(a', s_i) = x_i'$, then

$$a \succsim a' \Leftrightarrow \sum x_i P(s_i) \geqslant \sum x_i' P(s_i).$$

This is the decision criterion (3) (with p_i replaced by s_i).

The independence axiom certainly is not very plausible even if income x is replaced by its utility value $u(x)$ throughout the argument. However, it can be replaced by an equivalent axiom which requires the concept of a probability mixture: If a_1 and a_2 are two actions, we say that $a = a_1 \frac{1}{2} a_2$ is a probability mixture of a_1 and a_2 (with probability $\frac{1}{2}$) if it depends on an event with (objective) probability $\frac{1}{2}$ (like flipping a coin), whether the (state-dependent) consequence x is the one which results from a_1 or the one that results from a_2. With this concept we may state that if $a_1 \sim y_1$ and $a_2 \sim y_2$ then

$$a_1 \tfrac{1}{2} a_2 \sim \tfrac{1}{2}(y_1 + y_2).$$

If the consequences x and y are assumed to be N-M utility values, then this modified independence axiom makes much more sense. Its drawback is that it requires a concept outside the usual framework of the theory and depends on objective probabilities being given. This approach has been taken e.g. by Anscombe and Aumann (1963).

5.3. *Measuring Utility and Probability*

The axiomatic systems imply the existence of a utility function and of a probability measure, respectively. The proof is constructive, i.e. existence is proved by presenting methods of measuring these entities. Thus, utility is measured according to (14) on the assumption that probabilities are given. Alternatively, probability is measured according to (15) on the assumption that utility values are given.

In both cases one of the two dimensions of a decision problem can be measured, given measurements on the other dimension. It can be shown, however, that only very limited knowledge of one dimension is required in order to be able to measure the other dimension. E.g. assuming the existence of a continuous utility function on a continuum of consequences (e.g. money incomes), one need only know of an event with probability $\frac{1}{2}$ (e.g. a coin toss) and can use this event as a measuring instrument to construct the utility function (cf. Schneeweiss, 1967, p. 164; Ramsey, 1931; Krelle, 1968, p. 169).

On the other hand, only qualitative knowledge of a utility function like convexity is required in order to measure (subjective) probabilities (cf. Rosett, 1967).

The ultimate aim, of course, is to measure both dimensions without any prior knowledge. The subsequent section deals with this problem.

6. AN INTEGRATED AXIOMATIC SYSTEM

The two axiomatic systems presented above are only partial systems. They each refer solely to one of the basic concepts, either utility or probability, and take the other as given. What is needed is a set of axioms which can serve as a foundation of utility *and* probability theories, and hence of decision criterion (5). With such a system one might resolve the duality between utility and probability which we have found in our previous discussion, and one might find an ultimate synthesis of both these concepts.

The first such system was developed by Ramsey (1931). To some degree, it can be regarded as a combination of the two axiomatic systems considered previously (although v. Neumann and Morgenstern stated their axioms much later): Ramsey first constructs a utility function assuming the existence of an event with probability $\frac{1}{2}$. He then develops a method, similar to the one proposed before, of evaluating the probability of any other event with the help of the previously constructed utility function. For a more refined version of this approach cf. Pfanzagl (1967).

A different approach was taken up by Savage (1954), following some earlier work of de Finetti. His axioms permit measurement of probabilities without any reference to utility, and then, after the finding of a probability measure, construction of a utility function. This order – first probability, then utility – seems to be more appealing than Ramsey's approach, since it gives proper weight to the fundamental concept of probability. Also, Savage's axiomatic system seems to be the ideal synthesis of the partial systems considered before. From very few and rather simple and plausible axioms of 'rational' behaviour under uncertainty one can deduce the existence of a probability measure, as well as of a utility function. The ultimate source of the many analogies and similarities between these two concepts seems to lie in these axioms common to both.

E.g. an independence axiom (the Sure Thing Principle) plays a dominant role in the treatment of the theory by Savage. This axiom generalizes the corresponding axiom of the NM-theory (5.1) and also implies the independence axiom in our axiom system of probability theory (5.2). Similarly, a continuity axiom is needed to guarantee exact measurements of probability and utility, just as the two continuity axioms in (5.1) and (5.2) are.

It may help to look at a short and somewhat modified (and simplified) review of Savage's system in order to see its unifying power.

We make the same general assumptions as in (5.2). However, in order to allow for a continuity argument, S should be infinite. In spite of this, our examples will be constructed under the simplifying assumption of a finite S.

Savage's system permits the introduction of the concept of information, such that one may study its impact on preferences and, in particular, on the formation of probabilities (cf. also 2.2). Information is introduced in a very simple and most natural way: An information asserts that certain states of the world are ruled out because they are known to be impossible. It reduces the world S to some subset $A \subset S$ comprising all those states of the world not ruled out by the information 'given A'. Hence, if a decision maker has the information that only those states of the world obtain that lie in A, he can base his decision on those consequences of his actions which are influenced by only the states of A, disregarding all the consequences that are due to states of $\bar{A}$. A may be called a subworld (relevant to the decision maker given this particular information). Alternatively, A is also called an event.

The *first axiom* (ORDER) states that the set of actions, given A, can be ordered completely by a preference relation $\succsim_A$. This relation takes into account only those consequences $\varepsilon(a, s)$ that come from the states $s \in A$; i.e. if $\varepsilon(a, s) = \varepsilon(a', s)$ for all $s \in A$, then $a \sim_A a'$ (regardless of the consequences of a and a' on A).

This preference relation depends on the information 'given A'. It is called a conditional preference relation. The relation $\succsim_S$ is unconditional and is simply denoted by $\succsim$. (Note that the information 'given S' is an empty information since, by assumption, S is known to be the entire set of states of the world relevant to a particular problem.)

The *second axiom* (INDEPENDENCE) states that if $a \succsim_A a'$ and $a \succsim_{\bar{A}} a'$, then $a \succsim a'$ and if $a \succ_A a'$ and $a \succsim_{\bar{A}} a'$, then $a \succ a'$ unless A is considered to be virtually impossible.[5]

This axiom is (within the whole system) equivalent to Savage's famous Sure Thing Principle. It links conditional preference to unconditional preference, and vice versa, and thus restricts the possible forms of the latter. The unconditional preference relation $\succsim$ implies the conditional preference relation $\succsim_A$ for every $A \subset S$.

Consider e.g. the following example:

	A			$\bar{A}$	
	s_1	s_2	s_3	s_4	s_5
a_1	e_1	e_2	e_3	e_4	e_5
a_2	f_1	f_2	f_3	e_4	e_5
a_1'	e_1	e_2	e_3	g_4	g_5
a_2'	f_1	f_2	f_3	g_4	g_5

We have $a_1 \succsim a_2 \Leftrightarrow a_1 \succsim_A a_2$, since a_1 and a_2 have identical outcomes on $\bar{A}$ and therefore $a_1 \sim_{\bar{A}} a_2$. Hence, $\succsim$ implies $\succsim_A$. We also have $a_1 \succsim a_2 \Leftrightarrow a_1' \succsim a_2'$, because both relations are equivalent to $a_1 \succsim_A a_2$. Hence, $\succsim$ is restricted. (Allais (1953) gives a counterexample to this property.)

In order to have a link between the preference relation $\succsim$ on the set of actions and the preference relation on the set of consequences (denoted by $\succsim$, too) we need the following rather trivial and self-evident

third axiom (DOMINANCE): Let a_e denote an action that results in outcome e for all states of the world. (Thus, with action a_e one can be completely certain to receive e.) With this convention, the axiom states that for each $A \subset S$ and any two outcomes $e, e' \in E$:

$$e \succ e' \Leftrightarrow a_e \succ_A a_{e'}.$$

For S finite, this axiom, together with the independence axiom, implies dominance in the usual sense: If $\varepsilon(a, s) \succsim \varepsilon(a', s)$ for all $s \in S$ and $\varepsilon(a, s) \succ \succ \varepsilon(a', s)$ for some $s \in S$, then $a \succ a'$. For S infinite, one could add to the system a dominance axiom of this kind, if needed.

Although it appears very trivial and innocuous, the dominance axiom actually says (among other things) that a person's utility evaluation of an outcome $e = \varepsilon(a, s)$ does not depend on the state of the world s (nor on the action a). Stated otherwise, it says that all relevant aspects of the state s are already incorporated into the description of the consequence $e = \varepsilon(a, s)$. In practice, it may be difficult to find or even to perceive an action that has the same consequence $e = \varepsilon(a, s)$ for all s of some sub-world A. This difficulty pervades the whole theory, especially the definition of the probability relation below. For a penetrating analysis of this problem cf. Drèze (1961).

There is a natural way to infer a probability relation among events from the preference relation among actions. Consider the special action $a_{Ae\bar{e}}$ that results in consequence e if some state of the subworld A obtains and in consequence $\bar{e}$ if some state of $\bar{A}$ obtains. If $e \succ \bar{e}$, we call $a_{Ae\bar{e}}$ a bet on A with prize e and non-prize $\bar{e}$. Now suppose an individual may choose between a bet on A or a bet (with the same prize and non-prize) on some other event B. If he chooses a bet on A, say, we may infer from his choice that he thinks A to be more probable than B. In symbols:

$$A \succsim B \Leftrightarrow a_{Ae\bar{e}} \succsim a_{Be\bar{e}}.$$

Thus the preference relation generates a probability relation 'more probable than' (and 'as probable as') on the set of events. In order that this relation be uniquely defined, we must make sure that it is independent of the prize and non-prize chosen. In addition, there must exist at least one pair $(e, \bar{e})$ such that $e \succ \bar{e}$. These two properties, which are almost self-evident can be formulated as a

fourth axiom (UNIQUE BETTING): There exist $e, \bar{e} \in E$ with $e \succ \bar{e}$. If $f, \bar{f} \in E$ and $f \succ \bar{f}$ then (for any $A, B \subset S$):

$$a_{Ae\bar{e}} \succsim a_{Be\bar{e}} \Leftrightarrow a_{Aff} \succsim a_{Bff}.$$

It can be shown (with the help of the independence axiom) that this probability relation defines an ordinal probability in the sense of Section 3.1. In particular, (7) holds true. This can be seen by tracing back the probability relation to its origin: a preference relation between bets. Having fixed prize e and non-prize $\bar{e}$, we denote a bet on A simply by a_A instead of $a_{Ae\bar{e}}$. We have (with $A \cap C = B \cap C = \emptyset$):

$$A \succsim B \Leftrightarrow a_A \succsim a_B$$
$$\Leftrightarrow a_A \succsim_{\bar{C}} a_B \quad (\text{since } a_A \sim_C a_B)$$
$$\Leftrightarrow a_{A \cup C} \succsim_{\bar{C}} a_{B \cup C} \quad (\text{since no change occurs on } \bar{C})$$
$$\Leftrightarrow a_{A \cup C} \succsim a_{B \cup C} \quad (\text{since } a_{A \cup C} \sim_C a_{B \cup C})$$
$$\Leftrightarrow A \cup C \succsim B \cup C$$

which proves (7).

The following example may help to follow the proof more easily:

		B			C		
	s_1	s_2	s_3	s_4	s_5	s_6	s_7
a_A	e	e	e	$\bar{e}$	$\bar{e}$	$\bar{e}$	$\bar{e}$
a_B	$\bar{e}$	$\bar{e}$	e	e	$\bar{e}$	$\bar{e}$	$\bar{e}$
$a_{A \cup C}$	e	e	e	$\bar{e}$	e	e	$\bar{e}$
$a_{B \cup C}$	$\bar{e}$	$\bar{e}$	e	e	e	e	$\bar{e}$

The situation here is similar to the one in the previous example, and, by the same argument,

$$a_A \gtrsim a_B \Leftrightarrow a_{A \cup C} \gtrsim a_{B \cup C}.$$

Many interesting results can be deduced from (7) (and the transitivity of $\gtrsim$), e.g. the following useful generalization of (7):
If $A \cap C = B \cap C' = \emptyset$ and $C \sim C'$, then

(7') $\qquad A \gtrsim B \Leftrightarrow A \cup C \gtrsim B \cup C'.$

For a proof consider the following Venn diagram

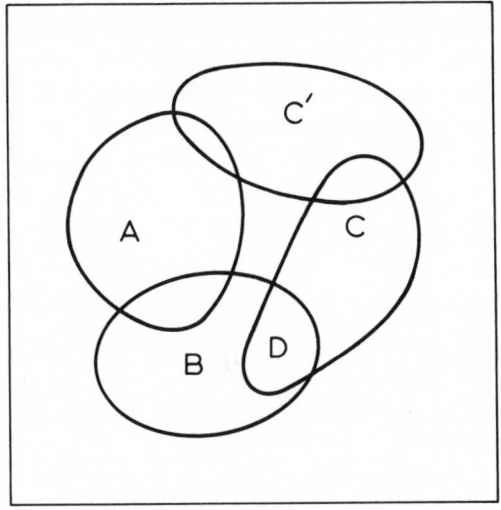

Fig. 3

Call $D = B \cap C$. Then, by (7):

$$
\begin{aligned}
A \gtrsim B &\Leftrightarrow A \cup (C-D) \gtrsim B \cup (C-D) = B \cup C \\
&= C \cup (B-D) \sim C' \cup (B-D) \quad \text{(because } C \sim C') \\
&\Leftrightarrow A \cup (C-D) \cup D \gtrsim C' \cup (B-D) \cup D \\
&\Leftrightarrow A \cup C \gtrsim B \cup C',
\end{aligned}
$$

which proves (7').

Restricting all our considerations to some subworld $C \subset S$, we can derive in the same way a conditional probability relation with all the properties we found for the unconditional one:

$$A \gtrsim_C B \Leftrightarrow a_A \gtrsim_C a_B.$$

Actually, $\gtrsim_C$ is related to $\gtrsim$ in a very simple way:

(17) $\qquad A \gtrsim_C B \Leftrightarrow A \cap C \gtrsim B \cap C.$

This is true because $a_A \gtrsim_C a_B \Leftrightarrow a_{A \cap C} \gtrsim_C a_{B \cap C} \Leftrightarrow a_{A \cap C} \gtrsim a_{B \cap C}$ since

$$a_{A \cap C} \sim_{\bar{C}} a_{B \cap C}.$$

Starting from the concept of a conditional probability relation, we could try to develop a concept of stochastic independence for ordinal probabilities. However, it seems to be difficult to carry out this programme in general. Instead, let us restrict our considerations to 'neutral' events, i.e. to events that are as probable as their complements $(A \sim \bar{A})$. All neutral events are equally probable.

Let A and B be neutral events. We say that A is independent of B if

$$A \sim_B \bar{A}.$$

Now, for neutral events A, B, we have $\bar{A} \cap B \sim A \cap \bar{B}$. For suppose $\bar{A} \cap B \underset{(\prec)}{\succ} A \cap \bar{B}$, then by (7') $\bar{A} \cap B \cup A \cap B \underset{(\prec)}{\succ} A \cap \bar{B} \cup A \cap B$ and hence $B \underset{(\prec)}{\succ} A$, a contradiction. Therefore, $\bar{A} \cap B \sim A \cap \bar{B}$ and likewise $A \cap B \sim \bar{A} \cap \bar{B}$. Now, if A is independent of B, we have $A \cap B \sim \bar{A} \cap B$. Combining all equivalences:

$$A \cap B \sim \bar{A} \cap B \sim A \cap \bar{B} \sim \bar{A} \cap \bar{B}.$$

In addition, it follows that $B \sim_A \bar{B}$, i.e. B is independent of A; also $A \sim_{\bar{B}} \bar{A}$ and $B \sim_{\bar{A}} \bar{B}$.

This concept of stochastic independence can be extended to more than two neutral events. E.g. we say that the neutral events A, B, C are independent if A is independent of $B \cap C$, $B \cap \bar{C}$, $\bar{B} \cap C$ and (hence) of $\bar{B} \cap \bar{C}$ and if analogous independence relations hold for B and C. (Actually independence follows from fewer independence relations.) It can be shown that for A, B, C independent $A \cap B \cap C \sim \bar{A} \cap B \cap C \sim A \cap \bar{B} \cap C \sim \bar{A} \cap \bar{B} \cap C \sim A \cap B \cap \bar{C} \sim A \cap \bar{B} \cap \bar{C} \sim \bar{A} \cap B \cap \bar{C} \sim \bar{A} \cap \bar{B} \cap \bar{C}$, and therefore also $A \cap B \sim A \cap \bar{B} \sim A \cap C \sim B \cap C$ etc.

In order to derive a cardinal probability for some person, it is necessary to get hold of an appropriate measuring rod. The simplest one might be a coin, or rather a multitude of coins, deemed to be fair by the person. If, in addition, the person thinks the outcome of a coin toss to be independent of the outcome of all the other coin tosses taken together, then all possible 2^k outcomes of k tosses are equally probable to this person. By comparing any event A with an event formed out of this coin tossing experiment, it should be possible to evaluate numerically the probability of A to any desired degree of accuracy, if only k is sufficiently large.

To make this precise let us assume that the world S can be represented as a direct product

$$S = S' \times S''$$

where S'' can be decomposed into[6] $n = 2^k$ equally probable[7] events $s_1'', s_2'', ..., s_n''$, and S' consist of all those primitive events $s_1', s_2', ...$ that the decision maker actually wants to know about. In other words, for all those actions a that pertain to the actual decision problem, the consequence depending on a and $s \in S$ does not depend on the event s'' that happens to occur but only on the event s', where $s = (s', s'')$:

$$\varepsilon(a, s) = \varepsilon(a, s', s'') = \bar{\varepsilon}(a, s').$$

S' may be called the relevant world and its elements s' the relevant states.

We may think of S'' as of the set of all possible outcomes of k independent coin tosses. These outcomes do not interfere with the consequences of the actions of an actual decision problem.

On the other hand, one can always construct (artificial) actions the consequences of which do depend on the outcome of a multiple coin toss s'', either solely or in connection with a relevant state s'. Such actions, although not directly relevant to the decision maker, may still be of great importance to him if he wants to analyse his own preference structure on the set of actions. In fact, an example of such actions naturally turns up if one wants to test the probability relation $s_i'' \sim s_j''$, which is done by putting to choice two appropriately constructed betting actions over S''.

S'' is our measuring rod. Thus the world S is composed out of a relevant world S' and a measuring rod S''. We want to measure probabilities of events of S' with the help of S''.

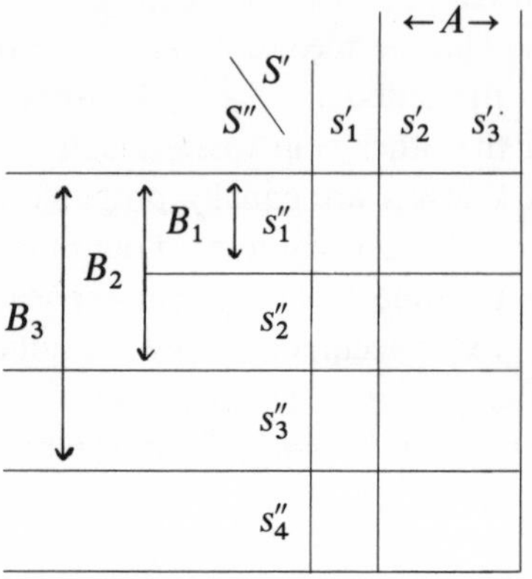

	ordinal	cardinal
E.g.	$s'_1 \sim B_1$	$P(s'_1)=\frac{1}{4}$
	$s'_2 \sim B_1$	$P(s'_2)=\frac{1}{4}$
	$s'_3 \sim B_2$	$P(s'_3)=\frac{1}{2}$
	$A \sim B_3$	$P(A)=\frac{3}{4}$

$S = S' \times S''$

Fig. 4

In order to do so, we first of all investigate the structure of S''. Let us define an m-event in S'' as any subset of S'' which consists of exactly m of the events s''. It will be denoted by B_m. By (7′), given m, all m-events are equally probable, and an m-event is more probable than an m'-event if and only if $m > m'$:

$$B_m \succsim B_{m'} \Leftrightarrow m > m'.$$

Therefore, by setting

$$(18) \qquad P(B_m) = \frac{m}{n}$$

we arrive at a (cardinal) probability measure on S'' which agrees with the probability relation $\succsim$ on S''.

This probability measure can be used to introduce a similar probability measure on S'. For any relevant state $s' \in S'$ one can find an m such that

$$B_m \precsim s' \prec B_{m+1}.$$

If n is sufficiently large, there is a good chance that one can even find an m such that (at least approximately)

$$B_m \sim s'.$$

For all practical purposes, this will always be possible and we may set (with sufficient accuracy)

(19) $$P(s') = P(B_m) = \frac{m}{n}.$$

For the sake of a precise theory it will be necessary, of course, to put forth further arguments to ensure the possibility of an exact measurement of $P(s')$. This can be done by appealing to some continuity arguments and by introducing a new continuity axiom (cf. Savage, 1954). First of all, S'' must be structured in such a way that a partitioning into n equally probable events is possible for any n (or at least for any $n = 2^k$). One may think of S'' as the (infinite) set of all possible outcomes of an infinite series of independent coin tosses. A partitioning into $n = 2^k$ equally probable events is realized by considering only the outcome of the first k tosses.

The continuity axiom, among other things, must make certain that for any two events C, D in S with $C \succ D$ there is a sufficiently fine partitioning (n) of S'' and an m-event $B_{m,n}$ of this partitioning such that $C \succ B_{m,n} \succ D$, so that C and D can be separated by an event with probability m/n. With the help of such a continuity axiom we can not only assign numerical probabilities to any event in S', but also to any event *in* S.

However, for our purpose it suffices to have a probability measure on S' [and also on S'' for any partioning (n)], and we assume that probabilities can be evaluated by applying (19) to any relevant state $s' \in S'$. Assuming, for the sake of simplicity, S' to be finite, it is clear, again by (7′), that the assignment of probabilities via (19) results in a probability measure[8] on S' which agrees with the probability relation $\succeq$ on S'. Again, drawing from the continuity axiom, one can prove that P' is unique.

All the arguments leading to a probability measure on S' can be applied in the same way to any subworld $A' \subset S'$. They prove the existence of a probability measure on A' which agrees with the conditional probability relation $\succeq_{A'}$ of events in S'. This probability measure is identical with the usual conditional probability measure $P(\cdot \mid A')$, as defined by

(6). For, by (17), the conditional probability agrees with the conditional probability relation and is uniquely defined by this property.

Having established the existence of a probability distribution, Savage goes on proving the existence of a utility function and verifying the Ramsey decision principle (5). This is done by proving the validity of the NM-axioms (5.1), from which, as we know, the rest follows readily. The proof is somewhat complicated, even within our simplified approach, and will not be restated here [9].

It may nevertheless be worthwhile to point out that the independence axiom of the NM-theory is a direct consequence of Savage's independence axiom.

For suppose that a' and a'' are two relevant actions inducing the probability distributions W' and W''' on E, and $W'' \underset{\sim}{\succ} W'$. Let $p = m/n$ be a probability and W another distribution on E induced by a relevant action a. Finally, let B_m be an m-event on the measuring rod S''. $P(B_m) = p$. Consider actions b' and b'' which result in $\varepsilon(a', s)$ and $\varepsilon(a'', s)$ resp. if $s = (s', s'')$ and $s'' \in B_m$, and in $\varepsilon(a, s)$ if $s'' \in \bar{B}_m$.

Then, assuming the events in S'' are independent of those in S' (the results of coin tosses are independent of relevant events), b' and b'' will induce the conditional distribution W' and W'' resp. on B_m and W on $\bar{B}_m$. Taking for granted that preferences (conditional or unconditional) between actions depend solely on the induced probability distributions [10] (order axiom of the NM-theory), it follows that $b'' \underset{\sim}{\succ}_{B_m} b'$ and $b'' \sim_{\bar{B}_m} b'$. Therefore, by the independence axiom (Sure Thing Principle), $b'' \underset{\sim}{\succ} b'$. But b'' and b' induce probability mixtures on E, for which we can conclude: $W'' p W \underset{\sim}{\succ} W' p W$. These arguments are exemplified in the following figure (cf. also Figure 4):

$$
\begin{array}{ccc}
s'_1 & s'_2 & s'_3
\end{array}
$$

$$P(B_3) = \tfrac{3}{4} = p$$

$$W' : \begin{cases} \tfrac{1}{4} & \tfrac{1}{4} & \tfrac{1}{2} \\ e'_1 & e'_2 & e'_3 \end{cases}$$

$$W : \begin{cases} \tfrac{1}{4} & \tfrac{1}{4} & \tfrac{1}{2} \\ e_1 & e_2 & e_3 \end{cases}$$

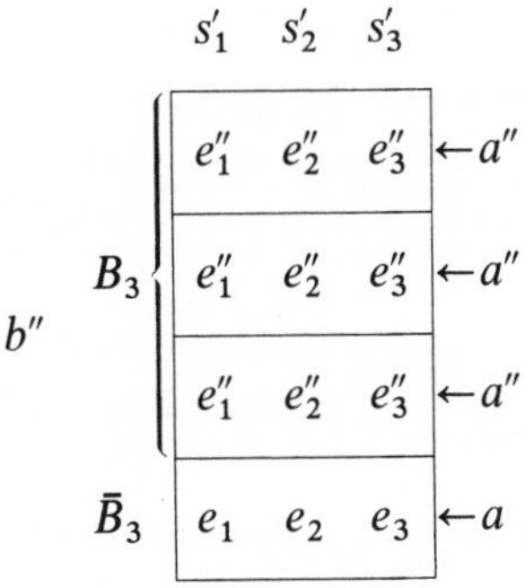

$$W'': \begin{cases} \frac{1}{4} & \frac{1}{4} & \frac{1}{2} \\ e''_1 & e''_2 & e''_3 \end{cases}$$

$$W'pW = \begin{cases} \frac{3}{16} & \frac{3}{16} & \frac{3}{8} & \frac{1}{16} & \frac{1}{16} & \frac{1}{8} \\ e'_1 & e'_2 & e'_3 & e_1 & e_2 & e_3 \end{cases}$$

$$W''pW = \begin{cases} \frac{3}{16} & \frac{3}{16} & \frac{3}{8} & \frac{1}{16} & \frac{1}{16} & \frac{1}{8} \\ e''_1 & e''_2 & e''_3 & e_1 & e_2 & e_3 \end{cases}$$

Fig. 5

The independence axiom (Sure Thing Principle) of the integrated theory is thus seen to be the common source of the independence axiom in utility theory and of the addition rule in probability theory and also (indirectly) of the independence axiom in Section 5.2. A similar account could be given of the continuity axiom in Savage's integrated theory (which we did not state here) as leading to the continuity axioms in both partial theories.

7. A SYNOPSIS

The analogies between utility and probability found in this investigation are seen to have their ultimate source in an integrated axioms system. The following synopsis is designed to display these analogies in the two dimensions of a decision problem.

	utility		probability
objective (1)	$x_i = x(e_i)$	$\to \sum x_i p_i \leftarrow$	$p_i = p(s_i)$
subjective (5)	$u_i = u(e_i)$	$\to \sum u(e_i)\,P(s_i) \leftarrow$	$P_i = P(s_i)$
special cases (2), (3)	$u(e_i) = v(x(e_i))$		$P(s_i) = \pi(p(s_i))$
	$\sum v(x_i)\,p_i$		$\sum x_i \pi(p_i)$
	$v(x_i) = x_i$	$\to \sum x_i p_i \leftarrow$	$\pi(p_i) = p_i$
ordinal	preference $\succsim$ on E		prob. rel. $\succsim$ on S ordinal addition (7)
dominance	in utility (8)		in probability (9)

	cardinal utility on E	numerical probability on S
cardinal		
conditional (6)	$u(e \mid e_0) = u(e+e_0) - u(e_0)$	$P(A \mid B) = P(A \cap B)/P(B)$
independent	$E = E_1 \times E_2$ (10)	$S = S_1 \times S_2$ (12)
components	$u(e_1, e_2) = u^1(e_1) + u^2(e_2)$	$P(s_1, s_2) = P^1(s_1)\, P^2(s_2)$

	cardinal utility (Alt)	numerical probability
axioms		(Koopman)
introspective		
axioms	Bernoulli principle (5.1)	Bayes principle (5.2)
behaviouristic	(probabilities given)	(utilities given)

ORDER	$\succsim$ on prob. distr. over E	$\succsim$ on actions
CONTINUITY	$e_3 \succsim e_2 \succsim e_1 \Rightarrow e_2 \sim e_3 p e_1$	$A \subset S,\ x \in E \Rightarrow a_{Ax} \sim y$
INDEPENDENCE	$W'' \succsim W' \Rightarrow W''pW \succsim W'pW$	$a_1 \sim y_1,\ \ a_2 \sim y_2 \Rightarrow$
		$a_1 + a_2 \sim y_1 + y_2$
axioms for	utility *and*	probability
	Ramsey: first utility	Savage: first probability
	then probability	then utility

independence axiom

$\swarrow$ $\searrow$

independence axiom   independence axiom

addition law

measurement	$u(e_i) = w_i$ (14)	$P(s_i) = y_i/x$ (15)
	with prob. given	with utilities given
	method with prob. $\frac{1}{2}$	method with qualitative properties of utility or with measuring rod S''

University of Munich

NOTES

[1] According to Ellsberg a third component, ambiguity, has to be added. For a critical appraisal of this view see Schneeweiss (1968a).

[2] Bernoulli norm, according to Marschak (1955).

[3] For a different view see Menges (1967, 1970).

[4] The consequence function $\varepsilon: A \times S \to E$ assigns a consequence e to each pair (a, s). $\varepsilon(a, s) = e$ is the consequence of action a when s is the true state of the world. If a is fixed, the partial consequence function $\varepsilon(a, .): S \to E$ assigns to each state $s \in S$ the consequence $\varepsilon(a, s)$, which would result as a consequence of action a if s were the true state of the world.

[5] No attempt is made to discuss this concept, which ultimately leads to events with probability zero (null events). Instead, reference is made to the work of Savage (1954), Koopman (1940) and Renyi (1962) (II. 11). In the following we tacitly assume that all events $A \subset S$ that we refer to are non-null events.

[6] Nothing important depends on our assumption that n is a power of 2. The only reason we make this assumption is that it is amenable to an easy interpretation (coin tossing). For the sake of the theory n may be any number (sufficiently large).

[7] The probability relation on S induces marginal probability relations on S' and on S'': If A' and B' are events in S' (i.e. subsets of S') then $A' \succsim B' \Leftrightarrow A' \times S'' \succsim B' \times S''$, and similarly if A'' and B'' are events in S''. Thus, saying that s_1'' is as probable as s_2'' is equivalent to saying that $s_1'' \times S'$ is as probable as $s_2'' \times S'$. The first statement $(s_1'' \sim s_2'')$ refers to the marginal probability relation on S'' whereas the second $(s_1'' \times S' \sim s_2'' \times S')$ refers to the joint probability relation on S. Both statements say the same thing.

[8] This probability measure is finitely additive. By introducing some further axioms it is possible to prove the existence of a countably additive measure (cf. Arrow, 1970; Villegas, 1964).

[9] Cf. Savage (1954), also Fishburn (1970), Chapt. 14. For a different approach see Arrow (1970).

[10] This can be proved with the help of the Savage axioms. The proof, which is somewhat involved, utilizes the independence axiom, too.

BIBLIOGRAPHY

Allais, M., 'Le comportement de l'homme rationnel devant le risque: Critique des postulats et axiomes de l'école Americaine', *Econometrica* **21** (1953), 503–546.

Alt, F., 'Über die Messbarkeit des Nutzens', *Zeitschrift für Nationalökonomie* **7** (1936), 161–169.

Anscombe, F. J. and Aumann, R. J., 'A Definition of Subjective Probability', *Annals of Mathematical Statistics* **34** (1963), 199–205.

Arrow, K. J., 'Exposition of the Theory of Choice under Uncertainty', in *Essays in the Theory of Risk-Bearing*, Amsterdam 1970, pp. 44–89.

Bernoulli, D., 'Specimen theoriae novae de mensura sortis', *Commentarii Academiae Scientiarum Imperialis Petropolitanae* **5** (1738), 175–192.

Debreu, G., 'Representation of a Preference Ordering by a Numerical Function', in R. M. Thrall, C. H. Coombs and R. L. Davis (eds.), *Decision Processes*, Wiley, New York, 1954.

Drèze, J. H., 'Fondements Logiques de la Probabilité Subjective et de l'Utilité', in *La Décision*, Centre National de la Recherche Scientifique, Paris, 1961, pp. 73–88.

Fishburn, P., *Decision and Value Theory*, Wiley, New York, 1964.

Fishburn, P., *Utility Theory for Decision Making*, J. Wiley, New York, London, Sidney, Toronto 1970.

Koopman, B. O., 'The Bases of Probability', *Bulletin of the American Mathematical Society* **46** (1940), 763–774.

Krelle, W., *Präferenz- und Entscheidungstheorie*, J. C. B. Mohr, Tübingen, 1968.

Marschak, J., 'Probability in the Social Sciences', in *Mathematical Thinking in the Social Sciences* (ed. by P. F. Lazarsfeld), The Free Press, Glencoe, Ill., 1955, 2. edition, pp. 166–215.

Menges, G., 'Über Thomas Bayes (1702–1761) und das Theorem-Versuch einer Würdigung', in *Geschichte und Zukunft* (ed. by A. Diemer), Meisenheim/Glan, 1967.

Menges, G., 'On Subjective Probability and Related Problems', *Theory and Decision* **1** (1970), 40–60.

144   HANS SCHNEEWEISS

v. Neumann, J. and Morgenstern, O., *Theory of Games and Economic Behavior*, Princeton, 2. ed., 1947.

Pfanzagl, J., 'Subjective Probability Derived from the Morgenstern-von Neumann Utility Concept', Chapter 18 in *Essays in Mathematical Economics, In Honor of Oskar Morgenstern*, Princeton, 1967, pp. 237–251.

Pfanzagl, J., *Theory of Measurement*, Physica-Verlag, Würzburg-Wien, 1968.

Ramsey, F. P., 'Truth and Probability', in *The Foundations of Mathematics and Other Logical Essays*, London 1931.

Rényi, A., *Wahrscheinlichkeitsrechnung*, Deutscher Verlag der Wissenschaften, Berlin 1962.

Rosett, R. N., 'Experimental Measurement of Subjective Probability and its Relation to Relative Frequency', Paper presented at the European Meeting of the Econometric Society, Bonn, 1967.

Samuelson, P. A., 'The Numerical Representation of Ordered Classifications and the Concept of Utility', *The Review of Economic Studies* 6 (1938), 65–70.

Savage, L. J., *The Foundations of Statistics*, New York 1954.

Schneeweiss, H., *Entscheidungskriterien bei Risiko*, Springer-Verlag Berlin, Heidelberg, New York, 1967.

Schneeweiss, H., 'Spieltheoretische Analyse des Ellsberg-Paradoxons', *Zeitschrift für die gesamte Staatswirtschaft* 124 (1968a), 249–256.

Schneeweiss, H., 'Note on Two Dominance Principles in Decision Theory', *Unternehmensforschung* 12 (1968b), 213–216.

Villegas, C., 'On Qualitative Probability σ-Algebras', *Annals of Mathematical Statistics* 35 (1964), 1787–1796.

MINAKETAN BEHARA

ENTROPY AND UTILITY

1.   Statistical decision theory is concerned with problems of making decision under risk. In case of total uncertainty, decision must be made following certain criteria. But, statistical decision theory makes use of some experimental evidence before reaching a decision. Experiments are supposed to be informative; more experimental evidence should reduce the amount of uncertainty associated with the states of nature. It is true that the measure of information as provided by entropy displays monotonic behaviour with respect to amount of experiment. Here we try to show that the value of information, a utilitarian concept, associated with experiments shows the same monotonic behaviour.

   This monotonicity, added with certain other obvious properties, may lead to the establishment of a theory of value of information independent of probabilistic concept.

2.   One of the major tasks of statistics as of many other sciences is to estimate the probabilities of the states of nature. The methods of classical statistics are designed to help in solving the above estimation problem. These methods include design of experiment, collection of samples, computation of statistics etc. and finally estimation of population parameters or testing of hypothesis regarding them. The approach is based on the frequency theory of probability and is called as non-Bayesian approach nowadays. The Bayesian approach, named after the eighteenth century English probabilist Thomas Bayes (who may not be held responsible for everything that goes under the term 'Bayesian') is designed to estimate the probabilities with or without the help of samples or experiments. The subjective Bayesian believes in the beliefs of a so-called rational person and uses his estimation (of probabilities) in making decisions. The objective Bayesian, on the other hand, begins with the assumption about the probabilities of the states of nature (known as the prior probabilities) before conducting an experiment and revises the prior probabilities into the posterior probabilities in the light of

Günter Menges (ed.), Information, Inference and Decision, 145–154. All Rights Reserved.
Copyright © 1974 by D. Reidel Publishing Company, Dordrecht-Holland.

newer evidences via Bayes theorem. Very often it is not possible to conduct the experiment extensively due to cost, time and other unavoidable factors and yet the probabilities of states of nature must be estimated for decision-making purposes. Wald's sequential decision theory is usually used in such cases and Bayes theorem aids such decision processes by estimating the probabilities sequentially. Bayes axiom, however, rests on the imagination, as Fisher (1936) puts it, that the possible types of population have themselves been drawn, as samples, from a super-population. Good (1965) calls the sampling from (i) a population, (ii) a super-population, (iii) a super-super-population etc. as (i) sampling of type I, (ii) sampling of type II, (iii) sampling of type III and so on respectively. The entire problem is, thus, transformed into a purely deductive one so that the Kolmogorov's axiomatic probability theory, of which Bayes theorem is a trivial consequence, becomes applicable.

3. Motivated by the very importance of the problem we are led to think if some illumination can be gained by the *information-theoretic* study of the situation. In decision making under uncertainty a rational solution is provided by Laplace by assuming the possible states of nature to be equi-probable; and in this case we find the Shannon's entropy to be maximum. At the other end, when the true state of nature is known with certainty, the above entropy becomes zero. This particular behaviour leads one to wonder if the measure of information can depict the problem of statistical decision theory completely. D. Gabor (see Barnard, 1951) remarks that in Shannon's theory one can calculate in advance, before any message has been sent, the expected rate at which information will be transmitted in a given code, in a given language. 'After' the transmission one can still ask, 'what was really meant?' – a question similar to Fisher's, 'what is the most likely value of some unknown parameter from these experiments and how accurately do we know it?' But this looking backward program is essentially the problem of statistical inference, which deals with the estimation of probabilities of states of nature. As a user of statistical inference, the decision theorist is interested in what is called the 'value of information received after certain event'. Gabor calls it as the attitude of 'looking forward after the event'. The value of information which incorporates the utility or loss function is a necessary component for the solution of a statistical decision problem.

The measure of information such as Shannon's entropy seems to solve the simple decision problem as described above. It would be of interest to investigate the relationship (if any) between the value and measure of information.

4.   In order to see if *Shannon's entropy* can be used for solving statistical decision problems, we formulate the decision problem in terms of utilitarian value of information (Raiffa and Schlaifer, 1961) instead of utility function. We proceed by giving the classical formulation due to Wald (1950). The components of statistical decision theory:

(1)   Space of experiments: $\mathscr{E} = \{e\}$
(2)   Space of sample outcome of experiment $e: \mathscr{X} = \{x\}$
(3)   Space of terminal decisions: $\mathscr{D}^t = \{\delta^t\}$
(4)   Space of states of natures: $\Omega = \{\theta\}$
(5)   Probability $p(x \mid \theta, e)$ of x given θ and e.
(6)   Utility function: $u(e, x, \delta^t, \theta)$ defined on the product space $\mathscr{E} \times \mathscr{X} \times \mathscr{D}^t \times \Omega$.
(7)   The a priori probability $p'(\theta)$ on Ω.

The utility $u(e, x, \delta^t, \theta)$ may be decomposed into

(6a)   Sampling utility: $u_s(e, x)$
(6b)   Terminal utility: $u_t(\delta^t, \theta)$

where, if

(4.1) $u(e, x, \delta^t, \theta) = u_s(e, x) + u_t(\delta^t, \theta),$

we may introduce the following concepts (Raiffa and Schlaifer, 1961),
A.   Opportunity loss
B.   Value of information.

A.   Opportunity loss: It is the difference between the gain actually realized and a higher gain that would have been realized if the true state of nature were known. The opportunity loss is zero or positive according as the true state of nature is or is not known with certainty. (We do not assume any negative value for the opportunity loss.) This situation arises when utility considerations are made over the product space $\Omega \times \mathscr{D}^t$ only, omitting the considerations of the cost of experiment.

Here the opportunity loss is the terminal one and is written as

$$(4.2) \qquad l_t(\delta^t, \theta) = u_t(\delta_\theta^t, \theta) - u_t(\delta^t, \theta)$$

where δ_θ^t is given by

$$(4.3) \qquad u_t(\delta_\theta^t, \theta) = \max_{\delta^t} u_t(\delta^t, \theta).$$

The generalized opportunity loss may be introduced by considering the utility over the product space $\mathscr{E} \times \mathscr{X} \times \mathscr{D}^t \times \Omega$. If e_0 denotes 'no experiment' which evidently has 'no outcome' denoted by x_0, then δ_θ^t may be defined by

$$(4.4) \qquad u(e_0, x_0, \delta_\theta^t, \theta) = \max_{\delta^t} u(e_0, x_0, \delta^t, \theta).$$

On the other hand, if an experiment e is performed whose sample outcome is x, and then a terminal decision δ^t is made, then the opportunity loss is given by

$$(4.5) \qquad l(e, x, \delta^t, \theta) = u(e_0, x_0, \delta_\theta^t, \theta) - u(e, x, \delta^t, \theta).$$

Note that an optimum decision function is defined as the one that minimizes the expected opportunity loss given by

$$(4.6) \qquad \bar{l}(\delta, e) = \iint l(e, x, \delta(x), \theta) \, p(x \mid \theta, e) \, p'(\theta) \, d\theta \, dx$$

with respect to δ, where $\delta : \mathscr{X} \to \mathscr{D}^t$.

Now assuming (4.1) to hold, we may write (4.5) as

$$(4.7) \qquad l(e, x, \delta^t, \theta) = u_t(\delta_\theta^t, \theta) - u_s(e, x) - u_t(\delta^t, \theta)$$

$$\text{(since, } u_s(e_0, x_0) = 0.\text{)}$$

$$= l_t(\delta^t, \theta) + c_s(e, x)$$

where $c_s(e, x)$ denotes the cost of sampling and is equal to $-u_s(e, x)$.

We may now write (4.6), by using Fubini's theorem, as

$$(4.8) \qquad \int dx \left\{ \int l(e, x, \delta^t, \theta) \, p(\theta, x \mid e) \, d\theta \right\}$$

$$(4.9) \qquad = \int dx \left\{ \int (l_t(\delta^t, \theta) + c_s(e, x)) \, p''(\theta \mid x, e) \, p(x \mid e) \, d\theta \right\}$$

(by (4.7) and decomposing the joint probability measure $p(\theta, x \mid e)$ into conditional and marginal probability measures denoted by $p''(\theta \mid x, e)$ (called the posterior probability by Bayesians) and $p(x \mid e)$ respectively)

$$(4.10) \qquad = \int p(x \mid e) \, dx \left\{ c_s(e, x) + \int l_t(\delta^t, \theta) \, p''(\theta \mid x, e) \, d\theta \right\}.$$

Once an experiment e is performed and x has been observed, we need only seek the minimization of

$$(4.11) \qquad \int l_t(\delta^t, \theta) \, p''(\theta \mid x, e) \, d\theta$$

with respect to δ^t. Let us denote the minimizing δ^t by $\delta_0(x)$ for given x. The expression (4.11) is known as the 'expected terminal opportunity loss'. The optimum decision, after an experiment, is the one that minimizes the expected terminal opportunity loss.

An optimum experiment is defined by taking that $e \in \mathcal{E}$ for which

$$(4.12) \qquad \int c_s(e, x) \, p(x \mid e) \, dx + \int \int l_t(\delta_0(x), \theta) \, p(\theta, x \mid e) \, d\theta \, dx$$

is minimized.

B.   Value of information: If we compare the experiments (see Blackwell, 1953) in the light of utility (or dually, risk) associated with the adopted terminal decisions, we get to the notion of the value of information. Ordinarily, it is the 'increase' in utility in passing from a less informative experiment to a more informative experiment.

Assume that an ideal experiment e_∞, with sample outcome x_∞, performed at a cost of $c_s(e_\infty, x_\infty)$ yields the 'perfect information' over the states of the nature. Assuming (4.1) to hold, the utility of making the decisions δ_θ^t with perfect information and δ_0^t with no information are respectively given by

$$(4.13) \qquad u(e_\infty, x_\infty, \delta_\theta^t, \theta) = u_t(\delta_\theta^t, \theta) - c_s(e_\infty, x_\infty)$$

and

$$(4.14) \qquad u(e_0, x_0, \delta_0^t, \theta) = u_t(\delta_0^t, \theta) - 0$$

where δ_0^t and δ_θ^t are defined respectively by

(4.15) $\int u_t(\delta_0^t, \theta) \, p'(\theta) \, \mathrm{d}\theta = \max_{\delta^t} \int u_t(\delta^t, \theta) \, p'(\theta) \, \mathrm{d}\theta$

and

(4.16) $u_t(\delta_\theta^t, \theta) = \max_{\delta^t} u_t(\delta^t, \theta).$

The terminal opportunity loss of the optimal decision δ_0^t is then given by

(4.17) $l_t(\delta_0^t, \theta) = u_t(\delta_\theta^t, \theta) - u_t(\delta_0^t, \theta).$

The value of the complete information on θ is then defined as identical with this terminal opportunity loss, that is,

(4.18) $V'(\theta) = l_t(\delta_0^t, \theta) = u_t(\delta_\theta, \theta) - u_t(\delta_0^t, \theta).$

Imagining the true state of nature to be a 'message' M_θ, we may say that (4.18) is the 'a priori value of message M_θ'.

The 'a priori expected value of message M_θ' may be computed as

(4.19) $V' = \int V'(\theta) \, p'(\theta) \, \mathrm{d}\theta.$

The value of perfect information is associated with an ideal experiment e_∞ which is perhaps impossible to conduct. In order to define the value of information associated with actual experiment we first define δ_x^t by

(4.20) $\int u_t(\delta_x^t, \theta) \, p''(\theta \mid x, e) \, \mathrm{d}\theta = \max_{\delta^t} \int u_t(\delta^t, \theta) \, p''(\theta \mid x, e) \, \mathrm{d}\theta$

where δ_x^t is based on the outcome of some actual experiment e. We may now write the 'a posteriori expected value of message M_θ' as

(4.21) $V'(x, e) = \int V'(\theta) \, p''(\theta \mid x, e) \, \mathrm{d}\theta.$

Let us now define the 'posterior value of message M_θ given x, e' by

(4.22) $V''(\theta \mid x, e) = u_t(\delta_\theta^t, \theta) - u_t(\delta_x^t, \theta).$

The 'a posteriori expected a posteriori value of message M_θ given x, e'

may be written as

$$(4.23) \quad V''(x, e) = \int V''(\theta \mid x, e) \, p''(\theta \mid x, e) \, d\theta.$$

Now the 'value of message M_x' may be defined by

$$(4.24) \quad V(x, e) = V'(x, e) - V''(x, e).$$

The 'expected value of message M_x' is then given by

$$(4.25) \quad V(e) = \int V(x, e) \, p(x \mid e) \, dx.$$

For a detailed study of various values of information, see Behara (1963). See also Marschak (1970) for his value of information associated with an experiment e.

5.   In this section, besides defining measure of information due to Shannon, we shall establish a *complete analogous treatment of measures of information* for the values of information discussed earlier.

Let M_θ denote the 'message' that θ has occurred. Let $\mathscr{I}'(M_\theta)$ or simply $\mathscr{I}'(\theta)$ denote the 'information content' of this message. A measure of this information content is given by

$$(5.1) \quad \mathscr{I}'(\theta) = -\log p'(\theta).$$

This may be called the 'measure of information of message M_θ'. Note that $\mathscr{I}'(\theta)$ depends only on the probability $p'(\theta)$. It is also possible to define a measure of information independent of probability. See Ingarden and Urbanik (1962).

Before θ is known, the measure of information $\mathscr{I}'(\theta)$ may be expected to be

$$(5.2) \quad \mathscr{I}' = -\int p'(\theta) \log p'(\theta) \, d\theta.$$

This may be called the 'expected measure of message M_θ'. The quantity $\mathscr{I}'$ is known as 'entropy'. With the increase of uncertainty, the entropy increases. We are in need of maximum information when θ's are equiprobable. Note that the measures of information in this section take values in the extended real line. Therefore an assumption regarding the restriction of the range is required.

The above measure of information involves only the marginal probability distribution $p'(\theta)$ and is independent of an experiment. But after making an experiment, the measure of information may be expected with respect to the a posteriori probability measure $p''(\theta \mid x, e)$ as

$$(5.3) \qquad \mathscr{I}'(x, e) = - \int p''(\theta \mid x, e) \log p'(\theta) \, d\theta.$$

This may be called the 'a posteriori expected measure of M_θ'. We may now define the 'a posteriori measure of message M_θ given x, e' to be

$$(5.4) \qquad \mathscr{I}''(x, e) = - \log p''(\theta \mid x, e).$$

A posteriori expectation of the above measure may be given by

$$(5.5) \qquad \mathscr{I}''(x, e) = - \int p''(\theta \mid x, e) \log p''(\theta \mid x, e) \, d\theta.$$

Now the 'measure of information contained in message M_x' may be obtained as

$$(5.6) \qquad \mathscr{I}(x, e) = \mathscr{I}'(x, e) - \mathscr{I}''(x, e).$$

Finally, the 'expected measure of information in message M_x' (that is, the average amount of information provided by the experiment e) is given by

$$(5.7) \qquad \mathscr{I}(e) = \int \mathscr{I}(x, e) \, p(x \mid e) \, dx.$$

For a detailed study of various measures of information and their properties, see Behara (1963).

6. We are now in a position to establish the *relationship between the value and measure of information associated with experiments.*

THEOREM. If the experiments $e^{(0)}$, $e^{(1)}$, $e^{(2)}$,..., admit an order such that $e^{(n)} \supset e^{(n-1)}$ for $n = 1, 2, 3, \ldots$, then

$$(6.1) \qquad \mathscr{I}(e^{(n)}) \geqslant \mathscr{I}(e^{(n-1)}) \Leftrightarrow V(e^{(n)}) \geqslant V(e^{(n-1)})$$

provided the a priori probability distributions are fixed.

Proof. Here we will only give a sketch of the proof. For a detailed proof, see Behara (1963).

Note that

$$e^{(n)} = (e_0, e_1, ..., e_n).$$

For $n = 1$, (6.1) may be written as

(6.3) $\mathscr{I}(e_1) \geqslant \mathscr{I}(e_0) \Leftrightarrow V(e_1) \geqslant V(e_0).$

This is true, since, when there is no experiment e_0, the joint probability $p(\theta, x \mid e_0)$ equals $p'(\theta)$. Putting this value in the formula for $V(e_0)$ and $\mathscr{I}(e_0)$ we find that each of these quantities are equal to zero. From the properties of the value and measure of information we then establish (6.3).

For $n = 2$, (6.1) reduces to

(6.4) $\mathscr{I}(e_1, e_2) \geqslant \mathscr{I}(e_1) \Leftrightarrow V(e_1, e_2) \geqslant V(e_1).$

But, we have always,

(6.5) $\mathscr{I}(e_1, e_2) \geqslant \mathscr{I}(e_1).$

After some calculations, we can show that

(6.6) $V(e_1, e_2) = V(e_2 \mid e_1) + V(e_1).$

But $V(e_1) \geqslant 0$ and $V(e_2 \mid e_1) \geqslant 0$, therefore,

$$V(e_1, e_2) \geqslant V(e_1).$$

Similarly, the results for $n = 3, 4, ...$ may be established.

It would be interesting to develop the value and measure of information associated with an experiment without probability following the arguments of Ingarden and Urbanik. We have already the property of monotonocity by the above theorem. The property of continuity may be easily achieved by converting the underlying Boolean algebra of events (on which the value and measure of information $V(e)$ and $\mathscr{I}(e)$ are to be defined) into a topological algebra.

McMaster University and University of Heidelberg

BIBLIOGRAPHY

Barnard, G. A., 'The Theory of Information', *Journal of the Royal Statistical Society, Ser. B.* **13** (1951) 46–64.

Behara, M., *Value and Measure in Statistics: an Information-Theoretical Contribution to Statistical Decision Theory*, Dissertation, University of the Saar, 1963.

Blackwell, D., 'Comparison of Experiments', *Proc. 2nd Berkeley Symposium Mathematical Statics and Probability*, Berkeley, 1953, pp. 93–102.

Fisher, R. A., 'Uncertain Inference', *Proc. American Academy of Arts and Sciences* **71** (1936) 245–58.

Good, I. J., *The Estimation of Probabilities*, MIT Research Monograph No. 30, Cambridge, Mass., 1965.

Ingarden, R. S. and Urbanik, K., 'Information without Probability', *Colloq. Math.* **9** (1962) 131–50.

Marschak, J., 'Economics of Information Systems', *Frontiers of Quantitative Economics* (ed. by M. D. Intrilligator), Amsterdam 1970, pp. 32–107.

Raiffa, H. and Schlaifer, R., *Applied Statistical Decision Theory*, Boston 1961.

Wald, A., *Statistical Decision Functions*, New York 1950.

MARTIN J. BECKMANN

ENTROPY, GRAVITY AND UTILITY
IN TRANSPORTATION MODELLING

1. This paper considers *alternative approaches to an analysis of decision making* by users of transportation. There is considerable interest at a practical level in methods of travel forecasting. In recent years there has been a surging concern with urban and environmental problems and how these are affected by transportation. As geographers, sociologists, economists and regional scientists have entered this field, this has become an area of lively contest. Different approaches and ideas tend to be advanced by different groups. There is far from general agreement even on broad methodological principles. The following exposition does not pretend to be a comprehensive review of all approaches. Rather it will touch only briefly on the basic ideas of entropy and gravity and focus on the use of utility models in the analysis of travel and spatial interaction.

2. The *classical way* by which entropy is introduced into spatial theory concerns the problem of individual trip making, say trips to work. Consider a set of locations or small regional subdivisions, i. For each i we know the number of trips originating A_i and terminating there B_i. We also know transportation cost between pairs of locations r_{ij}. On the basis of this information alone what is the most likely assignment of trips to given origins and destinations? This appears to be a purely statistical problem. In the absence of any theoretical effort at explaining human behavior that underlies trip making it is a statistical problem. But it is solvable as that only when we introduce one additional piece of information: Let us assume that we also know total miles of actual travel. The problem thus formulated has the convenient form of a classical assignment problem in thermodynamics: Given total energy transportation cost and the number of particles in each cell of phase space, assign speeds to particles so that the total energy is as observed. Entropy is the likelihood function that counts the number of ways in which each assignment can occur. The basic assumption is that each

Günter Menges (ed.), Information, Inference and Decision, 155–163. *All Rights Reserved.*
Copyright © 1974 by D. Reidel Publishing Company, Dordrecht-Holland.

assignment is equally likely provided the total energy constraint is satisfied. The result, expressed in terms of trip making is (Wilson, 1967)

(1) $X_{ij} = a_i b_j \, e^{-\lambda r_{ij}}$.

The constant a_i and b_j and c have to be so fitted that the three constraints are satisfied

(2) $A_i = \sum_j X_{ij} = a_i \sum_j b_j \, e^{-\lambda r_{ij}}$

(3) $B_j = \sum_j X_{ij} = b_j \sum_i a_i \, e^{-\lambda r_{ij}}$

(4) $C = \sum_{i,j} r_{ij} X_{ij} = \sum_{i,j} a_i b_j r_{ij} \, e^{-\lambda c_{ij}}$.

The resulting trip distribution is usually not a bad approximation to the observed one. It is strange though that before entropy became popular, the gravity law was invariably claimed to be the best general representation of the observed distributions. But what is an acceptable first approximation has become, by degrees, an accepted basic law of spatial interaction and the underlying principle of entropy as a measure of likelihood has been elevated to a general principle of universal validity in spatial analysis. This being so its proponents have become virtuosos in subjecting every problem to this approach and inventing ad hoc constraints to make entropy fit the case. This may not even be bad as long as it is taken for the challenge that it is: to set up better theories of spatial relationships. For nature abhors a vacuum and it is for that reason I claim that entropy has proved so persuasive. The only way, as I see it, to beat entropy is to supply alternative models or explanations that have superior virtues: that are more plausible, perhaps, but more importantly that suggests new questions, broader contexts, ways of testing and comparing hypotheses. At least they should suggest alternative explanations so as to make entropy less inevitable.

3.   If one wants to set up an *economic model of the choice behavior that underlies trip making*, one runs at once into the necessity of distinguishing trips by purposes. For the explanation turns out to hang very much on the purpose.

    Take work trips. In a North American context, work trips are really the result of more basic choices, to wit, where to live. Typically one accepts a job first and then looks for a suitable place to live. If we have no other information about residential possibilities, the supply of housing in an area, assume that it is equally likely that something suitable turns up in any regional subdivision. This vague notion has to be made more precise. A given household looking at various potential residences associates a rating or utility index with each. Let the ratings be normally distributed. The probability of something in location i having utility u or better is then

$$P(u) = \int_u^\infty \frac{1}{\sqrt{2\pi}} e^{-(x-\mu)/2\sigma^2} \, dx.$$

This utility includes rent, spaciousness, access to schools, and local shopping facilities, etc., everything except distance from work. For that is something depending on the particular situation of the place of work for the head of this household. In comparing different residences it is net utility that enters, that is, utility minus transportation cost. The household selects that residence for which net utility

$$u - kr$$

is largest. (k is a conversion factor of distance into utility units). If the city is large, it is too costly and time consuming to search for an absolute maximum: rather one settles for an acceptable (or satisfying) level

$$u - kr \geqq s \quad (s \text{ for standards}).$$

What is the probability that something in this class can be found at location i with a housing supply A_i and at distance r from work? It is

$$A_i P(s + kr) = \frac{A_i}{1 + e^{(s+kr-\mu)/\sigma}} = A_i \, e^{(\mu-s)/\sigma} \, e^{-(k/\sigma)r_{ij}}.$$

To generate a work trip distribution one must multiply with the number of B_j of persons employed in location j.

$$X_{ij} \sim A_i B_j \, e^{-(k/\sigma)r_{ij}}.$$

Thus we have reached the result of entropy analysis by another route. I suggest we have done more than that.

(1) We have shown the limited nature of the analysis; that it is based on ignorance of real conditions in the housing market and on homogeneity assumptions about acceptability of housing that are defensible only for lack of better information.

(2) The greater the disutility or cost of trips k the more rapidly do trip numbers fall off with trip length.

(3) The greater the variance σ of the quality or acceptability of housing, the more willing are people to make larger trips – or the more they are forced into it.

(4) As a refinement suppose that the mean value μ of the housing depends on location, $\mu = \mu_i$.

$$X_{ij} \sim A_i \, e^{(\mu_i - s)/\sigma} \, B_j \, e^{-(k/\sigma) r_{ij}}.$$

It turns out that not the raw supply of housing A_i (here also the aggregate of work trip origins) matters but in explaining work trips of a particular type of household, its acceptance level s and the mean standard μ_i of housing in i also enter. The quantity A_i is modified by a quality variable $e^{(\mu_i - s)/\sigma}$. These are examples of the way in which new hypotheses and new variables are brought into the analysis by an economic or utility approach.

4.   Now that the cat is out of the bag let us say a few kind words about *gravity*. These come naturally in the context of examining leisure and shopping trips. Unlike entropy, gravity does not even offer an underlying theory unless you call unwarranted analogies with theoretical mechanics a theory. All that gravity has to offer is a formula,

$$X_{ij} \sim \frac{A_i B_j}{r_{ij}^m} \quad m \geq 1.$$

The utilitists' approach is as follows: Assume that trip making serves purposes at the destinations, that there are alternative destinations serving the same purpose or purposes, but that their suitability or attraction as well as their distance matters. Even that is not enough. For a calculating housewife might then select only one destination, that with the highest return per cost ratio, when experience suggests that even one household makes a variety of shopping trips. In recreational trip making variety is even more apparent. To explain this diversification the element of saturation or in the fancier language of economics of diminishing returns to substitution must be introduced. Thus we arrive at a utility of trip purposes

$$u = \sum_j a_j \Phi(x_j)$$

x_j number of trips to destination j
a_j attraction of destination j
Φ a module (or element) of the utility function. In deference to Occam's razor it is assumed that this Φ function is the same for all destinations – but not necessarily the same for all purposes (say shopping versus leisure).

The Φ are increasing and concave: $\Phi' > 0$, $\Phi'' \leqslant 0$. Trip costs may be introduced in two ways. Either as a disutility to be subtracted from the gross utility of trip purposes or by way of a budget limit on total trip time or trip cost. We shall demonstrate the former. Let r_{ij} represent travel time from i to j. We introduce a utility of leisure $t\, a_0 \psi(t)$ where the function ψ may in special cases even be the same as Φ. As an example assume that

$$X_{ij} \sim A_i\, e^{(\mu_i - s)/\sigma}\, B_j\, e^{-(k/\sigma)r_{ij}}.$$

Now economic rationality is introduced, this time not in the satisfying but the maximizing manner

$$\max_{x_j} a_0 \left(T - \sum_j r_{ij}x_j\right)^\alpha + \sum_{j=1}^n a_j X_j^\alpha.$$

Differentiating

$$-a_0 \alpha \left(T - \sum_j r_{ij}x_j\right)^{\alpha - 1} r_{ij} + a_j \alpha x_j^{\alpha - 1} = 0$$

(5) $$x_j = \left[\frac{a_j}{a_0}\frac{1}{r_{ij}}\right]^{1/(1-\alpha)} \cdot \left[T - \sum_j r_{ij}x_j\right].$$

To eliminate x_j on the right-hand side let $R = \sum_{ij} r_{ij}x_{ij}$. Multiply Equation (5) by r_{ij} and sum over j

$$R = (T - R) \sum_j \left[\frac{a_j}{a_0}\frac{1}{r_{ij}}\right]^{1/(1-\alpha)} = (T - R)\, G_i, \quad \text{say.}$$

$$R = G_i T / (1 + G_i).$$

Let

$$g_j = \left(\frac{a_j}{a_0}\right)^{1/(1-\alpha)}$$

$$m = \frac{1}{1-\alpha} \geq 1.$$

Then

(6) $$x_j = \frac{g_j}{r_{ij}^m} \frac{T}{1+G_i}$$

where

$$G_i = \sum_j \left[\frac{a_j}{a_0} \frac{1}{r_{ij}}\right]^m.$$

This is, of course, the gravity formula. For a derivation using the budget constraint, cf. Niedercorn and Bechdolt (1969). Again a number of questions and hypotheses are raised by this approach beyond the mechanics expressed in the formula.

(1) The variable total time T – or equivalently a travel cost budget – is introduced suggesting that trip making depends on available time. The latter in turn depends on labor force participation, size of household, stage in life cycle, etc., and this suggests looking into these variables as important modifiers of trip making.

(2) It is not the absolute attraction a_j that matters but the attraction of trip destination relative to the attraction of time a_0. Different households even with the same time budget will show different sensitivity to travel time. Again this preference for leisure may be related to other socio-economic variables such as income or social class.

(3) Attraction of destinations might be measured directly from observed trip making. These measured values should be related in turn to variables attached to these destinations such as size, variety, comfort, parking convenience, etc., of shopping centers when analyzing shopping trips.

5.   My main selling point is, however, that the *utility approach* to travel *fits into a broader framework of household decision making* in an urban

context. The city dweller not only chooses a job and a residence but also the number of cars to own (possibly zero) the mode of travel to work and elsewhere, the number, distribution and mode and route of trips for various purposes, the size of his house, of his family, the number of hours to work, etc. In principle it should all fall out of one big model of household or family decision making. I will not be that ambitious. As an example I will show how the location and size of residence and the number of trips beyond the immediate neighborhood are determined by a representative household in a representative city of modest size where all jobs and shopping facilities (other than for convenience goods offered in the neighborhood) are concentrated in the central business district. For illustrative purposes I choose a utility function in terms of leisure, housing space, trips and consumption of other goods and services. To keep mathematical difficulties at a minimum I select the simplest mathematical form of a utility function, an additive logarithmic function

(7) $$u = a_0 \log t + a_1 \log s + a_2 \log c + a_3 \log x$$

where

t leisure time
s housing space
c consumption of other goods and services
x number of shopping trips
r distance from the center
y income
k work trips
p rent per unit of housing
T nonworking time.

The total number of trips is $k + x$ where k is work trips per household; k reflects labor force participation of the household.

Money is spent either on housing or consumption of other goods. The rent is $p(r)$. If money cost of commuting and shopping trips is disregarded, money available for consumption is $y - p(r) s$. Time available for leisure is $T - (k + x) r$. Substituting in (7)

$$u = a_0 \log(T - (k + x) r) + a_1 \log s + a_2 \log(y - p(r) s) + a_3 \log x.$$

Maximization with respect to x, s, r implies

(8) $\qquad \dfrac{a_0 r}{T-(k+x)\,r}=\dfrac{a_3}{x}$

(9) $\qquad \dfrac{a_1}{s}=\dfrac{a_2 p}{y-ps}$

(10) $\qquad \dfrac{-a_0(k+x)}{T-(k+x)\,r}=\dfrac{a_2 sp'(r)}{y-ps}.$

Solving (8)

(11) $\qquad x=\dfrac{a_3}{a_0+a_3}\dfrac{T-kr}{r}$

Solving (9)

(12) $\qquad s=\dfrac{a_1}{a_1+a_2}\dfrac{y}{p}.$

Substituting in (10)

$$\dfrac{(a_0+a_3)\,k}{r(T-kr)}+\dfrac{a_3}{r}=-a_1\dfrac{p'(r)}{p(r)}.$$

This differential equation in $p(r)$ is solved by

(13) $\qquad p(r)=cr^{-\beta}(T-kr)^{\gamma}$

$$\beta=\dfrac{a_0+a_3}{a_1}\dfrac{k}{T}-\dfrac{a_3}{a_1}$$

$$\gamma=\dfrac{k}{T}.$$

Assuming that $\beta>0$, land rent $p(r)$ falls off from the center for two reasons:

The decrease in leisure time due to time kr spent commuting.

The greater distance to be covered for shopping and recreation trips to the center.

The demand function (11) for trips is a simple variant of the gravity formula. The demand function (12) for housing agrees with bankers' recommendations: The house you can afford requires a fixed fraction $a_1/(a_1 + a_2)$(say 20%) of your income for mortgage payments.

This simple model is just an entering wedge into the flourishing field of urban geography and economics. It shows the close link between trip making and housing, a link that is also recognized by the entropy school. Entropy comes up with a density that declines exponentially with distance from the center. In this model density depends also on how incomes vary with distance. Assuming constant average income, density is proportional to rent and is thus described by the function (13). Notice that in (13) density becomes zero at a finite distance, that at which all time is spent commuting. But a different specification of the utility function would have produced an exponential density. A good utilitist will not be outdone by an entropist.

6.   To *summarize*, it is strange that spatial theory is dominated by concepts from physics, in the present context entropy, potential and gravity. This puts social scientists in a defensive position: The burden of proof is placed on them to show, e.g., that utility is a valid, useful, or promising approach to explaining spatial phenomena. This I hope to have done in the present paper. The question of empirically validating one approach (say utility) against another (say entropy) seems insoluble at this time since both entropy and utility can be adapted by skillful proponents to explain almost any observed form of spatial interaction by the use of either an appropriate utility function or of special constraints. The answer will have to come through Occam's razor. Before it can be applied, however, a great many more spatial phenomena will have to be subjected to an analysis by the competing approaches.

Brown University

BIBLIOGRAPHY

Beckmann, M., 'The Soft Science of Predicting Travellor Behavior', *Transportation Planning and Technology* 1 (1973) 175–181.
Niedercorn, J. H. and Bechdolt, B. V., 'An Economic Derivation of the 'Gravity Law' of Spatial Interaction', *Journal of Regional Science* 9 (1969) 273–282.
Niedercorn, J. H. and Bechdolt, B. V., 'An Economic Derivation of the 'Gravity Law' of Spatial Interaction: Reply', *Journal of Regional Science* 10 (1970) 407–410.
Wilson, A. G., 'A Statistical Theory of Spatial Distribution Models', *Transportation Research* 1 (1967) 253–270.

PART IV

SEMANTIC INFORMATION

JACOB MARSCHAK

PRIOR AND POSTERIOR PROBABILITIES AND SEMANTIC INFORMATION*

ABSTRACT. According to logicians, high 'semantic information' must be desired by a scientist. It is associated with 'surprise'. Indeed, if scientist is defined as one for whom all errors are equally undesirable and all correct statements are equally desirable, then it does follow that in the case of mutually exclusive propositions:

(A) the scientist (though not a decision-maker in general) receiving *perfect* evidence gains *least* when it is *a priori* most probable (and thus 'least surprising'); and

(B) he gains on the average *most* from that *imperfect* evidence which assigns to some proposition a higher probability *a posteriori* than that assigned to any proposition by any other such evidence.

Of these results, (A) is probably, and (B) possibly, an adequate rendering, in terms of decision theory, of the logicians' discussion related to 'semantic information' of non-compatible propositions.

1. INTRODUCTION

Logicians – Bar-Hillel (1964, 1968); Hintikka (1970) – have suggested to assign a 'semantic information measure' to individual propositions. A measure assigned to a proposition z_i depends on its probability π_i. A higher measure is attributed to the less probable – also called 'surprising' – propositions suggesting measures such as $1 - \pi_i$ or $\log(1/\pi_i)$, thus justifying, in the latter case, the entropy formula $\sum \pi_i \log(1/\pi_i)$ for the set $Z = (z_1, z_2, \ldots)$ of all considered propositions.

The motivation for such measurements is partly one of interpreting certain words of the natural language: what do people mean by 'knowing more', by 'more informative', etc.? But those measurements are also motivated by "the importance of information as an aim of scientific procedure," as was pointed out by Hintikka (1970, p. 9) in agreement with Popper (1934). Some propositions and some kinds of evidence fulfill, then, the scientist's needs better, are more desirable than others. He is a decision-maker. Hence, in Hintikka's words, "The appeal of ... 'Bayesian' approach to scientific method." In what follows, we shall define the scientist as a special kind of decision-maker. We shall then show that the scientist (though not a decision-maker in general) receiving *perfect* evidence gains *least* when it is *a priori* most probable. And he gains on the average most from that *imperfect* evidence which assigns some proposi-

Günter Menges (ed.), Information, Inference and Decision, 167–180. All Rights Reserved.
Copyright © 1974 by D. Reidel Publishing Company, Dordrecht-Holland.

tion a higher *posterior* probability than that assigned to any proposition by any other such evidence. (This result does not apply when the compared propositions are not mutually exclusive: see Footnote 1.)

As a matter of fact, Hintikka's challenge to the Bayesians was earlier met, to some extent, by none other than Rudolf Carnap, one of the founders of semantic information theory who, in some writings of his last decade – (1962a, p. xv; 1962b) – took the Bayesian position very explicitly. In (1962a) in particular, he works out a numerical example, to conclude that if

a practically acting man..., bases his choice either on content measure alone [semantic information measure defined in his own earlier writings. J.M.] or on probability alone, he will sometimes be led to choices that are clearly wrong.... We should choose that action for which the expectation value of the utility of outcome is a maximum (pp. 252, 253–4, 257).

Carnap does make a distinction between 'predictions' that, as I understand him, characterize the 'practically acting man', and 'laws and theories'. It is not clear whether the two cases are mutually exclusive or one is a special case of the other [1]. In the present paper I shall characterize the scientist by a particular type of utility function and thus as a special kind of a 'practical man'. The scientist is concerned only with the truth or falsity of his propositions not with further benefits and losses from applying them. This will turn out to be a sufficient condition for propositions with lower prior probabilities to be preferable, and also for the desirability of higher posterior probabilities.

The defining properties of utility and prior probabilities as revealed by a consistent decision-maker's choices between actions will be given later [in connection with (1.2)]. We state here that the utility obtained by him depends on his *action a* (which he controls) and on the external *situation z* (which he does not control). Action *a*, an element of a set *A* of available actions, will be also called *decision*; situation *z*, an element of a set *Z*. will be also called, interchangeably, *event*, or *true proposition*. In this paper, only finite sets $Z = (z_1, ..., z_m)$ and $A = (a_1, ..., a_s)$ will be considered, so that the utility function w from $A \times Z$ to the reals

$$(1.1) \qquad u = w(a, z)$$

can be represented as a $m \times s$ matrix. In general, the matrix is not a square one. For example Z may be the set (cancer, no cancer) and A may be the set (surgery, radiotherapy, no treatment), so that $m = 2$, $s = 3$.

A prior probability $\text{Prob}\,(z=z_i)=\pi_i$ is associated with z_i in $Z(i=1,\ldots,m)$ by the decision-maker obeying certain axioms of consistency, with the following property: if he chooses action a rather than a' then [2]

$$(1.2) \qquad \sum_1^m \pi_i w(a, z_i) \geqslant \sum_1^m \pi_i w(a', z_i).$$

It follows that the choice of action is not influenced by the change of the origin and unit of utility.

In the case of a scientist, z_i can be interpreted thus: 'proposition z_i is true'; and action a_i thus: 'he asserts that proposition z_i is true'. Because of this one-to-one correspondence, there are as many 'events' as 'actions', $m=s$. Moreover, let us define a scientist as a decision-maker for whom to have asserted any false proposition among the set A of alternative ones is equally bad, and to have asserted any true proposition in this set is equally good. We can then, without loss of generality (because of the freedom in the choice of origin and unit, as just mentioned) characterize the scientist by the following utility function (a 'Kronecker delta'):

$$(1.3) \qquad w(a_j, z_i) = \delta_{ij} = {}_0^1 \quad \text{as} \quad i\overset{=}{\underset{\neq}{\,}}j; \quad i, j = 1,\ldots,m$$

and thus represent it by a unit matrix of order m:

$$(1.4) \qquad [w(a, z)] = \begin{pmatrix} 1 & 0 & \cdot & \cdot & 0 \\ 0 & 1 & \cdot & \cdot & 0 \\ \cdot & \cdot & \cdot & \cdot & \cdot \\ 0 & 0 & \cdot & \cdot & 1 \end{pmatrix} = I_m.$$

In general [3], decision is based on some evidence y, an element of the set Y. Like the word 'information', the word 'evidence', used in law and in logic, does not admit of a plural. We shall therefore use, interchangeably with it, the word 'message' (received by the decision-maker). The decision-maker associates each y in Y with some a in A; this defines his 'decision function', α, from Y to A. An 'information system' is characterized by the conditional probability distribution of messages given each event, $p(y \mid z)$. If Y, too, is assumed finite, $Y=(y_1,\ldots,y_n)$, the information system, to be denoted by η, is a matrix of order $m \times n$,

$$(1.5) \qquad \eta = [\eta_{ij}], \quad \eta_{ij} = p(y_j \mid z_i), \quad i = 1,\ldots,m;$$
$$j = 1,\ldots,n.$$

Since every $\eta_{ij} \geqslant 0$ and $\sum_{ij} \eta_{ij} = 1$, η is a 'Markov matrix'. We say that the information system is (or the individual messages are) *perfect* when the decision-maker always receives true evidence. We say that the information is *null* (the case of 'ignorance') when, regardless of the event, he always obtains the same evidence. Thus, in the case of perfect information, we have, by properly labelling the messages,

$$(1.6) \qquad \eta_{ij} = p(y_j \mid z_i) = \delta_{ij} = {}^1_0 \quad \text{if} \quad {}^{i=j}_{i \neq j}; \quad i, j = 1, \ldots, m,$$

which, too, can be represented by the unit-matrix (of order m). On the other hand, in the case of null-information, η can be represented as a column-vector $(n = 1)$ with all elements $= 1$:

$$(1.7) \qquad \eta_{i1} = p(y_1 \mid z_i) = 1, \quad i = 1, \ldots, m.$$

We shall begin by expressing the utility yielded by a perfect message, and compare it with that obtainable under ignorance. This will be later generalized, replacing perfect by imperfect information; and also specialized, replacing the general decision-maker by a 'scientist'.

In the case of perfect information we can write $y_i = z_i$. Denote by $a^{(i)}$ the optimal response to (true) evidence z_i. That is,

$$(1.8) \qquad w(a^{(i)}, z) \equiv \max_{a \in A} w(a, z).$$

In the case of null-information, on the other hand – *but with the decision-maker's knowing the prior probabilities* $\pi(z)$! – the optimal decision, to be denoted by a^0, maximizes the expectation of utility, in accordance with the statement (1.2) about his choices:

$$(1.9) \qquad \sum_1^m \pi_j w(a^0, z_j) \equiv \max_{a \in A} \sum_1^m \pi_j w(a, z_j).$$

If the decision-maker has acted on the basis of null-information and the true event is z_i, he will earn the 'utility under ignorance' $w(a^0, z_i)$, which can be shown never to exceed the utility $w(a^{(i)}, z_i)$ earned under perfect information. Thus the gain derived from the perfect evidence z_i is

$$(1.10) \qquad g(z_i) \equiv w(a^{(i)}, z_i) - w(a^0, z_i) \geqslant 0.$$

As defined above, z_i is more surprising than z_j whenever

$$(1.11) \qquad \pi_j > \pi_i > 0.$$

We shall show that, in the case of the 'scientist' as defined,

(1.12) $[\pi_j > \pi_i > 0]$ implies $[g(z_i) \geqslant g(z_j)]$,

but that this is not true in general. In particular, we shall consider, in Section 2, the simple case of 2 actions and 2 events and derive conditions under which the more surprising event brings a greater or a smaller gain, and show that for the scientist the former case applies. We shall then, in Section 3, extend the case of 'scientist' to m events and m actions $(m \geqslant 2)$ and show that his gain from any true evidence with non-maximal probability is the same, and is equal to the gain from any maximally-probable evidence except one – a result that somewhat weakens the importance of the 'surprise' concept. We shall further show that the *expected* gain from perfect information, evaluated before evidence is available, is the smaller, the more probable is the least surprising possible evidence.

In Section 4, the expected gain from imperfect evidence will be shown to depend on the posterior probabilities of events (propositions), given that evidence. It will be then shown in Section 5 that the 'scientist's' excepted gain from given evidence increases with the posterior probability of the conditionally most probable event, confirming the previous simple result for the special case of perfect information. Besides summarizing the results, the conclusion will draw a parallel with the theory of communication where, too, two approaches have been used: a decision-theoretical and a 'linguistic' one.

2. THE CASE OF 2 ACTIONS, 2 EVENTS, PERFECT INFORMATION

Exclude as trivial the case when one of the two actions $(a_2$, say) is inadmissible (never yielding a better consequence than the other) or both are equally good (always yielding equally good consequences). That is, we exclude the case such as

(2.1) $w(a_2, z_i) \leqslant w(a_1, z_i)$ $i = 1, 2,$

for in that case, the same optimal action will be chosen, with or without obtaining evidence, and therefore

(2.2) $g(z_1) = g(z_2) = 0.$

With the trivial case excluded, the following utility matrix is completely general:

$$
(2.3) \quad
\begin{array}{c}
\quad \\
a_1 \\
a_2
\end{array}
\begin{array}{cc}
\overset{\displaystyle z}{\diagdown}\; z_1 & z_2 \\
\left(\begin{matrix} u_1 + r_1 & u_2 \\ u_1 & u_2 + r_2 \end{matrix} \right),
\end{array}
\quad r_i > 0, \quad i = 1, 2,
$$

The 'regret' r_i is also known as 'penalty for error of the ith kind'. Clearly the best response $a^{(i)}$ to perfect evidence z_i (as defined in (1.8)) is $a^{(i)} = a_i$, and the resulting utility is

$$
(2.4) \quad w(a^{(i)}, z_i) = u_i + r_i, \quad i = 1, 2.
$$

Now compute a^0, the optimal response under ignorance, as defined in (1.9):

$$
a^0 = {}^{a_1}_{a_2} \quad \text{if} \quad (u_1 + r_1)\, \pi_1 + u_2 \pi_2 \gtrless u_1 \pi_1 + (u_2 + r_2)\, \pi_2;
$$

hence

$$
(2.5) \quad a^0 = {}^{a_1}_{a_2} \quad \text{if} \quad r_1 \pi_1 \gtrless r_2 \pi_2.
$$

Without loss of generality, let z_2 be the more surprising message, i.e.:

$$
(2.6) \quad \pi_1 > \pi_2.
$$

Then by (2.5) we have the following sufficient conditions[4] for z_2 to bring a greater or smaller gain than z_1:

$$
(2.7) \quad 0 = g(z_1) < g(z_2) = r_2 \quad \text{if} \quad \pi_1/\pi_2 > \max(1, r_2/r_1)
$$

$$
(2.8) \quad r_1 = g(z_1) > g(z_2) = 0 \quad \text{if} \quad r_2/r_1 > \pi_1/\pi_2 > 1.
$$

Now, stronger than (2.7) is the sufficient condition

$$
r_2 = r_1 = r \quad \text{(say)},
$$

for it follows from (2.6) that then

$$
(2.9) \quad 0 = g(z_1) < g(z_2) = r.
$$

This presupposes a utility matrix of the special form (putting $r = 1$ without loss of generality by changing utility units appropriately)

$$
(2.10) \quad \begin{pmatrix} u_1 + 1 & u_2 \\ u_1 & u_2 + 1 \end{pmatrix}.
$$

Since the numbers u_1, u_2 do not appear in the sufficient conditions stated above, attention should be paid to the simple symmetric case – a unit matrix –

$$(2.11) \qquad \begin{pmatrix} 1 & 0 \\ 0 & 1 \end{pmatrix}$$

which we have proposed earlier to characterize the scientist see (1.4).

On the other hand, consider the utility matrix

$$(2.12) \qquad \begin{array}{c} \\ a_1 \\ a_2 \end{array} \begin{array}{cc} z_1 & z_2 \\ \left(\begin{array}{cc} 1 & 1-K \\ 0 & 1 \end{array}\right) \end{array}$$

With K very large, this can be interpreted thus:

$z_1 =$ 'all is well'; $a_1 =$ 'act as if all is well'

$z_2 =$ 'emergency'; $a_2 =$ 'act as if to meet emergency'.

This matrix was used by Shannon (1960) in another context [5]. We have

$$r_1 = 1, \qquad r_2 = K, \qquad r_2/r_1 = K, \qquad \pi_1/\pi_2 > 1,$$

so that by (2.8) $g(z_1) > g(z_2)$ provided $K > \pi_1/\pi_2$. Less formally: even if the probability of emergency is small but its potential damage is very large, it may be best to act in the absence of information as if there were emergency. This action (a_2) will still be best if the message 'emergency' were obtained; this message, though 'surprising' because of its small probability, would not increase the earned utility compared with the case of no message. A message 'all is well' on the other hand, would shift the optimal action from a_2 to a_1 and thus improve utility (from 0 to 1).

3. THE SCIENTIST'S GENERAL CASE UNDER PERFECT INFORMATION

Let us generalize the scientist's utility matrix (2.11) to the case of m events and m actions, and arrange the columns (i.e., label the events $z_1, z_2, \ldots$) so that

$$(3.1) \qquad \pi_1 \geqslant \pi_2 \geqslant \cdots \geqslant \pi_m; \quad \pi_1 > \pi_m.$$

Consider first the case when there is only one event with maximal probability, so that (3.1) becomes

(3.2) $\qquad \pi_1 > \pi_2 \geqslant \cdots \geqslant \pi_m$.

Then the unique optimal action under ignorance is $a^0 = a_1$ since it yields expected utility

$$\pi_1 \cdot 1 + (1 - \pi_1) \cdot 0 = \pi_1,$$

while any other action, $a_j (j \geqslant 2)$ would yield

$$\pi_j \cdot 1 + (1 - \pi_j) \cdot 0 = \pi_j < \pi_1.$$

If event z_i occurs, the action $a^0 = a_1$ would yield

$$w(a_1, z_i) = {}^1_0 \quad \text{if} \quad i {}^{\neq}_{=} 1.$$

On the other hand, the best response to message z_i is $a^{(i)} = a_i$, yielding

$$w(a_i, z_i) = 1.$$

Hence

$$g(z_i) = w(a_i, z_i) - w(a_1, z_1) = {}^0_1 \quad \text{if} \quad i {}^{=}_{>} 1.$$

For example, let

$$\pi_1 = \cdot 50; \qquad \pi_2 = \cdot 49; \qquad \pi_3 = \cdot 01;$$

then the gains are:

$$g(z_1) = 0; \qquad g(z_2) = 1; \qquad g(z_3) = 1;$$

that is, z_2 which can be said to be 'almost as little surprising as z_1 and much less surprising than z_3' brings actually the same gain as the 'very surprising' event z_3.

Now allow for more than one event to have maximal probability:

$$\pi_1 = \pi_2 = \cdots = \pi_k > \pi_{k+1} \geqslant \cdots \geqslant \pi_m, \quad k < m.$$

Then any action $a_j, j \geqslant k$, is optimal under ignorance, yielding as it does the expected utility

$$\pi_j \cdot 1 + (1 - \pi_j) \cdot 0 > \pi_h \cdot 1 + (1 - \pi_h) \cdot 0, \quad h > k.$$

We then have by the same reasoning as before

$$g(z_i) = {}^0_1 \quad \text{if} \quad i {}^{=}_{\neq} j \leqslant k,$$

where j is the label of that one of the k maximally-probable events that was picked out arbitrarily from the set $(z_1, \ldots, z_k)$ when choosing a particular one – viz. a_j – from among the set of equally optimal actions $(a_1, \ldots, a_k)$. Thus the gain from the most surprising message z_m (whose probability is the smallest one or is among the minimal ones) is equal, not only to that of all other messages with non-maximal probabilities but also to that of all the least surprising messages except one! Example:

$$\pi_1 = \cdot 45, \qquad \pi_2 = \cdot 45, \qquad \pi_3 = \cdot 09, \qquad \pi_4 = \cdot 01.$$

Then both actions a_1 and a_2 are optimal under ignorance. Suppose a_1 is chosen. Then

$$g(z_1) = 0, \qquad g(z_2) = g(z_3) = g(z_4) = 1,$$

so that the most surprising message, z_4, brings the same gain as one of the least surprising messages, z_2! (This and the previous example correspond to the case when, in (1.12), '$\geqslant$' is replaced by '$=$'.)

Using the notations of this section we can summarize the result in the following

THEOREM: For all h, i, k in $M = (1, \ldots, m)$ assume

$$w(a_h, z_k) = \delta_{hk},$$
$\pi_i > 0$; and without loss of generality
$$\pi_j = \max_{i \in M} \pi_i.$$
Then
$$g(z_i) = 1 - \delta_{ij}.$$

We can now evaluate the *expected gain*, G, from perfect information (i.e., averaging over all possible perfect messages) as it appears to the 'scientist' before the evidence becomes available. By the above theorem,

$$(3.3) \qquad G = E(g(z_i)) = \sum_i \pi_i (1 - \delta_{ij}) = 1 - \pi_j = 1 - \max_{i \in M} \pi_i.$$

Thus the scientist's expected gain from perfect information decreases as the prior probability of the least surprising message increases.[6]

4. GAIN FROM IMPERFECT EVIDENCE

In Sections 2 and 3, information was perfect so that the relevant Markov matrix $\eta = [\eta_{ij}]$, where $\eta_{ij} = p(y_j \mid z_i)$, was a unit matrix. In general, this need not be the case. In fact, the set Y of messages y may have more or fewer elements than the set Z of events. We may have

$$A=(a_1,\ldots,a_s), \qquad Z=(z_1,\ldots,z_m), \qquad Y=(y_1,\ldots,y_n).$$

In the scientist's case, $s=m\underset{<}{\overset{>}{=}}n$.

Given the information system's matrix η, the decisionmaker's problem is to find an optimal decision function α^* defined by

(4.1)
$$\begin{aligned}&\sum_j \sum_i p(z_i,y_j)\, w(\alpha^*(y_j),z_i)\\ &\equiv \max_\alpha \sum_j \sum_i p(z_i,y_j)\, w(\alpha(y_j),z_i),\end{aligned}$$

the maximum being taken over the set of all functions from Y to A[7]. Here $p(z_i,y_j)$ denotes[8] the joint probability of event z_i and message y_j. It is completely determined by the prior probability π_i and the conditional probability $p(y_j\,|\,z_i)=\eta_{ij}$ (both *given* to the decision-maker) since, by definition,

(4.2) $p(z_i,y_j)=\pi_i\eta_{ij}.$

We also have, by definition,

(4.3) $p(z_i,y_j)=p(y_j)\cdot p(z_i\,|\,y_j), \quad$ provided $\quad p(y_j)>0,$

a product of the marginal probability of message y_j and the posterior probability of event z_i, given that message. These two probabilities, too, are completely determined by the given π_i and η_{ij}, since $p(z_i,y_j)$ is so determined [(4.2)] and since

$$p(y_i)=\sum_i p(z_i,y_j).$$

By (4.3), the right side of (4.1) can be rewritten as

$$\begin{aligned}&\max_\alpha \sum_j p(y_j)\sum_i p(z_i\,|\,y_j)\, w(\alpha(y_j),z_i)\\ &=\sum_j p(y_j)\max_{a\in A}\sum_i p(z_i\,|\,y_j)\, w(a,z_i);\end{aligned}$$

that is, the optimal decision function is obtained by finding for each message y_j that action which maximizes the conditional expectation of utility, given that message[9]. This action is the optimal response to that message and can be denoted by

$$\alpha^*(y_j) = a^{(y_j)},$$

in a notation analogous to $a^{(i)}$ of (1.8). Thus (1.8) is generalized into

(4.4) $$\sum_i p(z_i \mid y_j) w(a^{(y_j)}, z_i) \equiv$$

$$\max_{1 \leqslant h \leqslant m} \sum_i p(z_i \mid y_j) w(a_h, z_i) \equiv W(y_j),$$

the expected utility yielded by the message y_j (averaged, that is, over all z_i, $i = 1, \ldots, m$)[10]. This amount is to be compared with the expected utility earned under ignorance, which by (1.9) is

(4.5) $$W^0 \equiv \sum_i \pi_i w(a^0, z_i) = \max_a \sum_i \pi_i w(a, z_i).$$

The difference

(4.6) $$G(y_j) \equiv W(y_j) - W^0$$

is the expected gain from imperfect message y_j.

5. POSTERIOR PROBABILITIES AND THE SCIENTIST

In the scientist's case, the utility function was defined in (1.3) so that (4.4) becomes, for $j = 1, \ldots, n$,

(5.1) $$W(y_j) = \max_{1 \leqslant h \leqslant m} \sum_i p(z_i \mid y_j) \delta_{hi}$$

$$= \max_{1 \leqslant h \leqslant m} p(z_h \mid y_j);$$

and (4.5) becomes

(5.2) $$W^0 = \max_{1 \leqslant i \leqslant m} \pi_i; \quad \text{hence by (4.6)}$$

(5.3) $$G(y_j) = \max_h p(z_h \mid y_j) - \max_i \pi_i.$$

Note that under perfect information as a special case, with $y_j = z_j$ for all j, $p(z_h \mid y_j) = \delta_{hj} = 1$ or 0, as in (1.6). Then by (5.1), (5.3)

(5.4) $$W(y_j) = 1, \qquad G(y_j) = 1 - \max_i \pi_i,$$

confirming the result (3.3) of Section 3.

The result (5.3) implies that, independently of the prior distribution π,

$$G(y_j) - G(y_k) \geqslant 0, \quad j, k = 1, \ldots, n$$

(5.5)   if and only if

$$\max_h p(z_h \mid y_j) \geqslant \max_h p(z_h \mid y_k),$$

i.e., if and only if the proposition (event) that is most probable *a posteriori*, given the message y_i, is not less probable *a posteriori* than any proposition, given the message y_k.

A counter-example can show that (5.5) does not apply if the utility function is of a general type. Let $n = 2$, $p(z_1 \mid y_1) = \frac{1}{4}$, $p(z_2 \mid y_2) = \frac{1}{3}$ so that

$$\max_h p(z_h \mid y_1) = \tfrac{3}{4} > \max_h p(z_h \mid y_2) = \tfrac{2}{3}.$$

Yet, assuming the utility function of (2.12) with $K = \frac{1}{4}$, by (4.4)

$$W(y_1) = \tfrac{5}{8} < W(y_2) = \tfrac{11}{12}, \quad \text{so that by (4.5)}$$
$$G(y_1) < G(y_2).$$

6. CONCLUSION

If the refutation of any of the scientist's alternative assertions is regarded by him as equally bad, and the confirmation of any of them as equally good, then the expected gain from a given message (evidence) is the larger the larger the maximal posterior probability derived from it.

Moreover, in the special case of perfect information, the scientist's gain from a message can have only two distinct values; and it can assume the lower value only if the message belongs to the least surprising ones, i.e., has the maximal prior probability. And his expected gain from perfect information (averaged over all possible messages) is the lower, the higher the prior probability of the least surprising message.

This justification of semantic information measures in terms of decision logic is quite independent of the attempts to justify them by appeals to the usages of natural languages. The situation is indeed similar to that in the theory of communication: the entropy formula is relevant to the decisions of the user of communication devices in that it measures, for long sequences of messages, the minimum expected number of symbols needed. This is quite independent of justifying the entropy formula by asking what people mean by the word information.[11]

For a more general analysis, including the case of compatible propositions, see the author's 'Information, Decision and the Scientist' in a forthcoming volume of this book series, edited by Colin Cherry.

University of California

NOTES

* I owe much to discussions conducted by Professor G. Menges in his Heidelberg Seminar in the summer 1972, and to his paper (1972), and to discussions which I had with Y. Bar-Hillel and D. W. Peterson in the same summer.

Acknowledgements are due to the University of Heidelberg and, for the general support of this work, to the U.S. Office of Naval Research.

[1] But see also De Finetti (1971).

[2] Reference is made to Marschak (1970).

[3] Reference is made to Marschak (1971).

[4] The sufficient and necessary conditions are somewhat more involved for, in the borderline case $r_1\pi_1 = r_2\pi_2$, $g(z_1) <$ or $> g(z_2)$ depending on which of the two actions, both optimal, is taken under ignorance: $a^0 = a_1$ or $a^0 = a_2$.

[5] In the spirit of pure communication theory, in which events and decisions are not considered explicitly, Shannon interprets the columns of the matrix as 'messages sent' and its rows as 'messages received', and our utility, $w(a, z)$, is called the 'fidelity criterion'. In the bulk of the literature on communication theory, and still in most textbooks, the fidelity criterion degenerates into the form (2.11) or (1.4) above: all communication errors are considered as equally bad, and the communication engineer behaves like our 'scientist'.

[6] It is worth noting that the quantity G in (3.3) is identical with that proposed by DeGroot (1962) to partially order – not to measure – 'uncertainty'. It satisfies two of the three axioms fulfilled by the entropy formula and claiming to express the properties associated with the word 'uncertainty' in natural languages. Since G depends only on the (prior) probability distribution we can write it as $G(\pi_1, ..., \pi_n)$. The two properties of 'uncertainty' satisfied by G can be expressed thus:

$$G(\pi_1, ..., \pi_n) \leqslant G(1/n, 1/n, ..., 1/n) < G(1/m, 1/m, ..., 1/m) \quad \text{if} \quad n < m.$$

A third property of the entropy formula – variously stated as 'splittability' or 'additivity' – is needed to make 'uncertainty' measurable. It is debatable – but perhaps it is unnecessary to debate – whether or not this property is required by natural language. In physics, the definitions of force and of energy, which have proved so useful, have not been derived from requests of our natural language. That the entropy formula has been useful in deriving the expected number of code symbols needed to convey long sequences of messages is, of course, beyond doubt, – regardless of 'what people mean by uncertainty'.

[7] In the case considered here all decision functions α from Y to A are feasible and of equal cost. See Marschak (1971).

[8] In the expressions $p(z_i, y_j), p(y_j), p(z_i \mid y_j)$ the same symbol p is used for different functions

180   JACOB MARSCHAK

without danger of ambiguity: the distinction is given by the different arguments within
the parentheses.
[9] See Marschak and Radner (1972), pp. 51–52.
[10] In the case of perfect information (4.4) is reduced, as it should be, to (1.8), using (1.6)
and the definitions of $p(y_j \mid z_i)$, $p(z_i \mid y_j)$, always assuming $p(y_j)$ positive.
[11] See also Wolfowitz (1961) and the author's 'Limited Role of Entropy in Information
Economics', *Proceedings of the 5th Colloquium on Optimization Techniques*, (Rome, 1973),
Springer, forthcoming.

BIBLIOGRAPHY

Bar-Hillel, Y., *Language and Information*, Addison-Wesley 1964.
Bar-Hillel, Y., 'Essence and Significance of Information Theory', *Information über Information* (ed. by H. V. Ditfurth and W. D. Bach), Hoffman & Campe, 1968, pp. 13–41.
Carnap, R., Preface to 2nd edition of *Logical Foundations of Probability*, University of Chicago Press, 1962a.
Carnap, R., 'Probability and Content Measure', *Mind, Matter and Method*, Essays in Honor of M. Feigl (ed. by P. Feyerabend and G. Maxwell), University of Minnesota Press, 1962b.
De Finetti, B., 'Probabilità di una Teoria e Probabilità dei Fatti', Studi in Onore di G. Pompilj. Gubbio 1971.
DeGroot, M., 'Uncertainty, Information and Sequential Experiments', *Annals of Mathematical Statistics* 1962.
Hintikka, J., 'On Semantic Information', *Information and Inference* (ed. by J. Hintikka and P. Suppes), D. Reidel, 1970.
Marschak, J., 'The Economic Man's Logic', *Induction, Growth and Trade*, Essays in Honour of Sir Roy Harrod (ed. by W. A. Eltis, M. F. G. Scott and J. N. Wolfe), Clarendon Press, 1970.
Marschak, J., 'Economics of Information Systems', *Frontiers of Quantitative Economics* (ed. by M. Intriligator), North-Holland, 1971 (Also: *Journal of American Statistical Association*, 1971).
Marschak, J. and Radner, R., *Economic Theory of Teams*, Yale University Press, 1972.
Menges, G., 'Semantische Information und Statistische Inferenz', Discussion Paper 21, Universität Heidelberg, Fachgruppe Wirtschaftswissenschaften, Lehrstuhl für Ökonometrie, 1972.
Popper, K. R., *Logik der Forschung*, Springer, Wien, 1934.
Shannon, C. E., 'Coding Theorems for a Discrete Source with a Fidelity Criterion', *Information and Decision Processes* (ed. by R. E. Machol), McGraw-Hill, 1960.
Wolfowitz, J., *Coding Theorems of Information Theory*, Springer, 1961.

HEINZ J. SKALA

REMARKS ON SEMANTIC INFORMATION

ABSTRACT. A concept of semantic information due to Belis and Guiasu is discussed. It is indicated how this concept can be extended to the infinite case by using devices of non-standard analysis. Moreover it may be considered as an appropriate measure for the average information which is supplied by an axiomatized theory.

1. SOME PREREQUISITES

A filter on a set I is a family $\mathfrak{F}$ of subsets of I such that:

(1) $\emptyset \notin \mathfrak{F}$,
(2)   if $X, Y \in \mathfrak{F}$, then $X \cap Y \in \mathfrak{F}$,
(3)   if $X \in \mathfrak{F}$ and $X \subseteq Y \subseteq I$ then $Y \in \mathfrak{F}$.

$\mathfrak{F}$ is called principal if $\bigcap \{X : X \in \mathfrak{F}\} \in \mathfrak{F}$. A maximal filter is called ultra-filter and characterized by the condition that whenever $X \subseteq I$, then either $X \in \mathfrak{F}$ or $I - X \in \mathfrak{F}$. It is well known that every filter can be extended to an ultrafilter.

For the following remarks we restrict ourselves to binary relational systems. It will be clear that everything we do can be extended to arbitrary relational systems.

Given an index set I, for every $i \in I$ let $\mathfrak{A}_i = \langle A_i, R_i \rangle$ denote a binary relational system. Let $A = \prod_{i \in I} A_i$ be the Cartesian product of the sets A_i and denote the elements of A by $f, g, h, \dots$. The ith component of $f \in A$ is written as $f(i)$.

If $\mathfrak{F}$ is a filter on I, then the relation $=_{\mathfrak{F}}$ on A defined by

$$f =_{\mathfrak{F}} g \text{ if and only if } \{i \in I : f(i) = g(i)\} \in \mathfrak{F}$$

is a equivalence relation on A.

We define a relation S on A by

$$\langle f, g \rangle \in S \text{ if and only if } \{i \in I : \langle f(i), g(i) \rangle \in R_i\} \in \mathfrak{F}.$$

One can easily prove, that $=_{\mathfrak{F}}$ is a congruence relation with respect to S, i.e. if $f =_{\mathfrak{F}} f'$ and $g =_{\mathfrak{F}} g'$, then $\langle f, g \rangle \in S$ implies $\langle f', g' \rangle \in S$.

Günter Menges (ed.), Information, Inference and Decision, 181–188. All Rights Reserved.
Copyright © 1974 by D. Reidel Publishing Company, Dordrecht-Holland.

For each $f \in A$ we denote by $f/\mathfrak{F}$ the equivalence class to which f belongs under $=_\mathfrak{F}$ and we let

$$\prod_{i \in I} A_i/\mathfrak{F} = \{f/\mathfrak{F} : f \in A\}.$$

Defining $\langle f/\mathfrak{F}, g/\mathfrak{F} \rangle \in R_\mathfrak{F}$ if and only if $\langle f, g \rangle \in S$, a relation $R_\mathfrak{F}$ on $\prod A_i/\mathfrak{F}$ is induced by the relation S on A.

We write $\prod \mathfrak{A}_i/\mathfrak{F}$ for the relational system $\langle \prod A_i/\mathfrak{F}, R_\mathfrak{F} \rangle$ and call $\prod \mathfrak{A}_i/\mathfrak{F}$ the reduced product over the filter $\mathfrak{F}$. If $\mathfrak{A}_i = \mathfrak{A}$ for every $i \in I$ we write $\mathfrak{A}^I/\mathfrak{F}$ and call this system reduced power of $\mathfrak{A}$ over $\mathfrak{F}$. In the case that $\mathfrak{F}$ is an ultrafilter one calls the above systems ultraproduct and ultrapower respectively.

Frayne *et al.* (1962) proved the following useful

THEOREM 1. Let $\langle \mathfrak{A}_i : i \in I \rangle$ be a sequence containing all finite subsystems of a relational system $\mathfrak{A}$. There exists an ultrafilter $\mathfrak{F}$ on I such that $\mathfrak{A}$ is embeddable in $\prod_{i \in I} \mathfrak{A}_i/\mathfrak{F}$.

This theorem is very useful to prove representation theorems. In order to show that a relational system $\mathfrak{A}$ can be embedded into an ultrapower of the reals one has only to prove that every finite sub-system of $\mathfrak{A}$ is embeddable into the reals.

Ultrapower constructions are a very useful tool. For example they can be used to prove that there exist non-standard models of the reals, i.e. (proper) ordered extension fields of the reals. These non-standard models do not have the Archimedian property. Thus they contain infinitely large and infinitely small numbers.

If we consider the set A which consists of all finite sets of real numbers then in a non-standard model of the reals A extends to A^*. A^* contains sets which have infinitely many elements, but every element of A^* has all the properties of a finite set. This fact has a very interesting consequence for we can extend concepts of finitary probability theory to the infinite case. Let us consider the following example: We choose arbitrarily an integer. If we are interested in the 'probability' of choosing an even integer, then it is not possible to proceed as in the finite case and use the ratio $\dfrac{\text{cardinality of the even integers}}{\text{cardinality of the integers}}$ as this ratio would be 1 when applying the classical concept of cardinality. But this ratio makes sense as, by the above remark, the cardinality concept for finite sets can be extended to infinite sets if nonstandard devices are used.

For details see Bell and Slomson (1969), Frayne *et al.* (1962), Luxemburg (1962) and Robinson (1966).

2. A CONCEPT OF INFORMATION DEPENDING ON UTILITY

Quite recently Belis and Guiasu (1968) introduced a concept of information depending on the notion of utility. As the concept of utility plays an important role in economics and statistical decision theory it is astonishing that it did not enter into information theory before.

Let us briefly reconsider the idea of Belis and Guiasu. We denote the (finitely many) events by $E_1, E_2, ..., E_n$, the probability of occurrence of these events by $p_1, p_2, ..., p_n$, $\sum_{i=1}^{n} p_i = 1$ and the utilities of the events by $u_1, u_2, ..., u_n$. The occurrence of an event with the probability p and the utility u results in an information $I(p, u)$ which depends on the probability of this event as well as on its utility.

Assuming for the first time, that all events have the same utility $u_i = c$, we have good reasons to demand, that the information supplied by two independent events E_1 and E_2 must be equal to the sum of the information supplied by each event alone. As the event $E_1 \cap E_2$ occurs with probability $p_1 p_2$, we have:

$$condition\ 1: \quad I(p_1 p_2, c) = I(p_1, c) + I(p_2, c),$$
$$0 \leq p_1, \quad p_2 \leq 1, \quad c \geq 0.$$

There are also good reasons to demand that an increase of the utility of an event E_1 should result in a directly proportional increase of the information supplied by this event. Thus we have:

$$condition\ 2: \quad I(p_1, ku_1) = kI(p_1, u_1), \quad 0 \leq p_1 \leq 1, \ u_1 \geq 0, \ k \geq 0.$$

It is now easy to prove, that a function $I = I(p, u)$ which satisfies condition 1 and 2, must have the form

(I) $\qquad I = I(p, u) = -a\, u \log p,$

where a denotes an arbitrary constant > 0.

We observe, that by setting $u = 1$ condition 1 results in:

(II) $\qquad I(p_1 p_2, 1) = I(p_1, 1) + I(p_2, 1).$

Moreover from condition 2 we get:

(III) $I(p, u) = uI(p, 1)$.

Let us put

(IV) $I(p, 1) = f(\log p)$,

then we get, because of (II), the functional equation

(V) $f(\log p_1 + \log p_2) = f(\log p_1) + f(\log p_2)$.[1]

It is well known, that the only continuous solutions of (V) have the form $f(\log p) = b \log p$ where b denotes an arbitrary real number. Thus we get (I) from (III) and (IV).

The analogue to Shannon's entropy measure due to Belis and Guiasu is now immediately seen to be

(VI) $H(p_1, ..., p_n; u_1, ..., u_n) = -a \sum_{i=1}^{n} u_i p_i \log p_i$.

The situation radically changes for the infinite case. To see this we consider the following example.

Let A consist of the set of all pairs (r_1, r_2), $0 \leqq r_1, r_2 \leqq 1$, and interpret the elements of A as commodity bundles, where r_1 denotes the amount of commodity 1 and r_2 the amount of commodity 2. Let the preference ordering P of an individuum be a lexicographic one:

$$(r_1, r_2) P(r_1', r_2') \text{ if and only if } r_1 < r_1' \quad \text{or}$$
$$r_1 = r_1' \quad \text{and} \quad r_2 < r_2'.$$

It is well known that this preference ordering cannot be represented by a real-valued utility function (Debreu, 1954). To prove this, we assume that there exists a real-valued utility function f and take two elements (r_1, r_2) and (r_1, r_3), $r_2 < r_3$. As f is a utility function it must hold $f(r_1, r_2) = r'$, $f(r_1, r_3) = r''$, $r' < r''$. But $r' < r''$ cannot hold for every r_1 as there are uncountably many different r_1's but only countably many non-void non-degenerated intervals of the real line. Thus the applicability of (VI) seems to be restricted to situations where a real-valued utility function exists.

Another limitation although not too severe is due to the use of real-valued probability measures. It is well known that in the above example there exists no strictly positive probability measure on the set of all subsets of A. Thus we cannot say for example that the probability that someone buys the commodity bundle (r_1, r_2) is half that of buying (r_1, r_2) or (r'_1, r'_2).

An example due to Diximier (Luxemburg, 1962, p. 148) shows that even complete non-atomic Boolean algebras may not admit a strictly positive probability measure.

The following two theorems show that, by allowing the utility function and the probability measure to take values in an ordered extension field of the reals $\mathfrak{R}^*$, undesired situations as indicated above may be avoided.

THEOREM 2. Let $\mathfrak{A} = \langle A, \precsim \rangle$ be a set (of events) where $\precsim$ is a transitive and connected preference relation. If $\langle \mathfrak{A}_i : i \in I \rangle$ denotes a sequence containing all finite subsystems of $\mathfrak{A}$ then there exists an ultrafilter $\mathfrak{F}$ on I and a utility function u on A with values in the ordered extension field of the reals $\mathfrak{R}^I / \mathfrak{F}$.

Proof. As every $\mathfrak{A}_i$ is finite it is evident that a real valued utility function f_i on A_i must exist. Thus Theorem 2 is an immediate consequence of Theorem 1.

Utility functions with values in an ordered extension field (non-standard model) of the reals have been introduced independently by Richter (1971) and Skala (1970)[2].

THEOREM 3. For every Boolean algebra $\mathfrak{B}$ there exists an ordered extension field of the reals $\mathfrak{R}^*$ such that $\mathfrak{B}$ admits a strictly positive probability measure with values in $\mathfrak{R}^*$.

This theorem is due to Nikodým (1956). A proof by means of an ultrapower construction may be found in Luxemburg (1962, 1962a).

If we wish to apply the above ideas to formal languages it is necessary to assign probabilities to the formulas of the language. Attempts to do so are mainly due to Carnap (1950). His ideas have been considerably expanded especially by Gaifman (1964) who succeeded to assign probabilities to formulas of arbitrary (finitary) first order languages[3]. We would like to remark in this connection that there might occur systems of statements which are so complex that they cannot appropriately be represented in a probability space. In this case the introduction of non-standard real valued probability measures seems unavoidable. Moreover the use of such measures might be preferable because of methodological points of view even if 'appropriate' real valued probability measures exist. We shall not go into these quite technical problems and turn to a question with which every experimenter is faced: What conditions must be satisfied in order that there exists a probability measure on a finite Boolean algebra? This question was originally raised by De Finetti (1937) who gave also necessary conditions for the existence of a probability measure. Necessary and sufficient conditions are due to Kraft *et al.* (1959) and Scott (1964).

Let $\mathfrak{B}$ be a finite Boolean algebra with the unit element Ω and let $\otimes$ be a binary relation on $\mathfrak{B}$. $E_1 \otimes E_2, E_1, E_2 \in \mathfrak{B}$, should be read: Event E_2 is not more probable than event E_1. We shall write $E_1 \oslash E_2$ for not $E_2 \otimes E_1$. For every E in $\mathfrak{B}$ the characteristic function χ_E of E is defined for all x in Ω as follows:

$$\chi_E(x) = \begin{cases} 1 & \text{if } x \in E \\ 0 & \text{if } x \notin E. \end{cases}$$

Scott (1964) proved:

THEOREM 4. For $\langle \Omega, \mathfrak{B}, \mu \rangle$ to be a (finitely additive) probability space such that

$$E_1 \otimes E_2 \text{ if and only if } \mu(E_1) \geq \mu(E_2) \text{ for all } E_1, E_2 \in \mathfrak{B}$$

it is necessary and sufficient, that the conditions

(1) $\Omega \oslash \emptyset$,
(2) $E \otimes \emptyset$,
(3) $E_1 \otimes E_2$ or $E_2 \otimes E_1$

hold for all $E, E_1, E_2 \in \mathfrak{B}$ and

(4)   for all sequences $E_0, \ldots, E_{n-1}, E'_0, \ldots, E'_{n-1} \in \mathfrak{B}$, if $E_i \otimes E'_i$ for all $i, 0 < i < n$, and if for all $x \in \Omega \sum_{i=0}^{n-1} \chi_{E_i}(x) = \sum_{i=0}^{n-1} \chi_{E'_i}(x)$, then $E'_0 \otimes E_0$.

If the conditions (1)–(4) of the above theorem are satisfied by all finite Boolean subalgebras of an arbitrary Boolean algebra then, by an application of Theorem 1, we have established the existence of a non-standard real valued probability measure.

If there exist both utilities [4] and probabilities for the outcomes (events) $E_1, ..., E_n$ of an experiment then the average information which supplies the experiment to the experimenter can be measured by

$$H(p_1, ..., p_n, u_1, ..., u_n) = -a \sum_{i=1}^{n} u_i p_i \log p_i.^{[5]}$$

This measure reduces to the well known entropy measure of Shannon when all events bear equal utilities. By allowing the utility function and the probability measure to take values in a non-standard model of the reals one can modify the above measure for the infinite case. The index i then ranges over non-standard positive integers. It should also be clear by the preceding remarks that H can be used to measure the average information which is supplied by an axiomatized theory, if appropriate utilities and probabilities (real valued or non-standard real valued) can be assigned to the formulas of the corresponding language.

University of Heidelberg

NOTES

[1] The functional equation $f(x+y)=f(x)+f(y)$ is called Cauchy's functional equation. See for example Aczél (1966, p. 31ff).

[2] For a thorough treatment of non-standard utility functions see Skala (1973).

[3] Loš (1962) proved that under very general conditions, the probability of formulas may be interpreted as a result of two consecutive drawings. Firstly one chooses at random a model out of a given class $\{\mathfrak{M}_i\}_{i \in I}$ following a given σ-additive probability measure μ on a σ-algebra of subsets of I. From the so obtained model $\mathfrak{M}_i$ a sequence of elements is selected at random following a probability measure v_i on a Boolean algebra of subsets of sequences of elements from $\mathfrak{M}_i$. The probability of the formula α is then equal to the probability that the so obtained sequence of elements satisfies α.

[4] If the preference relation $\precsim$ of the experimenter is transitive and connected then the existence of a utility function is evident in the finite case. It may be more realistic to allow the indifference relation $\sim$ to be intransitive as it is the case with semiorders. Also for finite semiorders real valued utility functions exist (Scott and Suppes, 1958). For further results on utility theory see Fishburn (1970) and Skala (1973).

[5] As H depends on a specified utility function we could appropriately call it a measure of the average goal-oriented information.

BIBLIOGRAPHY

Aczél, J., *Lectures on Functional Equations and Their Applications*, New York, Academic Press, 1966.

Belis, M. and Guiasu, S., 'A Quantitative-Qualitative Measure of Information in Cybernetic Systems', *IEEE Transactions on Information Theory* **14** (1968), 593–594.

Bell, J. L. and Slomson, A. B., *Models and Ultraproducts*, Amsterdam, North-Holland, 1969.

Carnap, R., *Logical Foundations of Probability*, Univ. of Chicago Press, 1950.

De Finetti, B., 'La prévision: Ses lois logiques, ses sources subjectives', *Ann. de l'Inst. Henri Poincaré* **7** (1937), 1–68.

Fishburn, P. C., *Utility Theory for Decision Making*, New York, Wiley, 1970.

Frayne, T., Morel, A., and Scott, D., 'Reduced Direct Products', *Fund. Math.* **51** (1962), 195–228.

Gaifman, H., 'Concerning Measures on First Order Calculi', *Israel J. Math.* **2** (1964), 1–18.

Kraft, C. H., Pratt, J. W., and Seidenberg, A., 'Intuitive probability on Finite Sets', *Ann. Math. Stat.* **30** (1959), 408–419.

Loš, J., 'Remarks on Foundation of Probability', *Proc. Int. Congress of Mathematicians* (1962), 225–229.

Luxemburg, W. A. J., *Non-Standard Analysis*, Pasadena, Math. Dep. CIT, 1962.

Luxemburg, W. A. J., 'Two Applications of the Method of Construction by Ultrapowers to Analysis', *Bull. Amer. Math. Soc.* **68** (1962a), 416–419.

Nikodým, O. M., 'On Extension of a Given Finitely Additive Field-Valued, Non Negative Measure, on a Finitely Additive Boolean Tribe, to Another Boolean Tribe More Ample', *Rend. Sem. Math. Univ. di Padova* **26** (1956), 232–327.

Richter, M. K., 'Rational Choice', in J. S. Chipman *et al.* (eds.), *Preferences, Utilities, and Demand*, Harcourt Brace Jovanovich, New York, 1971, pp. 29–58.

Robinson, A., *Non-Standard Analysis*, North-Holland, Amsterdam, 1966.

Scott, D., 'Measurement Models and Linear Inequalities', *J. Math. Psychol.* **1** (1964), 233–247.

Scott, D. and Suppes, P., 'Foundational Aspects of Theories of Measurement', *J. Symbolic Logic* **23** (1958), 113–128.

Skala, H. J., *An Application of Model Theory to the Theory of Measurement*, 2nd Int. Game Theory Workshop, Berkeley, 1970.

Skala, H. J., 'Über einige Grundprobleme der Nutzentheorie – Nichtarchimedische Nutzentheorie', Habilitation-Thesis, Heidelberg 1973.

INDEX OF NAMES

INDEX OF SUBJECTS

THEORY AND DECISION LIBRARY

An International Series in the Philosophy and Methodology
of the Social and Behavioral Sciences

Editors:

GERALD EBERLEIN, *Universität des Saarlandes*
WERNER LEINFELLNER, *University of Nebraska*